FROM
THE CENTER
OF THE EARTH

FROM
THE CENTER
OF THE EARTH

The Search for the Truth
about China

RICHARD BERNSTEIN

Little, Brown and Company — Boston — Toronto

FIRST EDITION

LIBRARY OF CONGRESS CATALOGING IN PUBLICATION DATA

Bernstein, Richard.
    From the center of the earth.

    Includes index.
      1. China—Social life and customs—1976–
    2. China—Social conditions—1976–
    I. Title.
DS779.23.B47   1982   951.05′7   81-23647
ISBN 0-316-09194-4   AACR2

MV

Designed by Susan Windheim

Published simultaneously in Canada
by Little, Brown & Company (Canada) Limited

PRINTED IN THE UNITED STATES OF AMERICA

To my parents

They knew themselves as the residents of the Celestial Empire; their ruler they called the Son of Heaven. Surrounded by peoples less culturally advanced, they felt that they were a kind of chosen people, chosen not by God but by virtue of their superior attainments. Foreigners were known as barbarians. And the land of China was called *Zhongguo,* or Central Kingdom. It was a luminous domain, the global seat of civilization and of ethical conduct; it was, quite simply, the center of the earth.

A Note on Romanization

EVERY SYSTEM ever devised for rendering the Chinese language into the Roman alphabet has its imperfections. The Communist Chinese in 1979 put into use an alphabetization called *pinyin* (literal meaning: combine sounds) that has gained international acceptance. It is the system that I have used for most Chinese names and phrases. It has a couple of idiosyncrasies. The initial *x* is pronounced like the English *sh*; for example, *Deng Xiaoping* might be more phonetically rendered as *Deng She-ao Ping*. The letter *q*, which in *pinyin* is sometimes not followed by a *u*, sounds like the English *ch*, as in the Emperor *Qianlong* (pronounced *Chee-en Loong*). The letter *c* is pronounced *ts*, as in *Cao Yu*, the famous dramatist, whose name was formerly spelled *Tsao Yu*. Otherwise, *pinyin* gives a pretty close idea of the way Chinese words are actually spoken.

In two kinds of situations, however, I do not use *pinyin*. First, for two well known figures, Mao Tse-tung and Chou En-lai (*pinyin* would be Mao Zedong and Zhou Enlai), I have stuck with the old alphabetization for reasons of greater familiarity. The second case concerns some words that by common practice have for decades been spelled in a way that conformed to no standard system of romanization. These include the place-names Peking (*pinyin:* Beijing), Canton (Guangzhou), Nanking (Nanjing), Chungking (Chongqing), and Hong Kong (Xianggang), as well as a few historical figures, like the ancient philosopher Chuang-tse and Nationalist leader Chiang Kai-shek. These alphabetizations are more likely to be recognized by the nonspecialist than are the standardized *pinyin* spellings.

Acknowledgments

NO BOOK on contemporary China could be written without a lot of help. Unfortunately, in the case of this book, it is not possible publicly to acknowledge many of those whose assistance was crucial. I speak of the many Chinese people who took the considerable risk of befriending me, a foreign reporter in China, and, beyond that, who accepted the even greater risk of telling me about themselves and their experiences. To announce their names would almost certainly invite the attention of the Public Security Bureau, which has interrogated and even arrested many people for no more than having close, frank relations with foreigners. It is thus necessary to protect my friends and informants by using pseudonyms for them rather than their real names and, in some cases, to insert small falsities about them into the text — an erroneous place of residence here, a fictitious profession there — none of which will distort the meaning of what they told me. I apologize to the reader for these little white lies even as I thank those unnamed people who provided the information on which much of this book is based.

There are others outside China who also helped and whom I can thank: Professor Andrew Nathan of Columbia University for his shrewd, informed reading of the manuscript and for his many suggestions; Oscar Chiang of *Time* magazine for his comments on parts one and two; Roger Donald of Little, Brown, for his timely encouragement and excellent, critical advice; Melissa Clemence, also of Little, Brown, who wields as skillful an editing pencil as I have ever seen. Linda Jaivin, now with *Asiaweek* magazine in Hong Kong, dug up materials that bring to life the long and complex historical context of Chinese communism. Eileen Wu typed long segments of the manuscript as an act of friendship. René Vienet provided hospitality and a desk and a refuge from other demands when I took some time off from my duties at *Time* magazine to write. And, by no means least, Dick Duncan and my other editors at *Time* graciously gave me that time so that I could get the book done.

I take some strong positions here. My experiences in China and my conversations with my unnamed Chinese friends did not lead me to look on Communist rule with much favor. I think that many Chinese inside the country would agree with the views that I have formed. For those, in China or elsewhere, who do not, I should make clear that I, and none of those who helped me, bear entire responsibility for any errors of fact or judgment that might appear.

R.B.
Peking, October 14, 1981

Contents

FROM
THE CENTER
OF THE EARTH

Introduction

A Bicyclist and the Truth

THE IDEA for this book came to me on a warm summer afternoon while I was riding a bicycle behind the crenellated ramparts of the Imperial Palace in Peking. I was having a casual look around the city, just enjoying the rare good weather, heading south down Xiban Bridge Street toward the northern side of the palace moat, where the northwest guard tower rises up wonderfully into the clear blue sky. Somewhere along the road, I stopped for a minute to read a street sign, and as I began to pedal again, I discovered I had a companion.

He was about thirty-five to forty, mounted on the usual black, one-speed Flying Pigeon–brand bicycle, a clump of green vegetables tied to the rear frame indicating that he had just been to the market. He had on the standard men's summer dress, a white cotton shirt worn loosely outside his baggy blue trousers. He wore round, yellowed plastic glasses and was, for a Chinese, rather floridly complexioned. A fine stubble of mustache and beard was growing on his face, reflecting the enviable Chinese unconcern for daily shaving. He had extremely crooked, tobacco-stained teeth.

The man on the Flying Pigeon asked me if I was able to read the sign I had been looking at just before.

"Yes, I could read it," I said. "But slowly." We pedaled side by side a few meters. "Nice day, isn't it?" I said, in a weak attempt to keep the conversation going.

"Oh," he said predictably, "your Chinese is very good."

I told him that it was still rather poor, mainly trying to think of some way to keep this unexpected, fragile contact alive. In China, it often happens that people will approach a foreigner, rather shyly, with wonderment and hesitation, fascinated and at the same time intimidated by the possibility of contact. This is a welcome contrast to years past, when a man talking to a foreigner outside of official auspices could expect a swiftly following interrogation by agents of the Public Security Bureau.

In any case, I seized every opportunity to talk that came my way. On this particular day I was feeling rather expansive and at ease, enjoying the warmth of the sun, the pale green of the locust leaves filtering its light gently onto the street, the tinkling of a thousand bicycle bells. "Are you just out for a ride or do you have some business today?" I asked, furthering my effort to initiate some small talk.

What ensued in the way of conversation was out of the ordinary, yet, at the same time, typical of the frustrating plight of the foreigner in China trying to understand the country. My new friend told me that he was returning home from work in one of the machine-building ministries, where he was a minor official. He said that he was married with one child and, having been born and raised in Peking, knew the city very well. He asked me what embassy I worked for and I told him I didn't work for an embassy but for *Time* magazine. He had heard of it, he nodded knowingly, and had even read some of my articles in *Reference News*, the daily translation summary of the foreign press distributed to about twenty million Chinese but, for some inexplicable reason, forbidden to all foreigners. Then, entirely unprovoked, his anarchic teeth flashing yellow in the sun, the light glancing off his round glasses, he delivered himself of a stunning condemnation of his fellow citizens.

"You know," he said, nodding vaguely at the stream of bicyclists, "they are afraid. They won't tell you what they really think. They are frightened of talking to foreigners. But I want to tell you what the real thoughts of the Chinese people are."

We were passing the Beihai Park on the right, its lake full of afternoon boaters. The man on the Flying Pigeon continued, "After all these years of oppression, we have developed the habit of keeping our real opinions to ourselves. It's a bad habit. You foreigners have no way of understanding the real nature of China. In fact, I feel sorry for you. All you read is propaganda. You talk only to officials. But we common people, we people of the old hundred surnames, have different opinions. I'm not afraid. I want to tell the foreigners what is the real nature of life in China."

Though taken aback by the ferocity of these remarks, I knew that the man on the Flying Pigeon was right. For the most part, we foreigners did read propaganda and we did talk mostly to officials and we suspected that there were vast mountains of truth to which all the "old hundred surnames" (the ordinary term for the common Chinese), and none of us, were privy. Indeed, for me then — and even now, though to a far lesser extent — Peking was a city that yielded up its true nature with extreme reluctance. Even physically, the city suggests secrets, with its unmarked buildings, their long, concealing walls covered by whitewash or brick and interspersed with dark doorways, that give little hint of what lies within, whether ordinary residences or governmental palaces. In China, information is privileged. It is parceled out like the best tea, in small cups from which one sips very daintily. And so, a man on a bicycle who, unsolicited and eager, wants to disclose the secrets of life, the secrets that other people are afraid to tell — this is not common to the Chinese experience.

What the foreigner, especially the foreign journalist, learns very quickly in China is that the free and ready flow of news, opinion, statistics, and other data that exists in the West is largely absent in China. As a journalist, I became very familiar with this fact, having lived through dozens of experiences wherein the Chinese demonstrated how carefully and cautiously they manage the resource called information. One example:

In the summer of 1980, the Chinese press published a couple of brief articles dwelling on the fact that the famous Great Wall had, in many places, been ravaged by local peasants and army units looking for good stone building material. This great treasure of China, the articles said, should be protected against such vandalism. A team from the Bureau of Cultural Relics had, moreover, just departed on an inspection tour of the entire wall and would return to recommend ways of preserving it.

There was, I decided, a good minor story in this for me, so I called the Bureau of Cultural Relics and asked if I could talk to somebody about the state of the Great Wall. "Since we have just sent out our inspection team," came the cordial reply, "it would be better for you to wait a couple of weeks for them to come back. Then we will be glad to answer your questions."

That was clearly reasonable. I waited two weeks and then called again. "Since the inspection team has just returned, they are very busy making their recommendations," said the man at the other end of the line, adding vaguely, "Please call again later."

Just at that time, I left Peking for ten days or so. When I returned, I called a third time. This time, the man from the Bureau of Cultural Relics said he had "no comment" to make regarding the Great Wall.

"But," I protested, "you have told me twice already that you would give me some information."

"We have no comment."

"Are you going to make public the results of the special team's investigation?"

"No comment."

"Look." I was exasperated. I was trying to keep in mind that when dealing with the Chinese, if you get angry, you are lost. "All I want is a little information on the Great Wall. Can't you help me with that?"

"Sorry, we have no comment." The man hung up.

The Bureau of Cultural Relics is a central government organ. I decided to carry my inquiry to the Peking municipal government, which, as a local government, had jurisdiction over a hundred-mile portion of the Great Wall, including that very well maintained stretch that is visited by thousands of tourists every week. I sent over a written request for help and then telephoned the municipal government's foreign-affairs office.

"Sure," came the helpful response to my call. "We'll set up a meeting for you with responsible persons [a bureaucratic euphemism for a functionary who does not enjoy a high title like vice-director but who might know something] of our Bureau of Cultural Relics and Museums."

"Good," I replied. "As I indicated in my written request, I am primarily interested in the Great Wall."

The day arrived, and at the municipal government offices — located in a beautiful, guarded compound that was the Japanese legation in pre-Communist Peking — there were no fewer than four "responsible persons" of the "unit concerned."

"Would you like to ask questions right away or shall we give you a brief introduction first and you can ask questions later?" I was asked.

In fact, there is no way to avoid the "brief introduction" so I asked for that first. But, I said by way of a preemptive move, "I am primarily interested in the Great Wall."

The most responsible of the responsible persons nodded, gave me a warm welcome on behalf of his colleagues (no meeting starts without a "warm welcome on behalf of"), turned to his voluminous materials, and then plunged into the brief introduction. It lasted for forty-five minutes of our one-hour meeting. We skimmed lightly over the entire history of the Bureau of Cultural Relics and Museums since the liberation of Peking — "with its long history and glorious revolutionary tradition" (every Chinese city has a "long history and glorious revolutionary tradition"). We touched on the various measures adopted in various years "to do the work of cultural preservation well." We learned the precise number of artifacts dug up over the years and the number of sites designated for protection — all of this, by the way, in blatant contradiction of the obvious fact that many of Peking's most beautiful artifacts have been systematically destroyed since 1949. The brief introduction drew at last to a conclusion and I was asked if I had any questions.

"Yes," I said. "I wonder if you can tell me something about the state of the Great Wall?"

"Oh, the Great Wall. We're not very clear about the Great Wall."

I tried to be diplomatic. "Well, there was a special team that finished an investigation of the wall about a month ago. Can you tell me something about the results of that investigation?"

"We've not been given any information about that. You see, that was a central government bureau. We are only a bureau of the municipality."

To be fair, the responsible persons did have a few minor bits of information about the wall in the environs of Peking, in particular that many sections of the wall were in poor condition — exactly how many and where, they could not say. In any case, as the weeks passed I became absorbed in other matters and did not pursue the Great Wall, which had been at best a minor feature story anyway. To this day, I haven't written it. The special investigating team has disappeared into oblivion.

I have experienced many other such failures either to get information or to gain access to sources of information, some of them involving the most trivial aspects of life. Once I wanted a list of all of the places in China that had been officially opened for visits by foreigners. The New China News Agency had said that there were 114 such places, but it did not report which places they were. The China Travel Service had no list, nor did the Public Security Bureau's foreign-affairs office or even the branch of the Foreign Ministry that handles all requests by journalists, the Information Department. (In Peking we had other names for this outfit, like the Disinformation Department, the Interference Department, the Anti-information Department.) Moreover, whenever I presented my request, I elicited a response of wonderment, as though there was something bizarre and inexplicably foreign about wanting such a list. "If you want to go someplace," more than one person informed me, "you just apply. If it's open to foreigners we will give you permission."

All this indicates the precisely contrary conceptions China and the West hold regarding information. In the West, we assume that everything should be part of the public domain — except for that small portion of things that needs to be secret on the grounds of national security or personal privacy. In China it is the opposite. In China everything is secret, except for that small proportion of things that the authorities decide needs be put into the public domain. There is no right to know in China any more than there is a free and independent press.

And so, it was against that background of bureaucratic obstructionism and officially enforced secretiveness that a man willing to be incautious, to talk straight from the heart, approached me. In fact, even astride my bicycle I remained a bit skeptical about how much I would learn from this total stranger, though, despite experiences like those just recounted, I had by that time in China been privy to confidences. I knew that there was an enormous reserve of anger and disillusionment toward the regime, especially among the youth. We rode along for a while, the man on the bicycle beginning to get a bit monotonous in his insistence on the cowardice of everybody else, I trying gently to encourage him to move into what he promised to tell me — the real nature of life in China. Then, in front of the Beihai Park at the beginning of a gentle slope upward that led over the bridge to the other side of a lake, I slowed down, nodding at him to do so as well, thinking that we could talk more easily if we got off the damned bicycles. I made my way past the stream of bikes passing between me and the curb. When I reached the sidewalk, my friend was nowhere in sight. Finally, I recognized him from the clump of green vegetables strapped to the rack behind his seat. He was gathering speed up ahead. I resisted the temptation to set out in pursuit, figuring that he had had a sudden attack of prudence and would prefer that I not impose any more friendship or conversation on him. I watched his white shirt, sparkling in the sun, blend into the broad weave of other white shirts until there was nothing but an indistinguishable sea of sunlit white shirts streaming ahead up the slope and over the bridge. And even then, I had to suppress the temptation to call plaintively out to him: "Wait. Wait. Where are you going? Tell me. What is the real nature of life in China?"

Of course I knew better. I did not hinder his escape.

A lot of time has passed since that unfruitful encounter behind the Forbidden City. I am now in New York City, having returned from China for a few months at home, but still sufficiently under the influence of that faraway place to be mesmerized by the extraordinary spectacle of America — by its flamboyance, its variety, its overt sensuality, its extravagant hairiness, its often reckless and even dangerous degree of freedom. I am struck by the contrast between the easy accessibility of this place, its tendency to gush forth information, to spill its secrets, and the image of the man on his Flying Pigeon taking abrupt flight from me, escaping from the responsibility that he at first seemed to want to incur.

Even now that quite a lot of time has passed, I cannot claim since that emblematic encounter to have discovered the real nature of life in China. Probably no Chinese knows it either, not in a country as old, as big, and as complicated as China is with its one billion people and three thousand years of history. I remain keenly aware of the sound, cautionary wisdom of the London *Times* correspondent, George Wingrove Cooke, who preceded me to China by more than 120 years. No subject, Cooke said, "could offer wider scope for ingenious hypothesis, profound generalization, and triumphant dogmatism" than the character of what was then, as it is now, the most populous and the least accessible country on earth. "No single individual," declared the American missionary A. H. Smith in 1894, after twenty-two years in China, "whatever the extent of his knowledge, could by any possibility know the whole truth about the Chinese."* And yet, Smith, notwithstanding his becoming modesty, did write his classic book entitled *Chinese Characteristics*. I too find it impossible to resist the temptation to write down the results of my own sojourns in China and, indeed, with the specific purpose of trying to shed some light on precisely that question which the man on the bicycle raised but failed to answer: What is the real nature of the place? What is the nature of life there?

I have not tried for comprehensiveness. This is no encyclopedia that will run down, only a few years short of a century after Smith, all Chinese characteristics, from their frugality to their concern with face to the way they make careers in the governing bureaucracy. I do not claim to have discovered the whole truth about China and I would be a bit suspicious of any who did. Nonetheless, I hope that this book will deal with a significant part of the truth. It consists of some approaches to a place that is not only big but also secretive and many-layered, like one of those intricate series of concentric spheres that Chinese craftsmen carve from solid blocks of ivory.

In addition, all this is undertaken in concert with two undeniable and significant facts: one, that the Chinese have, after a long period of self-imposed seclusion, once again entered into our world; two, that their experience, particularly their experience in revolution, is meaningful to us.

The first of these is very simple. Even here in New York, the Chinese are visible, generally as rather prim, subdued figures in the colorful streets — students at the universities, participants in international conferences, members of performing arts troupes, diplomats, or reporters for the official New China News Agency. What has come to be called "normalization" between the United States and China has blossomed into a greater exchange of people than at any time since the 1930s, with the various U.S. consulates in China (there will soon be five of them) issuing in the area of one thousand to fifteen hundred nonimmigrant visas a month to citizens of the People's Republic.

At the same time, America has reentered the consciousness of the Chinese, not least as a place to escape to. Since 1972, when Richard Nixon opened the way, the chance of emigrating to America has become a fervent ambition for millions of Chinese. They plot and scheme to find some way to come here. They apply to Ivy League schools or to fly-by-night

* Arthur H. Smith, *Chinese Characteristics*, Introduction, p. 1 (New York, Fleming H. Revell, 1894).

language academies to come as students, in the hope of eventually changing their visa status to permanent resident; they write to long lost relatives already in the United States, trying to benefit from reunification
with this suddenly rediscovered family; they make claims to the Chinese
government of property — sometimes real, sometimes fictitious — owned
in Cincinnati or Los Angeles that they now want to recover. The bilateral
relationship between Peking and Washington is far more than part of a
global anti-Soviet strategy. It is an interaction involving the personal ambitions and aspirations of millions of people.

The second fact, that the Chinese experience is meaningful to us, is
more elusive, more abstract. I remember how, during the rebellious years
of the 1960s when I was a graduate student, China was going through the
Cultural Revolution, Mao's destructive, radical effort to cleanse the enormous governing bureaucracy both of those who stood in the way of his
absolute power and of those he felt were not sufficiently imbued with
proletarian ideals. At the time, the event seemed, to trendy students and
faculty alike, to be a great alternative, a heroic effort to force the country's
leaders to humbly "serve the people." Even before it was possible for
Americans to go there in significant numbers, China was the focus of various romantic imaginings that served the dual purpose of providing a political model and proof of one's racial and cultural open-mindedness as
well. Ironically, the Chinese themselves have now repudiated the reckless
Maoism that inspired revolutionary youths all over the world — and not
only revolutionary youths. There was a host of other strange bedfellows
who saw in the vague shadows cast by China across the globe something
different and valuable. For the jet-setters it became the ultimately fash-
ionable destination, an adornment of radical chic, an opportunity for
what David Caute has called "commitment at a distance." For geopoliti-
cal strategists, most notably of the ordinarily conservative, anti-Communist stripe, Peking became a part of the great global game whose
power — or perhaps more accurately, potential power — needed to be
harnessed to the anti-Soviet cause. Businessmen saw the prospect of a
huge new market opening up — and indeed, a small number of this last
group made lots of money. In 1980, Bloomingdale's mounted a well-publicized sales blitz for the products of chinoiserie. Designer bed sheets
were photographed in front of rice paddies in Jiangsu Province and made
to appear — with good commercial sense but a complete absence of verac-
ity — as though they had somehow been inspired by the reality of contemporary China.

From advertisements for Lindblad tours to dry scholarly papers in the
academic journals, an entirely nonexperiential and generally rather
breathless picture of China emerged as part of the commonplace wisdom.
Not surprisingly, it was an abstraction, replete with various glib clichés

about a giant country throwing off the past, making monumental changes, usually while emerging from a harrowing period of misguided turmoil, seething with near unanimous fervor to become great again. These well-meaning abstractions are not totally wrong. They are, rather, incomplete, bloodless, bleached dry by the harsh, sunny stares that came from outside the country, based often more on wish than on hard, empirical observation. Like the literature and theater encouraged by the Peking regime, they are short on subtlety, on complexity, ultimately on plausibility. Still, the attention that we as a society have paid to our image of China is a measure of the importance we attach to the place — as a partner in our battles with the Russians, as the repository of an enriching experience, as a moral and political lesson, either positive or negative, for us in the West who are beset by grave problems of our own.

Of course, there is a complex and rich world that shimmers just on the other side of our abstractions. There is a world of inner conflicts and personal strivings, nasty ambitions, lusts and melancholias, frustrations and dissatisfactions that belong to the individuals who comprise China. That may seem obvious; yet, these things have been missing from the "luminous portraits," in Simon Leys's aptly sarcastic phrase, that have been done of China. And inevitably so, given the energetic strivings of the regime to present the individual as little more than an enthusiastic participant in its grand national schemes. Often missing also from these portraits is the nature of that regime itself, as a still intrusive, controlling, terrifying, and irresistible force. When we in the West examine the Soviet Union or Eastern Europe, we are appropriately obsessed with the plight of the puny individual in his confrontation with the awesome clumsiness of totalitarian power. For some reason, when we look at China, the challenges of courage that the individual faces are rarely considered. Yet, they exist.

The Chinese themselves have two new slogans, the latest in a long series of such slogans, which say "seek truth from facts" and "take experience as the sole criterion of the truth." These are welcome practical epigrams in a country that has often been swept away by the madness of pure ideology. They are also useful to the visitors and analysts of China who have often been carried away into the formless seas of abstractions. This book is a personal experience with China. It is a search for at least a part of the reality that the man on the bicycle swore no Chinese would dare reveal to me — and then proved his point through his own evasive actions. To illustrate the dilemma of the foreigner in China, I began here with him, blending prudently under the bright springtime sun of Peking into the indistinguishable, amorphous crowd. But my hope is to pursue the question that he impetuously raised, to search for the mosaic of forms that comprises the China, not of theory or of hope, but of experience.

I

IN THE HEART
OF THE KINGDOM

1

Soft Sleeper to Chungking

THE TWELVE-HOUR JOURNEY by train from the city of Chengdu to the city of Chungking cuts a southeastern diagonal across endless miles of rural Sichuan Province. I was to make the trip twice, the second time during the day. But the first trip took place on a moonless night, in the fall of 1979, just before I was stationed as a reporter in China. I felt cheated that first time. I wasn't able to see the train's passage from the verdant, black-soiled reaches of the plains to the poor, red-clay hills that roll southward toward the Yangtse River, a passage from relative rural wealth to poverty through a region that had always lived in my imagination as the very heart of China — the country that for three millennia regarded itself as the center of the earth.

Several months later, duly accredited by the Information Department in Peking as a correspondent for *Time* magazine, I made the trip again, this time sitting all day under a sulfurously hot summer sun, while the train clattered through the heart of China. Irrigated fields and sturdy villages near Chengdu gave way to hundreds of miles of rugged, stony hills, dotted by villages that were barren even by Chinese standards. In the plains, the flooded paddies, glinting in the sun, were thick with green rice. They were lined with long rows of mulberry trees (Sichuan is China's leading producer of raw silk). Persimmons, banyans, and gracefully bending clumps of bamboo surrounded large thatch-roofed farmhouses constructed around private courtyards. But in the hilly areas, the rice was planted only in the narrow fingers of bottom land that followed streams and small rivers. The stony hills themselves were planted in circular patterns with less desirable corn. The train passed small huts, pressed against red laterite hills baking in the summer heat. There was no glass or, in many cases, even paper for the windows, only narrow, oblong holes cut into the thick clay walls. The scenery was poor but no less beautiful than the scenery of the plain.

Inside the train, the loudspeaker crackled a propagandistic exhortation to build socialism, climaxed by a few bars of heroic music. By one of those ironic coincidences that abound in China, I saw just at the end of the musical peroration an old peasant man below the railbed who might well have been seen at that spot centuries earlier in much the same condition. He was dressed in black; he was bareheaded, sunburned, squatting on his haunches next to a small hut of dried mud and reed matting. Alongside him on the red clay ground was a wooden night-soil bucket fitted with a harness that could be carried on the back like a crude camper's pack. A hundred meters farther down a group of swans floated in a small stream, incredibly white, mystically lovely, against the drab mud brown of the river itself.

Why was I so anxious to make this journey a second time, to sweat on an uncomfortable seat for twelve hours in hundred-degree heat between Chengdu and Chungking? Because Sichuan, with its three thousand years of recorded history, its ninety-six million people, its contrasts between agricultural affluence and agricultural poverty, had always seemed to me representative of China itself. Sichuan had everything. If it were an independent country — which it nearly was at many times in its history — it would rank as the eighth most populous in the world. In Sichuan, Emperor Qin Shi Huang, who first unified China, created a vast irrigation system called Dujiangyan, which, though fully twenty-three hundred years old, is still the main element in the network of rivers, dikes, and canals that today irrigates the Chengdu Plain. As the so-called Shu Kingdom, Sichuan was one of the principal locales of the famous *Romance of the Three Kingdoms* set in the third century A.D. that had thrilled that idealistic young man who changed the course of history, Mao Tse-tung. Much later, Sichuan was the home of the Nationalist government-in-exile during the war against Japanese aggression. The city of Chungking had in my mind a near legendary quality as the place where Vinegar Joe Stilwell did battle with the Nationalist Generalissimo Chiang Kai-shek, and the Communist Chou En-lai charmed a generation of American reporters and diplomats who would later be attacked in witch-hunts of the McCarthy period.

There was also a certain exclusivity to Sichuan, which was another reason why I was anxious to go there. It was among the last provinces opened to foreign visitors. The province was known to have been the scene of terrible fighting during the Cultural Revolution of 1966 to 1969 and, after that, it had come under the firm control of the central government only with great difficulty. Still later, at the end of the seventies, it emerged as a model province for a series of untested policies that a newly pragmatic leadership wanted to try out for the entire country. Thus, Sichuan Province seemed very much at the heart of the great Communist experiment in China, an experiment that, even before arriving in China to live, I had come more and more to regard as a tragic failure. Sichuan was deeply implicated in the power struggle. It was overpopulated. It struggled to feed itself. It once consisted in itself of an ancient civilization filled with poets and inventors that had entered upon a long period of decline, lasting not decades but centuries. It was trying, like the rest of China, to find some new dynamic formula that would arrest that decline and restore the wealth and power that the country, the empire, once had. I tended to see in Sichuan one of the great interior regions of the earth, fifteen hundred miles from the sea, blocked off in the north by rugged, treeless mountains, and in the west by the tallest peaks in the world, the Tibetan-Nepalese Himalayas. In that sense, it emblematized the idea of China as an inward-looking, self-contained giant, a great world to discover. I felt that Sichuan was China and that to understand it would be to understand China itself.

In all, I went to Sichuan four times in the course of eighteen months, both before and after I became a permanently accredited correspondent in Peking, and each time I observed and scribbled in my notebook obsessively. But, like trips to all places, the first one, the one of the nighttime train ride, remained the most exciting. Everything that I saw that autumn of 1979 took on portentous dimensions; everything was a possible clue to the reality of China. I had had a night of partially successful sleep, interrupted by constant crackings, rumblings, bangs, and whistles, followed by long periods of total, eerie silence when the train would stop altogether on, I supposed, various forlorn and remote village platforms, there to wait for still, lonely eternities before creaking into motion again.

My night was also interrupted by the stentorian snoring of one of my traveling companions, a somewhat idiosyncratic and at the same time rather classical Italian diplomat, who, as though out of respect for the vast silences of the Sichuan plain, would fall still himself in the bunk above mine when the train was stopped. But then, once the train began to roll again, he would accompany its repertoire of noises with an infernal bellowing that temporarily erased in me the affection that I actually felt for him.

In the months ahead, I would have many chances to travel in China by myself. But on this first trip to Sichuan, I was in a group, a dependent group whose every move was monitored and controlled by friendly but firm guides from the China Travel Service. In this particular case, the group consisted of some twenty-two diplomats and journalists based in Hong Kong and invited to China for eighteen days (at a cost of nearly twelve hundred dollars for each invitee) by the local branch of the New China News Agency. The Japanese were the largest nationality in the group, followed by the Americans. The snoring diplomat was the only Italian, a common fate for him. Despite the extraordinary noise that emanated from his unconscious being during the night, he was also my favorite in our group. While I took notes, looking for hidden political-economic clues and indications to the real China, he concentrated on the aesthetic side of things, finding the remaining graceful contours of a now dilapidated portal, noticing a spark of talent in the one student whose Klimt-inspired paintings hung, next to all that socialist realism, in the Institute of Art. I learned something from him.

But that morning, his snoring got me up at five o'clock. I picked up my notebook and looked out the window for some impressions, for some data about China. The sun was just beginning to rise. Beyond an embankment lined with trees it cast its reflection into the Yangtse River, which, this far west, while rapid and muddy, is only a rumor of the grandiosity and lordliness it will attain as it flows farther on into south central China. Beyond, on the other side of the Yangtse, were wooded slopes, the occasional isolated rough shed that probably belonged to some production brigade. But for the pale glint of red sunlight in the water, the landscape consisted of the sere, monochromatic brown that overwhelms the countryside in China from late September to early April. In the spring and summer, the landscape would become green again. But now, in the fall, nothing was growing but the bare trees that, like halberds and pikes, lined the riverbanks. Dirt tracks on the other side led over the far embankment, conveying the impression that, if you could only get off the train and walk at will, you would discover on the other side pretty, secluded villages, untouched by time. But here, along the river, there was only the occasional mud-brick house, covered with stained whitewash, standing lonely in the morning chill.

There was a knock on the door. Mr. Yang, known more affectionately as Little Yang, one of the Travel Service guides, was going from compartment to compartment waking everybody up. Guides in China seem never to sleep or, at least, they seem never to experience any discomfort in getting up extremely early in the morning. While the diplomat and the others in our "soft sleeper" four-person compartment began reluctantly to stir, I walked out into the surprisingly cold air of the corridor and then through four or five "hard sleeper" cars to the dining room. The night before, when we arrived at the dining car for dinner, we were kept waiting for nearly half an hour by a contingent of green-uniformed People's Liberation Army (P.L.A.) officers, the only others on the train who seemed to be traveling soft class. The less privileged Chinese passengers eat cold rice and hot water and a bit of pickled vegetable by their bunks in the hard-sleeper cars. The hard-sleeper cars are a kind of dim netherworld, smelling of dirty laundry and unbathed bodies. On the other side of the dining car — a portion of the train that is normally kept apart by locked doors — is still another element of the traveling hierarchy, the so-called hard-seat section. If hard sleeper is a dim netherworld, hard seat is a living hell, consisting of straight-backed benches packed with far more people than they were built to accommodate. The passengers squeeze together on the benches; they sit on boxes in the aisles; they pack the clattering airy space between the cars. And, showing the long-suffering qualities for which the Chinese are famous, they do so for days on end. Most of the passengers are ordinary Chinese citizens, factory hands and middle-school teachers, office workers and university students, who are visiting relatives, often wives and children, in distant parts of the empire, after having been randomly assigned to work by the employment bureaucracy in places far from their homes. I have had many trips by train in China lasting two nights or more, and on each of those trips, I have always viewed with mixed pity and admiration the densely packed mass of humanity that patiently sits on those hard, uncomfortable planks while the train makes its stately passage from one end of the country to another.

Normally, soft sleeper is placed directly adjacent to the dining car, so its privileged passengers need not push their way through the lesser quarters of the train for their meals. The dining car, in any case, is off limits to all but the foreigners, the generals, and the high officials. The classes are determined, not by how much each passenger is willing to or can afford to pay, but by his station in life, his rank. In the nineteenth century and earlier, foreigners admitted into China — like court astronomers or customs officials or even missionaries — were accorded the status of officials with all of the privileges and immunities that that designation carried with it. In China today, tourists and journalists and visiting capitalists from Europe or America or Africa are also made officials of a high rank. They thus travel soft class. But ordinary Chinese visiting relatives or taking their annual trips to their native cities are required to go hard seat. Most of those on official business get the luxury of a place to lie down for the night in hard sleeper. And those of high rank, whatever their purpose in traveling, have access to soft sleeper. The difference between the classes, between the P.L.A. officers and the rest of society, reflects the elitist nature of Chinese society, the importance of position in the governing bureaucracy. Soft class has a good deal of the comfort and elegance of European first class, carpeting on the floor, crisp white sheets and pillowcases on the comfortable bunks, lacy curtains covering the window, often even a rich wood paneling, though, on the Chengdu-Chungking train, there was a kind of off-white laminated plastic on the walls rather than wood. Hard class, whether of the seat or sleeper variety, is dingy and Spartan, grimy and brooding and unkempt, just as crowded with people as third class in India if, perhaps, a bit more orderly and far less colorful.

Breakfast was uncharacteristically terrible. I noticed one table of overseas Chinese eating steaming bowls of noodles that looked fine. For us, there was a well-intentioned Western breakfast that even Little Yang and his colleague Old Li ate with unconcealed distaste: two ice-cold eggs, one arranged atop the other on a tiny plate intended for use as a saucer, some cold damp bread flecked with dead ashes, and tasteless lead-colored coffee.

Soon, the sun was higher and the shaft of light streaking the misty Yangtse became a brighter red. The far bank was turning from opaque brown to a translucent shade of gray. A couple of peasant men stood stock-still on the riverbank, wheelbarrows at their sides, watching as everyone in every country watches when a train goes by. They were the first signs of life stirring in the cold barren outside. I downed what remained of the tepid coffee and made my way back through hard seat to my compartment. The soldiers and the common folk were astir, gathering together their belongings, jamming the aisle, making the passage a slow, bumpy affair.

By the time I got back to the compartment, the rural scenery had given way to scattered bits of urban sprawl. A few warehouses were interspersed with the bare trees that lined the far bank of the river; there was an occasional small factory building, its chimney issuing black coal smoke into the cool air. On the far bank, climbing the slope of the hill, a small city, colored black against the gray of the hill, took shape in the early morning light. I could make out the dim outline of a cement plant, a tramway extending to the river, a small jetty with low-slung wooden boats. Gradually, the widely spaced buildings gathered into clusters. There was a lime kiln, a rock quarry, a collection of ramshackle sheds and huts in front of a carved-out hillside, more smokestacks issuing black pollution into the air. The train passed a boat repair yard, a cinder-block plant, long stretches of brick wall broken here and there to reveal factory yards strewn with piles of concrete slabs. Then, after a railway yard lined with five, six, seven shiny black steam locomotives, came rows of housing blocks, squat, ugly rectangles of brick or concrete, reminiscent of the mill towns of nineteenth-century Lancashire. On the left, on the high hills dominating the railbed and the river, were the silhouettes of still larger buildings; on the right, more sheds, houses of crumbling brick pressed against the track, a thick succession of barracks and factories, a lumber-yard, more piles of concrete slabs, more stretches of brick wall, more huts, more sheds, more smokestacks, a disorderly, seedy, entirely random collection of urban artifacts that, suddenly, at 6:30 A.M. gave way to the station platform.

Chungking — the last place on mainland China where Americans had played a decisive role, an emblem of the lost past. I got out onto the platform and began to take notes:

The station: people pouring out of train in great numbers, P.L.A. soldiers with bedrolls on their backs, others carrying clothing, food, etc., in torn plastic bags or bulging string-mesh sacks. Much pushing, shoving, scrambling for advantage. An ancient woman with bound feet, dressed entirely in black, is carried off the train on somebody's back and lowered with painful bump onto blue quilt laid out on platform.

Smell of coal smoke overwhelming. It invades the sinuses, attacks the eyes. Station platform covered with so much grime I don't want to put my bag down. Chungking stinks the way Blackburn, Lancashire, must have stunk a hundred years ago in the English industrial revolution. Hills tower up into the mist on the other side of station from Yangtse. Dramatic sight. Occasional windows high above reflect red sun in brilliant flashes of light that emerge from the mist-shrouded hills. Vague shapes of buildings up there like river sentinels. Black smoke billowing out of unseen chimneys. The scuffling of thousands of feet as multitudes in monotonous blues and greens head with controlled haste down platform toward gates where tickets are examined as they pass through. Old woman still lying on quilt. Mailbags being unloaded from baggage car. Sound of riverboat foghorns drifts up from Yangtse side of station. Weather: cool, still misty, sky gray with pollution but red sun of early morning striving mightily to break into the clear.

2

Knowing and Not Knowing

TWO WEEKS AFTER that arrival in Chungking, I was at a rowdy, good-natured farewell banquet hosted by the New China News Agency, which had organized our tour. *Mao-tai,* China's potent sorghum-based distilled whiskey, flowed freely with the frequent toasts. Fellowship reigned supreme. Chinese banquets, as regular as the legendary three-martini lunch in the United States, can be stiff, predictable, tedious ordeals, hours of wooden conversation interspersed between plates of heavy corn-starchy food. But this one was conviviality itself. Faces reddened, laughter filled the room, glasses clinked together. Then, suddenly, the Chinese host commanded speeches from us, the guests. Before I knew it, some malicious conspiracy had determined that I would make the first speech — in Chinese.

I protested to no avail and rose to face five tables of flushed and expectant faces. There was nothing on my mind other than the throbbing produced by several glasses too many of *mao-tai.* What to say? I bought some time by observing that I was nervous to be giving my first speech ever in Chinese. I hesitated, an alcoholic storm exploding behind my eyes and beneath my temples. Finally, I resorted to what I have done at times when I've had nothing particular to say in a story I've had to write: I searched for a quote. Socrates made his way through the mental mist. "Centuries ago," I began, "there was a certain Greek philosopher who is very famous in the West. He once said that the difference between other men and him was that other men didn't know and they didn't know that they didn't know; while, as for him, he also didn't know, but he knew that he didn't know."

It is entirely possible that my Chinese version of this complex bit of syntax came out as so much gibberish. Still, as my hosts nodded approvingly (no Chinese would be so uncivil as to express utter confoundedness), I was emboldened to plunge ahead. "Before," I went on, "I and many of my colleagues in the American press had to watch your great country from outside in Hong Kong. But we are poised now to come to live in Peking as reporters. After these three weeks traveling in Sichuan and other places in China, I am at least beginning to know what it is that I don't know. Living in Peking, American reporters should begin for the first time to truly understand something about China."

I continued in this vein for a few more minutes, thanked our hosts for their meticulous hospitality, for the banquet, for the *mao-tai*, and for the fellowship, and resumed my seat amid loud applause and louder hurrahs for my extraordinary Chinese — another example of unfailing Chinese courtesy, extended in the case of my serviceable but imperfect Chinese in gross contradiction of self-evident facts. At the time, of course, it didn't matter what I said. Anything in Chinese would have gone down well. But later, I began to think that that desperation quote from Socrates was in fact an appropriate bit of wisdom for foreigners in China.

My two weeks in Sichuan and the southwest, culminating in my Peking banquet peroration, was not my first trip to China. I had been in the country three times before, to no fewer than twelve provinces and regions, as delegation member, tourist, and reporter for *Time* magazine covering visits by American officials. And, of course, there were many others like me, as China, in the months and years after the country opened for Americans in 1972, became one of the world's most trendy destinations. Thousands of journalists, celebrities, and politicians flocked to the once hermetically sealed Middle Kingdom; there were clothing designers, movie actresses, conservative anti-Soviet European cabinet ministers, youthful would-be revolutionaries; there were Beautiful People, filmmakers, stand-up comics, athletes, economists, violinists, international bankers, oilmen, and other capitalists, and group after group of garden-variety tourists. Almost every step by these foreign hordes was controlled by the army of guides and handlers trained for the purpose by the barbarian-reception departments of the Chinese bureaucracy. Still, dozens of books were written, documentaries made, television spectaculars produced. It seemed that everybody was duty bound to propagate in one way or another his personal discovery of China. And, looking back on it all after my accidental banquet reference to Socrates, it seemed to me that with a very few notable exceptions, this helter-skelter burgeoning of material proved that most people didn't know that they didn't know.

It happens that I entered into the complex and rather consuming world of sinology near the beginning of this blossoming love affair with China, a love affair that started in what was then called the New Left, centered mostly at the universities in the United States, but that, within a few short years, had spread to encompass an extraordinary assortment of bedfellows all across the political and social spectra. The year was 1966 when I arrived at Harvard to do graduate work in Chinese language and history under Professor John K. Fairbank, long the grand and justly respected mover and shaker in the field of sinology in America. It may seem strange that I had very little exact idea at that time of why I wanted to subject myself to the rigorous task of learning the Chinese language, especially since it then seemed very unlikely that I would ever be able to set my foot on any real Chinese soil — except for that on the island of Taiwan. But I had a general sense that to know something about this gigantic and faraway place would prove useful at some time in the future. And, in any case, at the time I began trying to speak in tones and distinguishing one ideogram from five thousand others, China was a subject of great attention, scrutiny, and puzzlement to most of the rest of the world. I arrived in graduate school almost exactly at the beginning of what soon became known as the Great Proletarian Cultural Revolution, one of the most massive political upheavals of the twentieth century.

Years later, when I had the chance to talk to people in China itself, I would hear horrific personal tales (of which more in later chapters) of sufferings, persecutions, and suicides, of the utterly mindless, superstitious fanaticism that characterized that event. And every time I talked about the Cultural Revolution in China later, I also experienced a hidden embarrassment about the way we in American universities had misconstrued that terrible episode — now repudiated as a "catastrophe" by the Chinese Communist party itself. But misconstrue it we did, led astray as we were by a number of distorted perceptions — most important, that it was a heroic effort by the great, iconoclastic Mao Tse-tung to rid China of a stodgy, privileged bureaucratic elite, of the newly risen antipopulist "new class" with its limousines and villas and disdain for the common people.

This view, combined with revulsion at the American war effort in Vietnam, produced visions of revolutionary societies in general, and of China in particular, that at many universities in both America and Europe were boundless in their wishfulness. There are many such examples of this, but I remember in particular a group of liberal Protestant clergy and divinity-school students around Cambridge, Massachusetts, in those days who used to participate in the informal conversations on China that often took place. Those people actually proclaimed Maoism and the Cultural Revolution to be a new kind of Christian goodness, devoted, as they were in theory, to eradicating selfishness from the human heart and serving "the people." I thought of these well-meaning theologians in 1981 when I talked with Chinese Christians who had lived through the Cultural Revolution. They told me how they had been made to stand on the streets outside their houses for entire nights while they held placards to their chests by pressing down on them with their chins — an effort that would force them to keep their heads bowed in humiliation. I once tried to hold a placard to my chest using only my chin. I found it, for even just a few minutes, a very uncomfortable form of Christian goodness.

What were the reasons for this roseate view of the Cultural Revolution? Perhaps it is helpful to bear in mind that China for centuries has inspired a whole series of cults among Westerners who were on the lookout either for curiosities or, in the case of the serious sinophiles, for some sort of alternative model for their own troubled societies. Such a cult existed in eighteenth-century France (and again in twentieth-century France), the chief *objets* of which were cloisonné, porcelain, and silk, as well as parasols, paintings, and lacquered boxes. The frivolous side of this earlier cult was represented by the likes of otherwise sober French aristocrats who used to show up in Chinese costume to sit for their portraits, or perhaps in the habit of the Prince de Condé, who around 1735 had monkeys dressed *à la chinois* to play about his grounds.

But there was a serious side as well. No less a man than Voltaire saw in eighteenth-century China, and in particular in Emperor Qianlong an oriental model for the kind of rationalist-secular society governed by a powerful and wise philosopher king that he longed for back in France. Voltaire believed of the Chinese that "the constitution of their Empire is in truth the best in the world, the only one which is completely based on a paternal power . . . the only one which has established rewards for virtue whereas all others confine their laws to the punishment of crime." Voltaire judged the emperor himself to be wise, literate, and sensible. He even suspected that this emperor's subjects were the "most just and humane people in the universe." He evidently did not suspect, looking on China from afar (from much farther than we do today), that his idol Emperor Qianlong used to enjoy eating monkey brain while the monkey was still alive (this is still done in some places), that he burned thousands of books, and that, while he had to pay lip service to the virtuousness of Confucian philosophy, he had a powerful disdain for Confucian scholars, many of whom he cruelly persecuted. He also mixed his rewards for virtue with some gruesome punishments for crime — execution by a thousand cuts was one.

In the years that I spent at Harvard — five altogether, from 1966 to 1970 and again from 1972 to 1973 — there could be heard a resounding latter-day echo of the eighteenth-century French cult of chinoiserie. It even came with its own latter-day *objets:* high-collared silk tunics for the jet set, collections of Mao badges and Little Red Books of Mao quotations for the revolutionary true believers; Han dynasty tombstone rubbings, Manchurian rabbit's fur hats, cotton Mao jackets, and even a new kind of panacea for mankind's physical ailments, Chinese medicine. I once examined the shelf on Chinese medicine in a standard, large bookstore and found no fewer than thirteen titles on acupuncture alone, including *Acupuncture: A Layman's View, The Incredible Healing Needles, Sexual Acupuncture, Acupuncture Energy,* and *Acupuncture and You.* What made the acupuncture craze all the more ridiculous was that, in the early 1980s, China itself began to suggest that the whole thing had been a bit of a fraud. For years, one of the standard parts of the tourist trip to the magical Middle Kingdom was to witness a surgical procedure — the removal of an ovarian cyst was the most common one — during which acupuncture was the sole anesthetic. Now, Chinese journals have discreetly published articles by doctors saying that they had been forced to use acupuncture anesthetic; Chairman Mao, after all, had proclaimed it a great advance. The patients were carefully selected beforehand; they were given lots of sedatives; and, poor Maoist guinea pigs, they experienced great, intense pain.

In academic circles during these years of fascination with China, there used to be a bit of commonplace wisdom that accounted for the relatively favorable view of Chinese communism and the persistingly unfavorable view taken of the Soviet variety of the Communist system. Most Kremlinologists hated the Soviet Union; the specialists on Peking by contrast loved China. The reason for that, went the usual explanation, was that the scholars of the Soviet Union were more often than not refugees from the actual experience of communism. They had fled Russia after the revolution, often during the era of Stalin; or, in many cases, they were Eastern Europeans, Poles, Lithuanians, and others, not inclined to look favorably either on the Russians as a people or on the Soviet domination of their native lands.

Russia had been for years an imminent threat, a powerful, militaristic giant with thousands of tanks on the borders of Western Europe and bristling arrays of nuclear missiles pointed toward America. Russia, moreover, was an essentially Western civilization made up of people who had religions like our own, who wrote novels we could understand, who talked in the same language of political ideals that we ourselves used. Perhaps, by comparison with culturally distant, oriental China, it was largely for this reason that when the Soviet Union — a menace to all of us — suppressed Jews, dissidents, artists, and ethnic minorities, it struck Western sensibilities more harshly than did the suppressions in China. There is, I believe, racism in this, an unconscious and unexamined inclination to see the imprisonment of a writer in Russia as more of an assault against human dignity than the exile of a Chinese intellectual to a forced labor camp in northern Manchuria.

The people who studied China had only in rare cases escaped from the region of their study. They were by and large gentle, scholarly men who had grown up in China as missionaries before the revolution, or who had lived as students with servants around courtyards in Peking, or who went there as liberators from the Japanese occupation during World War II. The younger generation that these founders of sinology nurtured — of which I was a member — had for years no direct contact with China at all. For them, the place had a magical quality. It existed in books. It was a fascinating abstraction. To study it was a kind of intellectual game, such as that played by the greatest master of translation into English of both Chinese and Japanese literature: Arthur Waley mastered oriental languages as few foreigners ever have but never once in his life set foot in China or Japan itself.

True, there were some now nearly forgotten years when what was called "Red" China was thought to be a grave threat, linked to the even graver threat of the Soviet Union. The Korean and Vietnamese wars were both fought with the expansionist hordes of brainwashed Communist Chinese very much in mind. For some, like *Time* magazine founder Henry Luce, who was born in China of missionary parents, the fall of that beloved country to Communist rule was the source of eternal chagrin and regret. More than any single factor, the much mourned "loss" of China to communism generated the McCarthy witch-hunts of the early 1950s, when many of the best sinologists in the United States were inexcusably and brutally persecuted. Much later, in the mid-1960s, there was still plenty of animosity against the Red peril, still plenty of well-organized support for the Nationalist party on Taiwan as the sole legitimate government of all China. Even so, by then the tide was already turning. As the post–Nixon trip explosion of interest in China showed so graphically only a few years later, the American public was by and large ready to forgive and forget the unpleasantness of the past and to restore the friendliness of the pre-Communist era — this particularly as China showed itself to be much less a threat to American security and much more the poor, struggling giant in need of help that it is.

Once, in the mid-1970s, I visited the home of a prominent northeastern senator who, along with his wife and family, had just finished a brief sojourn in China. The senator confined himself to political-economic observations along the lines that while China had not made much headway in industry, its age-old agony of agricultural production had largely been solved. That, we now know, was not entirely correct, though it was understandable and even intelligent as an observation at the time. His wife's version of China, however, was far more interesting. She couldn't get over the people. "They're so warm," she gushed. "They've created a whole new way of dealing with one another. They have," she went on rhapsodically, "eliminated hatred from the human heart. I would love to have a chance to live there."

Clearly, it was a benevolent impulse on the part of the senator's wife to find in the Chinese an eradication of hatred from the human heart. Similarly, the search for wisdom, for exotic charms, for startling comparisons with the awful Chinese past — all these habits of mind of Western travelers in China spring from such goodwilled cultural relativism that it is hard to feel anger for them. One phenomenon of the period of China rediscovery was what might be called the rhapsody in pictures. Professional photographers, and amateurs suddenly turned professional after their voyages to China, began to turn out coffee-table volumes that showed the country in all its glossy charm and few of its horrors. Adorable kindergarten tots and sturdy peasants in terraced rice fields were the subjects of this parade of photographers, who dutifully shot what they were allowed to see by their Travel Service guides. There were Uighur girls in colorful costumes lying in the midst of vast grassy plains; there were character shots of old men and women who had really seen life. One favorite was of fishing boats casting eerie lights into the Li River of Guangxi Province while behind towered the spectacular mountains of Guilin. And, of course, there were such other standbys as the "barefoot doctor" administering treatment to robust-looking commune members, urban crowds doing slow-motion *tai ji quan* exercises in the misty air of early morning, laboratory technicians peering intently at test tubes. It is not that these images are false. It is, rather, that they are only a small part of the truth. A photographer or an editor selects photographs that reflect their underlying concepts. Nobody who visited Stalin's Russia or Hitler's Germany would have been satisfied to take pictures of fishing boats with mountain backdrops or of kindergarten children, who are, no doubt, as cute in Germany or the Soviet Union as they are in China. And yet, in the case of China, the photographers, like those other Western pilgrims to the revolutionary wonderland, seemed to be driven by a benevolent, but wrongheaded, quest for the good China, rather than the real China.

The senator's wife and the picture takers who went to China after 1972 failed to realize that only a few years before, during the Cultural Revolution, the country had gone on a wild rampage of hate and irrationality, in which millions had been unjustly imprisoned or murdered. China, like the Soviet Union, was a place where hundreds of thousands, perhaps millions, were dispatched to labor reform camps in the cold and sparsely inhabited regions of the country. Where, in these Westerners' conceptions of the country, was the massacre of China's once great culture, the mind-numbing repetitiveness of the propaganda machine, or even the stout generals and senior officials who ride like banana-republic dictators in their huge black limousines? Just at the time that the senator's wife was proclaiming the withering away of human hatred, a courageous young dissident in Guangdong Province named Li Zhengtian was jailed after writing about what he called "the realities of lawlessness and recklessness, the gangsterism and killings, the kidnapping of males and the molesting of females, and the total rejection of the rule of law."

It is possible that the adoring cardboard images of China, both contemporary and historical, tell us more about ourselves than they do about the Chinese. Voltaire was looking for a philosopher king and he thought he had found him in Emperor Qianlong, a man who was one of the great monarchs of world history but both more and less than what Voltaire hoped for in a philosopher king. In the 1970s, the West was caught up in its own sort of despair, and China from afar looked like an unspoiled society that was free of the crime, the dropouts, the crass materialists and spoiled brats of the West. It seemed to be a country fired by a mission of self-recovery. When James Reston went there for the first time in 1972, he compared China's discipline and orderliness to what he called "the hairy costume party" of the youths back home. The Chinese, he said, accepting the illusion of a great unanimity among the people, were "engaged in one vast cooperative barn raising." China inspired the wishful thinking of all sorts of romantics, including some whose romanticism seemed capable of inspiration only by China and nothing else. When former French Minister of Justice Alain Peyrefitte went to China in 1973, he wrote a 419-page book, a runaway best-seller in France, based on his visit of a few short weeks and called *When China Awakes*. It was filled with just about every half-baked cliché capable of being generated by a little bit of knowledge. "I should like," he says in his opening chapter, "to help the reader understand how the oldest civilization in the world is striving — by passing through a period of great turmoil — to become the newest."*

Here, in one brief phrase, are all the grand notions, all the elements of that satisfying vision that places the Chinese into some gigantesque homiletic mural of the imagination. There is the Grand Sweep of Time, China as the world's oldest civilization, which can then be contrasted with that

* Reston quote cited in Sheila Johnson, "To China with Love," *Commentary*, June 1973, p. 37. Alain Peyrefitte, *The Chinese: Portrait of a People*, p. 5 (Indianapolis: Bobbs-Merrill, 1977), translated by Graham Webb from *Quand la Chine s'éveillera* (When China Awakes).

opposing concept, so well understood by the purveyors of washing suds and toothpaste, the concept of the New. There will be a new, improved, and totally different China, a transformed nation. Then there is the wonderfully romanticized idea of "passing through a period of great turmoil," the notion that out of the revolutionary crucible, from the ashes of the old will rise a transformed phoenix. How ironic that Peyrefitte, the very epitome of bourgeois France, could so admire a China remade in the image of Mao when, in all probability, he would not welcome a similarly sanguinary transformation were it to take place in France.

What are these grand notions compared to the Chinese reality? What is true in the conventional wisdom about China: that, yes, it was not very free but that it had made staggering strides in shaking off its age-old poverty and was advancing at breakneck speed toward great power status? At the very least, even if you rejected the silly sentimentality of the senator's wife or the equally silly *grandes illusions* of Alain Peyrefitte, there was reason to believe many favorable things about China. Maoism did seem to have brought considerable material benefits to the Chinese people. It had eliminated some of the worst injustices of what had been a very antidemocratic, hierarchical society.

Or had it? During the course of the 1970s, I began to doubt even the more reasonable claims made on China's behalf by Western analysts and visitors. During that period, there was too much countervailing information to be ignored. There were rumors of the terrible destructiveness of the Cultural Revolution. There were thousands of refugees in Hong Kong who had risked their lives to escape from China by swimming. I met some of them during my visits to Hong Kong between 1971 and 1979 and they told tales of astonishing poverty, of horrific abuses of power by local party despots, of ruined lives, sadness, tyrannical political control. Still, thinking about China remained a little like deliberating on the dark side of the moon or speculating on the possibility of life in other solar systems. It was impossible to know. Until, finally, in March and April 1972, just weeks after the breakthrough Nixon visit to Peking, I was able to make my own first trip to the fabled Kingdom of Mao. After that, almost any easy generalization about the country became for me well-nigh impossible.

I spent five weeks in the country on my first trip, in the company of another of the inevitable China tour groups, made up this time of graduate students from various American universities. We traveled (soft sleeper, of course) from Canton in the south to Manchuria in the northeast. We paid the *de rigueur* calls on such revolutionary shrines as Mao's birthplace in Hunan Province, lived in very simple peasant homes in Henan, sleeping on straw mattresses atop the north China brick platform called the *kang*, eating an unvarying diet of gluey, leadlike dumplings and sweet potatoes, and not bathing for a week. As one of the early student groups to go to China, we were even granted an audience with the revered Chou En-lai, who served us green tea and French cakes and asked us questions in the Great Hall of the People from about midnight to 5:00 A.M., working hours for him.

Of course, I was impressed, and I wrote a now somewhat embarrassing series of articles about the trip for the *Washington Post*, my first published stories on China. And yet, despite the friendly people, the superb hospitality, and the expressions of revolutionary enthusiasm from every corner, what disturbed me was the stage-setting quality of the experience. It was hard to tell whether the China that we were carefully guided through corresponded to reality or whether we had seen only meticulously constructed but misleading models; whether the people were real people or had been called up by the millions from central casting. I remember one incident in particular, a long talk with a history professor at Wuhan University in Hubei Province, a man who had, before "the liberation," gone to Harvard. He seemed sincere as he expressed his support for the party and the Cultural Revolution, and for the policy by which professors like him were sent for years to do hard physical labor on collective farms so they could, as he put it, "stand on the side of the masses." Yet, while the words (or was it the script?) were perfect, the old professor expressed these alleged happy convictions with such nervous timidity, such irrepressible sadness, that even at the time I regarded his life in China as a thinly veiled tragedy. A few years later I thought of the history professor when a story began making its way around journalistic circles after Vice-premier Deng Xiaoping took his celebrated trip to the United States in 1979. According to this tale, an American actress breathlessly told Deng how impressed she had been on her visit to China sometime before, when an old Chinese scholar reported to her on the joys of doing physical labor alongside the peasants. Deng, who had been twice purged and twice returned to power, mercilessly replied, "He was lying."

The story may be apocryphal. But it suggests well some important things about the China of 1972. On my trip there that year, it was troubling, not inspiring, to hear people attribute everything good to the study of Mao's supposedly brilliant "thoughts." It was simply not credible that people disclaimed any personal ambition and repeated with numbing predictability the same approved phrases in places thousands of miles apart. If you asked a student what he wanted to do after he graduated, his reply inevitably was: "Whatever the state requires of me." Ask someone else how he liked to spend his free time and the answer had something to do with studying the works of Chairman Mao. Ask a man what he was look-

ing for in a woman and he would reply: "A good ideological outlook."
They were all lying. When I used to tell Chinese in 1980 and 1981 that I
had gathered my first impressions of their country in 1972, they generally
responded that I must have gathered the wrong impressions.

The most suspicious aspect of traveling in China in those days was the
complete absence of spontaneous contact with any Chinese people. Diplomats I met in Peking on that trip complained that they were losing their
Chinese language skills because they had nobody to talk to. Even trying
to stop somebody on the street to ask directions was likely to produce an
embarrassed evasion, an awkward quickening of the step, or, perhaps, a
nod in the direction of a police box as the appropriate place to get the desired information. I found this palpable terror on the part of the local
people both astonishing and inexplicable. I decided to try a little experiment. In other Chinese places — Taiwan, Singapore, Hong Kong — I
used often to eat my meals in the simple, casual noodle restaurants that
those places have in great abundance. I had almost never failed to get a
warm and hospitable reception from my fellow diners, especially when I
demonstrated to them the efforts I was making to learn their language.
But when I tried to do the same thing in Peking, I initiated only a memo-
rably disturbing experience.

At about 5:30 P.M. (the Chinese dine early), I set off from my hotel
and, after a considerable search, found a noodle shop (the first lesson of
this expedition was how few restaurants there were at all). This restaurant consisted of a modestly sized room with eight long tables, each capable of accommodating ten or twelve people. The customer stood on line,
placed his order at the counter, paid, and then sat down to wait for one of
the staff at the restaurant to serve the meal. I followed this procedure and
then, filled with the milk of human kindness, ready to exchange a few
pleasantries in the furtherance of Sino-American friendship, sat down at a
table with some five or six others. Within about one minute, all of the
people at my table had quickly gobbled down their noodles in desperate
haste as if they had all suddenly remembered a terribly important appointment. I was left in awkward and embarrassed isolation, not knowing
whether it would be better simply to leave without eating or to tough it
out and stay. I stayed. The restaurant filled up. People were standing,
waiting for seats. It took an excruciating length of time for them to deliver
my humble bowl of noodles. When finally they arrived, I wolfed them
down, sitting at my table in unwanted solitary splendor while dozens of
people stood silently and watched until I finished. Then I fled.

That experience provided more than intense embarrassment. It was
also my first confrontation with an inevitable aspect of the foreigner's lot
in China. Official Chinese are gracious, civilized, hospitable: they over-

whelm the foreign visitor with the warmth of their reception, with their scrupulous attention to detail, with their ready smiles and good humor. Yet, they also want to place us, the outsiders, in positions where it will be hard, if not impossible, to find out many things about them. To some extent, this national reclusiveness, this desire to remain unknown, has its roots in history. But the tendency had, at the time of my 1972 visit, been intensified to the point of absurdity by the country's Communist government, so that virtually any private contact was avoided as a dread menace by the average person.

My noodle-shop experience provided me with an important example of China's controlled secretiveness. Thus, when I went back on subsequent trips, and particularly when I came to be stationed at Peking as a reporter, it was pleasant to see that the totalistic nature of the country's exclusiveness was slowly becoming a thing of the past. To be sure, the regime still felt uncomfortable about nonofficial contacts between foreigners and Chinese, and many private citizens remained understandably cautious about friendships with outsiders. Yet, at the same time, by the late 1970s and early 1980s, I discovered that, while difficult, it was nonetheless becoming possible to have real conversations, unhindered by the presence of some smooth-faced functionary from a government ministry. People began to talk believably. They began to neglect Chairman Mao, politics, serving the people, as they expressed individual hopes, aspirations, disappointments. The cacophony of real life became audible above the droning, monotonous Muzak of the regime. It was possible to learn something of the Chinese, to sense real life shimmering just beneath the highly polished surfaces of the propaganda. When I arrived in Sichuan in 1979 — knowing that I would soon come to China as a permanent resident — I wanted to take full advantage of the new opportunity, to begin to know what I didn't know. Chungking was a good place to start.

3

The Proletariat–Imperial Style

FROM THE TEEMING, grimy station platform, we were taken to two Japanese-made minibuses, which the China Travel Service seemed to have bought by the score to provide transportation for the thousands of tourists who were expected to arrive in China in the years ahead. We drove through hilly streets, lined by the usual low-slung buildings of weather-beaten concrete, the drab and always somewhat aimless strolling crowd in blues and greens, the ramshackle department store, the movie theater, a series of advertising posters — new since the fall of the Gang of Four — colorfully publicizing a spy film and some local products like fountain pens, rubber gloves, Maxam-brand toothpaste. And then, looming out of the still misty morning, there was a gigantic, multicolored circular building crowning the summit of one of the city's hills. A central, domed portion was a replica of Peking's lovely Temple of Heaven, but larger and with none of the Ming dynasty building's proportioned delicacy and grace. It was a bad, swollen copy. Two immense wings of imperial red and jade green extended outward from the round central portion, like a Chinese version of the Capitol in Washington. The middle of the building was a vast multitiered meeting hall used mainly for party congresses and mass meetings. The right wing was the People's Hotel, where our group of twenty-two would be staying.

The entire complex was like a time capsule of the mid-1950s, combining as it did a Chinese architectural cliché with Soviet-inspired gigantism. It was large; it was showy; it was what might be called Proletarian-Imperial and it dominated Chungking as cathedrals used to dominate muddy medieval European villages. It was, I guessed, inspired by a very similar building, constructed a couple of years before it, the Sun Yat-sen Memorial Hall in Canton. And it contained some of the same disappointments. On another trip just a year before coming to Chungking, I attended a concert at the Sun Yat-sen hall. From the outside, it is the same: a large, circular, domed structure in Temple of Heaven hues, better proportioned than the People's Hotel in Chungking. Inside it is unkempt and unmaintained, with chipped cement walls, naked light bulbs hanging from the ceiling, grimy concrete floors, ancient, hard, well-worn, wooden-slatted seats, a strong odor mixing dust and stale sweat and age and neglect.

In fact, that is the smell of China's cities, dust and sweat and age and an admixture of smoke from a thousand tiny braziers fired by coal-dust briquettes that are themselves stamped in absolutely satanic-looking workshops found in the small alleys of many neighborhoods. One of the overwhelming impressions of China is of a country that maintains itself very badly, where dilapidation is near rampant, where paint and whitewash seem never to be applied to surfaces worn and streaked and crumbling from the years, where things break and are never repaired, where they are allowed to remain uncared-for and filthy for years. A prolonged experience in China teaches that the old anti-Soviet symbol, the leaky toilet, that infernal, infuriating contraption with the cracked plastic seat that gurgles and drips drips drips all night, at times not flushing at all, is an apt metaphor for socialism. After months and years in China, I have myself become something of an expert in the dank interiors of Chinese toilet tanks, of deft repairs or manipulations of the levers and plungers whose unattended malfunction is causing the leak.

It is important to note that the vast majority of the people for whom the People's Hotel is named do not have flush toilets at all. In some places where, after 1978, Americans began to teach in Chinese schools, they discovered that they were blessed with one of the few modern sanitation facilities in town. In the countryside, most Chinese have slit trenches lined by stones and usually situated in some rear courtyard, surrounded by a not very high mud wall, from which the night soil, as the accumulation of feces there is called, is collected for recycling on the fields. In the cities they have common facilities down the lane or around the corner from residential blocks. In the spirit of thorough investigation, I have looked into several such facilities for men (the ones for women are next door). Along the wall there will be a long, filthy concrete urinal that seems never to have been cleaned. Elsewhere, often running through the center, is a row or two of open, unpartitioned latrines, squatted over by the young, the middle-aged, and the old, who grunt through their exertions in total, unaesthetic, and apparently unembarrassed, nonprivacy.

Of course, the smell of these places is awful. It is, in fact, quite asphyx-iating to the uninitiated. But it is the smell of almost any impoverished society, the rank odor of almost any place that has not yet been suffi-ciently industrialized for flush toilets to become a normal part of life. In-door plumbing is the preserve of the tiny minority in China — and of the pampered foreigners.

Once, on a later visit to Chungking, I asked to see the old wartime American embassy. I was taken by my China Travel Service guide to a building that was not what I was looking for — since I knew from my history books that it was on the other side of the river from Chungking proper — but that nonetheless may at one time or another have been used by the American government. It was a large, two-story building that now served as the research unit of Chungking's best hospital. It was a sham-bles of broken windows, chipped and unpainted walls, and grimy wooden floors, looking much more like an abandoned warehouse than a medical research laboratory. One room, cruelly labeled a "clean room," was piled with pieces of broken furniture and old dust-covered volumes of Ameri-can medical journals.

Not all buildings are in such a sorry state as that classic example, but almost all of them — airports and train stations, hotels and hospitals, kin-dergartens and textile mills — seem to suffer to one degree or another from a lack of basic maintenance.

This inattention is puzzling, if only because inattention in general and to economic matters in particular is decidedly not a characteristic of Chi-nese socialism. Indeed, the economy of urban Sichuan, like that of most places in China, has received near constant scrutiny, attention, and con-cern from central leaders and their provincial appointees for the entire three decades of Communist rule. The results of this attention are often impressive. Chungking when the Communists took over in 1949 was in every sense an economic backwater, ravaged by the Japanese bombings of the long Asian war, equipped with, at best, only the rudiments of an in-dustrial infrastructure. Now, there is an impressive bridge across the Yangtse River (one of the most difficult rivers in the world to build across because of the swift currents and silt deposits). There is an impressive array of industries from cotton spinning to tractors to seamless steel tub-ing. From 1949 to 1979, Sichuan Province as a whole increased its indus-trial output by 1500 percent — from about one billion to fifteen billion dollars — while Chungking itself was, when I was there in 1979, clearly in the midst of a construction boom. From that balcony of concrete and lacquer at the People's Hotel, I could count a good dozen and a half large cranes, each of them peering down on a slowly rising edifice of bricks or concrete.

Given this elaborate attention to building things, the lack of maintenance is even more of a puzzle, though there are a number of often expressed possible reasons, most of them having to do with the nature of socialism itself: its insufficient incentives and rewards, its bureaucratic listlessness, the fact that the people in charge got to their positions by manipulating the levers of political power, not by showing practical economic skills. But whatever the case, the People's Hotel in Chungking was a good example of the phenomenon of neglect. Its ornate balconies lined by black lacquer offered a splendid view of the city, including, down below and directly in front at a distance of about half a mile, a recently demolished building that had once been the presidential office-in-exile during the anti-Japanese war of Generalissimo Chiang Kai-shek — though on the road leading up to the hotel, half hidden by underbrush, was a pile of rusting steel junk. Inside, it was lugubriously quiet, the gleam of the hotel's lacquered exterior brilliance belied by dinginess. In a building of that splendor, fabulous carpets and rich, polished wood would have been appropriate. Yet, it seemed as though the Chinese designers of the hotel had contented themselves with getting the gross features right but few of the details. Floors were utilitarian and unaesthetic concrete. The rooms were shabby, the curtains smelled of mildew; they seemed never to have been washed. The bathroom tiles were stained. A layer of grime coated the windowpanes. Prissy little pink-shaded lamps adorned the room (as they do most hotel rooms), equipped with twenty-five-watt bulbs guaranteed to induce eyestrain if you tried to read at night. Corridors and staircases were dim and gloomy. Tin pails with filthy mops stood before the closed door of the maids' closets. We had been brought directly to our rooms by the Travel Service guides and no service personnel were about. The place was empty, still; it was like moving into a once grand but now abandoned, neglected, misused mansion of the sort that abound in gothic mysteries or Transylvanian thrillers.

A year later, I stayed again at the People's Hotel, and, while most of it remained the same, this time a reception desk and souvenir shop had been created in the bottom center of the hotel wing. That was a welcome addition, a sign that more guests were anticipated, which was in itself indicative of China's opening to the outside world. But that first time, in the fall of 1979, the People's Hotel reflected a great deal about the state of China in the early days of Sino-American normalization. Here was *the* hotel in a city of three million that for eight years had been the national capital, and it was eerily empty. Like those equally empty tarmacs with one or two Soviet-built Ilyushin 18's or British Tridents that one finds at such once bustling airports as those in Canton and Shanghai, the People's Hotel was a garish reminder of China's self-imposed isolation, the country's willful removal of itself from the crosscurrents of the international world. The bare tracts of airport asphalt, the depopulated lodgings, the empty, echoing for-foreigners-only handicrafts emporiums that had to be specially opened as each customer arrived — these were the artifacts of the Maoist attitudes to the rest of the world that Peking was slowly trying to change.

The hotel in Chungking also exemplified still another feature related to the country's long isolation, namely, that in most public buildings — hotels, government offices, hospitals, and the like — there is rarely any sort of central focal point to orient the newcomer; there is no obvious place to announce your presence, state your business, or ask how to find someone. Outside, at the far gate, there will often be an unsmiling, uniformed, armed guard of the People's Liberation Army whose main function seems to be to stare suspiciously, perhaps ask your nationality and your profession before waving you inside. It is a common occurrence to have made an appointment with somebody — say, at a major newspaper like the *People's Daily* in Peking — and then, once past the P.L.A. guard, to wander through empty foyers and dim corridors until, by chance, you bump into somebody who can tell you where to go for your meeting. The absence of reception desks derives from the fact that in China there is virtually no provision for the wayward voyager, the person who arrives alone or, even less usual, without advance notification. One is expected to arrive in the company and under the supervision of somebody who belongs, a "responsible person" who already knows the way and who has made all the arrangements beforehand.

The result for the Western visitor is a sensation of formlessness, a feeling of organizational disarray. On that first visit to the People's Hotel in Chungking, after being installed in my room by my Travel Service guide, I ventured out in search, one, of a bit of breakfast, and two, of someplace where I could send a cable informing *Time*'s Hong Kong bureau of my whereabouts. There was no breakfast — that need apparently having been theoretically satisfied by the icy eggs of the train hours before. The dining room doors were locked shut. Giving up on breakfast, I began to search for some sort of office where I could send my cable. The hotel seemed entirely empty. I wandered into its central, domed portion thinking that that would be a logical place to find, if not a reception desk, at least a service person or two, but instead, I discovered the cavernous, seedy cathedral of a meeting hall, absolutely empty and echoing loudly with my footsteps. Finally, I bumped into a man who seemed to belong to the hotel and, after asking him for the reception area, was directed down several flights of stairs into a gloomy, subterranean passage.

Deep in the bowels of the hotel, I came across a tiny, untidy office with three or four attendants sprawled out on chairs drinking tea. This, it seemed, was the reception room and the cable office and the billing room and the place where you could make long-distance telephone calls or even buy bottles of iced Sichuan beer. I stated my business and the attendants rummaged through heaps of paper in desk drawers to produce a cable form for me. I needed the hotel phone number to put into the cable and this request produced among the attendants a long consultation in the Sichuanese dialect before the desired information was finally procured. It often happens in China that what you expect to be the most ordinary request generates long moments of confusion, whispered conferences, episodes of indecision as though the people to whom you have made the request are facing some challenging and unprecedented situation. At last, they found a form and I gave them my text, made some conversation about what there was to do in Chungking, and departed, not at all confident that my telegram would ever arrive. But in this, I was wrong. It did.

4

Shang jie kan re nao

CHUNGKING HAS EVERYTHING that other Chinese cities have but with an elaborate, Byzantine quality that suggests more than most cities some of the romance of the mysterious East. Perched on bluffs overlooking the confluence of the Jialing and the mighty Yangtse, the city is layered like drawings showing architectural elevations. Roads wind up hills and through tunnels. Above and below the main streets are twisting narrow lanes that make their way past a disorderly mosaic of two- and three-story houses of stone, wood, and rusted tin sheeting. The houses lean, pitch, and roll in all directions as if bobbing on the surface of the sea. Inside the lanes, away from the street, the blaring of truck horns and the roar of buses give way to quieter village sounds, clothing being washed, the murmur of invisible voices, babies crying and laughing, the sawing and hammering and cutting that goes on continuously around these ancient habitations. From here and there, one or the other of the great rivers makes an appearance down below through some abrupt aperture or from the edge of a lane, while the sound of foghorns and the grinding of diesel engines drifts up over the city. Winding stone staircases disappear beneath portals and make their way downward toward the water.

On our first afternoon in Chungking, I went out for a long walk with my notebook and camera in hand and, by my side, my aesthetician friend, the Italian diplomat. I started out in search of vistas and found them by the dozen, wonderfully photogenic scenes near Renmin (People's) Road — abrupt hillsides covered with random geometric arrangements of old houses. In one large lot overlooking the Jialing we came upon a construction site and at the back of that a large, sturdy, soot-blackened stone church. I made a beeline for it. At what was once the entry foyer, there were some desks covered with papers and a few people sitting at them. "This is not a place for visiting," said an officious young man of about thirty. "Go away." I tried a gentle remonstrance. "Can't we just take a quick look inside?" I pleaded. The answer was a firm no, so I began to withdraw in defeat.

But the diplomat was not burdened by any knowledge of Chinese. While I was retreating, he was bestowing Latin charm on the other office workers and exploring the foyer itself, casting an observant eye over portals, walls, desks, paper, people. The women giggled. The men — all but the officious one — smiled. The diplomat called me back inside and together we were able to pry open the heavy main doors, which were manacled together with a metal chain, for a look into the main vault of the church.

Moist air smelling of earth and the past flowed out through the two-inch crack. Inside, dim slants of light from the high windows illuminated the bare pillars of a central apse that had died of neglect and misuse. Broken paving stones mixed with earth lay scattered over the ground, revealing here and there a shard of cracked, colored tile. I felt a sense of sorrow, of loss, while peering like a voyeur into that dank, stale chamber. Christian missionaries may have been the cutting edge of Western imperialism, as the Chinese were once fond of pointing out. I am even prepared to believe with Karl Marx that religion is the opiate of the masses. Even so, if the opiate is taken away, something needs to be put in its place. But here in Chungking this old stone building stood as mute testimony to the fact that communism prohibited without providing. If the empty church had stood in the midst of a roaring, vibrant city — lost in the folds of secular modernism, like a medieval ruin in Europe — I would have felt no sadness. I experience no nostalgia for medieval antiques. But here, it was emptiness surrounded by emptiness.

Turning back to the people in the foyer — and noticing that the officious cadre had disappeared — I learned that the church was to be restored and reopened in the months ahead, though nobody was sure when. Meanwhile, the office, which belongs to the Chungking Department of Cooperative Food Enterprises, would move to other quarters, though nobody knew exactly where.

On my second trip to Sichuan, about eight months later, I learned that, in fact, the church had been reopened, even though the entry foyer was still occupied by government functionaries from Monday to Saturday. The chapel had been swept clean. A rather chintzy altar had been built. The smell of mildew still pervaded the large hall, which was open for one mass a week on Sunday, attended by two hundred to three hundred people. There were five priests, one in his middle fifties and all the others in their seventies and eighties. The young priest, a courteous, even deferential, likable man named Liu Dungyu, ordained in 1945 at the Saint Sulpice Seminary in Kunming, talked to me in a bare little rectory situated down a narrow alley from the church. Beside him sat another man, who identified himself only as a parishioner (you almost never get to talk to anybody in China one on one; there is always somebody else who sits and listens). The priest said that proselytism was not allowed. There was no religious school or community center. The church stayed closed except for the mass on Sunday. He added: "It's hard for foreigners to understand that the government supervises the church. But the fact is that the government is really sincere in letting the Catholics and Protestants run their own affairs inside the church."

The diplomat and I left to try and find a market. We picked our way through the litter of the construction site, and stopped to take some pictures of youthful workers who were digging out the foundation of some future building with shovels, carrying out the excavated earth in baskets suspended from bamboo balancing poles. Up on the street there were a few signs of individual enterprise, mostly in the form of private sellers of tiny odds and ends like buttons and plastic watchbands. One woman tended an ancient scale on which you could weigh yourself for one fen, two-thirds of a cent. On one street directly overlooking the Yangtse, an old woman in patched blue stood beside a small table on which were arranged six plain glasses filled with amber-colored tea.

We decided to try to buy some fruit and asked some pedestrians where we could do that. The fruit market was "just down the road, over there," according to one youth who gestured westward along one of Chungking's main avenues where in the distance there seemed to be only featureless, low brick buildings lining both sides of the street. We set off in that direction and in doing so unintentionally initiated one of those quests that should be simple but in the end turn out to contain all sorts of hidden obstructions, unexpected and unsolved mysteries.

Yes, there is a fruit market, other people told us as we headed down the main street. But the market never seemed to materialize. Nonetheless, we continued to look along the wide avenue, dragging in our wake an ever growing entourage of the curious. Still we found no fruit. Someone then directed us elsewhere, to just over someplace else. Our entourage grew still larger, turning quickly from hundreds into literally thousands of people in their late teens and early twenties just moving along with us, filling up the sidewalk, pouring out into the street, blocking intersections, staring quietly, not with astonishment, certainly not with hostility, but with the slightly soporific interest of one looking at the less compelling animals in the zoo.

There were animated discussions among the people about where some fruit might be found. Along the way I noticed a candy shop and decided to satisfy a craving for chocolate that had been building for several days. I entered the shop and several hundred onlookers entered behind me. Pressed against the counter by an extraordinary weight, I bought ten bars. I had not been able to find it elsewhere and wanted to stock up, but to the onlookers it must have been an amazing purchase. It cost a bit over three yuan (two U.S. dollars) altogether, which meant that I had just spent nearly 10 percent of the average monthly industrial wage on chocolate.

The air was redolent of sweat and dust as I twisted around and leaned back against the crowd to get out to the street. It is amazing how quickly a great mass of people, all in various shades of faded blue, slip out of the consciousness as individual human beings, how you stop noticing them, and at the same time lose the sense of being observed even as you are the sole object of the attention of a crowd that has now swelled into the tens of thousands and fills the entire street. What I noticed mostly was that the diplomat was nowhere in sight, so, forgetting the fruit for a while, I asked instead, "Where is my friend?" The people in the crowd directed me first here and then there, and here and there I went, borne along by Chungking's sea of overpopulation until finally I located the Italian, surveying a state fruit shop.

What remained in my mind of that afternoon jostle through the streets of downtown Chungking was the most inescapable and sobering fact of life in China: the vastness of the country's population, the sense of this caldron of humanity spilling out onto the roadway, of this ceaseless, restless, dispirited search for something to do, particularly in a society where the implements of recreation are as much monopolies of the state as the implements of production and distribution are. In the summertime, Chungking teems; it roars; its crowds take on veritably epic dimensions. I went back late one June for another visit, this time in the company of two other Western journalists, and spent my few days there in rapt fascination at the spectacle of China's population. My recollections of evening activities in particular are overwhelmed by the pervasiveness of those restless crowds on the streets, participating in an activity that even has a name — *shang jie kan re nao* — or, idiomatically translated, "hitting the streets in search of some action."

On the first evening of our June visit, we went to the city's main square, not far from the fruit stand that I had found on my first trip.

Thousands shuffled along on the streets, their plastic sandals creating a cacophony of scratches against the pavements. Young men perched in long rows, like sparrows on telephone lines, on the curved iron railings that line the main streets. They crowded into the few, big, noisy, smoky restaurants of the city to eat bowls of hot noodles and drink bottles of warm, treacly soda pop.

We went into one such restaurant filled up with listless and yet at the same time noisy youths, packed on little stools around rickety wooden tables. A sign greeted the guest at the doors threatening fines of twenty-five yuan (seventeen dollars) and "administrative detention" by the Public Security Bureau for "disorderly behavior, fighting among the people, and infringing on the democratic rights of others." My two friends and I sat at one table, and drank the saccharine orange soda accompanied by bowls of coarse, fiery-hot noodles. The high windows of the restaurant were steamed. Ceiling fans beat uselessly against the air. The room's ocher walls were scuffed and stained. The crowds of young people, about five boys to each girl, sat and smoked or slouched over their bowls. The chopsticks were grimy. Waitresses and waiters moved slowly, like beadles among the crowd, speaking to them, it seemed rather angrily, in the Sichuan dialect.

We took a look at the little plastic suggestion book that hung on a nearby pillar. It contained praise or criticism of service people, who were indicated by number ("Number 77 and 78 are very good; the leaders should pay attention to this when it comes time for promotions"). One scrawled note complained that the red dumplings smelled bad ("You don't notice it when they're hot but you can tell when they've cooled down. This does not conform to the sanitation requirements."). We put the suggestion book back on its hook, and for the first time noticed another moral exhortation pasted up next to it: "Respect the law and the regulations. Everybody should be conscientious." That was the second law-and-order slogan we had seen, a hint that the bored youth of Chungking were sometimes prone to disorders. We saw none, but the density of the crowd, its sullen dispiritedness, had a dangerous smoldering quality, a latent tendency toward violence, especially in the humid heat of Chungking.

On the next night, we went to an open-air restaurant near the market that, operated collectively by some thirty unemployed young people, served an unseasonable hot pot. It consisted of a huge iron container placed over a gas burner and holding a rich assortment of red-pepper oil, soup broth, garlic, and great gobs of melted, viscous sesame-seed paste. Into this foaming mixture we dropped slices of pig stomach, intestine, liver, and kidney, as well as chunks of cabbage, green onions, strips of freshwater eel, and bunches of watercress, all of which we ate in steaming tropical heat to the accompaniment of warm bottled Sichuan-brand beer that we had brought ourselves from the hotel. But again, what stuck later in the memory was not the food or the sultry heat or even the few dozen local people who stood in a semicircle around us to enjoy the spectacle of foreigners eating. The drama of that evening came again from the oceanic dimensions of the crowd in the streets, from the visual and audible sense of the numberless masses of China who must be fed and clothed, educated and inoculated, entertained and housed and brought technologically into the twentieth century.

That sultry summer evening in Chungking was infused with a truly Conradian atmosphere, with the sense of being close to something awesome and unknowable. The humid streets near the market were choked with humanity, with old bent women and young bucks with long hair, with schoolgirls and P.L.A. soldiers, and ragged, grizzled peasants from the surrounding countryside in sleeveless undershirts. The main street of town extended outward and up a slight grade from a traffic circle and, except for a narrow, ragged parting in the middle for the occasional car, it too swarmed with Sichuanese. At the end of the main street were the alleys of the free market, dark, narrow, mysterious, and also dense with humanity. Peasant peddlers were seated on the ground or stood beside bicycles fixed with baskets, and tens of thousands of shoppers or browsers milled about. The crowd flowed through the broad avenues and narrow, perpendicular lanes like blood cells coursing through vessels. It undulated and spread. Most of all, it generated a mid-range roar that rose up into the air and hung over the hot city like a cloud of gas. Chungking's sound is not at all the sound of a city in the West that comes from the hum of machines and engines and the whoosh of tires on pavement. It is an entirely human sound, created only by the friction of feet and by voices, the vague, unfocused sound that fills a stadium or amphitheater as the crowd waits for some spectacle to begin. It is the sound of idleness, the sound of waiting. It is the muffled cacophony of overpopulation, of masses of people who throng the city's streets and alleys, its bright spots and its dark crevices, but who, besides escaping the airless heat of their tiny homes, really have nothing to do.

Too many people, cramped, stuffy living quarters, an enforced idleness — these are the conditions of daily life in most Chinese cities, where the phenomenon of *shang jie kan re nao* stops only from late at night until early in the morning. When I got to Peking as a resident, I used, in the summer, to walk after dinner down the *hutung*, or narrow lanes, that wind through the residential neighborhoods. The young, the old, the middle-aged, stroll through the streets. They sit on small portable chairs or on the elevated sills of the entryways smoking or talking. They play chess or read newspapers in the feeble yellow cones of light cast onto the ground by the streetlamps. They cluster, like swarming bees, around the few places that sell summer refreshments — cool yogurt in returnable crockery pots, or ices on sticks.

Every place has its own version of these long, hot summer nights as millions pour out of houses too small, too stuffy, too unventilated to endure until it is time to sleep. In Shanghai, crowds of young people mass in front of movie-house marquees, trading and scalping tickets. (In that city alone, 300,000 people go to the state-produced movies every day; as in other cities in China, they are the only readily available activity aside, perhaps, from watching television's state-produced programs.) The crowds are most conspicuous at night but they are there during the day as well, from early in the morning. Once, in the city of Kunming, in Yunnan Province, I noticed how clumps of people stood outside the doors of the for-foreigners-only antique shop, waiting to catch a glimpse of the *terra incognita* within whenever somebody opened the door to enter or to leave. In most cities, the outsides of the bookshops are places of concentrated loitering, where people form tight knots around the few who often come to sell their used volumes, their thrice-read magazines. "It is like the fruit," an intellectual in Peking once told me. "We have no better fruit so the markets can easily sell the bruised and rotten stuff. We have no better books or magazines, so whatever they put out, we read."

Perhaps my strangest experience of China's crowds took place in Amoy in coastal Fujian Province. Probably half or more of the population in Amoy has relatives overseas, so the entire region is afloat in the radios and watches, the color TVs, the imported sunglasses, the Taiwan-made shirts and musical cassettes that are brought in as gifts by these Chinese from other lands. In the middle of town, down a lane from a department store, is the resulting black market, seething with activity, most of it carried out, not so much by people buying and selling, as by the greater numbers just watching and waiting. Mean-looking teenagers loiter under ancient, crumbling columned porticoes on either side of the street. Younger kids run through the area, making skillful swipes at the wallets of passersby.

As in Chungking, when I visited this part of Amoy late one afternoon, I soon gathered behind and alongside me a huge accompanying throng that (the pernicious influence of foreign materialism?) seemed rowdier, more implicitly menacing than the one in Chungking. But what I remember most startlingly about my stay was an early morning manifestation of the search for something to occupy the mind. On my last morning in Amoy, I was out on the city's streets about 6:00, walking through quiet neighborhoods. In the small lanes, night-soil collectors with long-handled shovels were scooping up their harvest from holes in the ground. People were lining up already to buy (with ration tickets) the wheat crullers that are delivered from some central cruller plant (rather than being fried fresh on the spot as they are in other Chinese places like Taiwan and Hong Kong). By about 7:30, I found myself in the city's central square, dominated by the People's Theater, where a large, milling crowd had already gathered. As I took a look at the billboards in front of the theater entry, I could make out the sound of tinny orchestral music flowing out from someplace inside. I followed the sound through the dim entry foyer and into a huge movie hall. A silly 1940s-vintage Austrian musical about ice skaters was showing on the screen. As my eyes adjusted to the light I could make out the vague form of a head above every seat. "This showing is sold out," whispered an attendant who came over to ask me to leave. Maybe, he added helpfully, I could buy a ticket for the second show at 8:00. What time did the first show begin, I asked, nodding at the glittering image of a couple waltzing on the ice. "Six o'clock," came the reply. Six o'clock in the morning, I reminded myself, and the theater was sold out.

5

The Market
and the Malthusian Dilemma

THERE IS A BIZARRE DISCREPANCY between the mass, dispirited boredom evident on the streets of China and the epic-heroic tone of its self-description. During my several visits to Chungking, the provincial radio's reports on Sichuan were filled with more than the usual number of phrases about "holding high the great banner of Marxism-Leninism–Mao Tse-tung Thought," and doing our work with "great enthusiasm and a militant attitude." The bombastic press, drawing, as it always does, on the metaphors of guerrilla war, spoke in a vocabulary of struggle and victory, of the "front lines of production," the "fight for the Four Modernizations," the various "weapons of analysis" and "glorious revolutionary traditions." There is more here than an Orwellian degeneration of language into utter meaninglessness (though, unfortunately, there is that too). It's also as though China's leaders are hoping that the country's bare, drab circumstances can be obscured, or maybe even transformed, by melodramatic prose. For those who read about China from the outside, the constant repetition of these pumped-up clichés inevitably gives rise to images of a nation struggling as one to transform itself through some sort of cathartic violence, to become the newest thing under the sun. But the revolutionary war, which occurred thirty years ago, is one thing. Governing is another. And, in Chungking, there is a dose of dull reality about the latter in the armies of the idle and unemployed who fill the streets from morning to night. Chungking brings one face-to-face with China's great agony, its swollen, undereducated, underutilized population.

It is that simple but compelling aspect of things that also belies much of the Western romanticism about China that followed the country's rediscovery in the early 1970s. The population — combined with the trials, the errors, and the inadequacies of Chinese socialism itself — explains much about the plight of modern China and its afflictions: its unemployment, its controls, its cramped living quarters, the spare, rationed diet of the vast majority of its people. In this sense, the greatest Maoist misadventure of all was the failure to deal effectively with the slowly ticking population bomb, a failure that has annulled the country's often considerable absolute economic advances.

In the early days of Sino-American rapprochement, none other than Joe Alsop, the famous columnist and commentator who had been in Yunnan and Sichuan during the war and whose anticommunism was thought to be unshakable, went to China for a visit of a few weeks. Upon his return he wrote a series of articles for the *New York Times Magazine* in which he fairly glowed with the discovery of how wrong he had been for all those years. His main finding was that China was so well organized into its new, efficient agricultural communes that it would almost literally bury the rest of the world in grain production in just a few more years.

In fact, it didn't work out that way. Far from burying anybody in grain production, China to this day carefully rations rice and wheat, millet and sorghum at what seem to be ample but not overabundant amounts. Not surprisingly, it is a dramatic statistic about population that tells the reason why. In 1953, China took the only census of the entire Communist period. The population then was found to be 583 million — meaning that it must have been at the most 550 million when the Communists took power in 1949. Early in 1980, Peking claimed — as did most foreign demographers — that the population had gone over the one billion mark. That means that during the three decades of Communist rule, the population of the country has increased by over 450 million people, or roughly the entire current population of the United States and Western Europe combined. Today, nearly 70 percent of that immense population is under thirty, so that they are just beginning to produce babies themselves, or, in the case of 50 percent of the entire population, have not yet even reached the age of reproduction, or, in the case of many millions, not yet arrived on the already strained job market.

With that kind of population, to increase the food supply substantially, China would have had to run twice as fast just to keep up. But China didn't run twice as fast. We now know that during the years from 1959 to 1961, there was starvation on a mass scale, that many people survived on the boiled bark of trees or on rats that they searched for in the cellars and sewers. Even today, rationing remains a way of life for just about everybody. Rice is bought with little tickets. Even if you want a bowl of sweet "eight treasures" glutinous rice in a tea shop or a bowl of noodles in soup you have to hand over a postage-stamp-sized ration coupon along with your money. In early 1980, I asked a young Cantonese how many times a month he ate chicken or duck. "You ought," he replied, "to ask me how many times I eat chicken a year. Maybe once for the Spring Festival [the Chinese New Year], a second and third time to celebrate mother's and father's birthday. That's about it." A chicken or duck, when one can be found on the market, costs about four yuan, a significant chunk out of the average monthly salary.

This sort of personal testimony is acknowledged now by the government. After 1978, as Peking began retroactively to tarnish the reputation of the preceding decade, the propaganda machinery began to admit that for ten years China had been "on the brink of chaos," even though, of course, during all that time the same propaganda machine had continued its ritualistic claim that "the situation is excellent." In a startlingly truthful series of statements during 1978 and 1979, Chinese leaders began to report for the first time that, in fact, for more than twenty years, China as a whole had not fundamentally improved its agricultural standard of living. Articles in the Chinese press admitted that on some two-thirds of China's collective farms, per capita annual income was less than 75 yuan (U.S. $48), and that as many as 100 million people were not assured of enough food despite the fact that over 80 percent of the population was engaged full time in farming. Yields per hectare ranged from one-half to one-third of those normally attained in Japan, the United States, and Western Europe. "The farm situation is still serious," said Hu Qiaomu, the president of China's Academy of Social Sciences, in 1978. "In 1977, the average amount of grain per capita in the nation was the same as it was in 1955." At that same time, American government economists estimated that China's per capita income was roughly $380. Late in 1979, several Chinese leaders said that as of 1978, the per capita income was in fact less than half that figure, or roughly $150, which would have put China one hundred twenty-fifth among the nations of the world.

All of this adds up to a stunning indictment of the man who was once worshiped in China with all the fanaticism that a secular religion can generate — Communist Party Chairman Mao Tse-tung. The Communists under him at times rejected outright any kind of population-control policy until the 1970s, and when population control first became the policy, it was only hesitantly enforced. In general, Mao saw in China's population a great virtue; it excited his own romantic imaginings about the unlimited potentiality of the masses, well motivated politically to accomplish great feats of labor. In 1957, one of China's leading economists, Ma

Yinchu, at the time president of Peking University, proposed at the Fourth Session of the First National People's Congress (the representative rubber-stamp body that passes for a parliament) that a birth-control campaign become part of the mass-education curriculum. Ma, for his pains, was branded a "rightist." He was disgraced and driven from the university and remained for twenty years an object of official contempt. As late as 1974 at a world population conference in Belgrade, China's representatives angrily denounced birth-control policies as a wicked imperialist plot designed to hold down populations in the Third World, a policy that, the Chinese illogically claimed, would help to perpetuate imperialist mastery of the developing world.

It was, in fact, not until 1978 that China implemented in earnest the population-control program for which it is now famed. Its essential elements include rewards — salary bonuses and educational and housing priorities — for those couples who sign an agreement to have only one child, combined with penalties for those who have two or more. For violators of the policy, abortion has been made all but mandatory. But even if the one-child policy is successful all over China, the country's demographers say that by the year 2000, the population will "level off" at about 1.2 billion. That's 200 million people more than the population of 1980, a figure that falls not very far short of the total current population of the United States. "Because of the mistake of one man," a Chinese intellectual once told me, "we have half a billion more people than we can comfortably support. In that sense alone, Mao is our greatest tragedy."

The tragedy impinges on every aspect of day-to-day life. On that first afternoon stroll through Chungking's streets with the Italian diplomat, I had asked people if they had jobs or if they were "awaiting employment" — China's euphemism for unemployment. Nobody admitted to not having a job (or not being a student); yet, I knew that what many of them had were jobs without work. In interviews with Sichuanese officials in Chengdu, I had already been told that to soak up jobless youths, many enterprises are simply required to take on new employees and pay them salaries equivalent to fifteen to twenty-one dollars a month — whether they need new workers or not. Since there are not nearly enough state enterprises to provide jobs for all, the government in the late 1970s began first to tolerate, then to encourage, so-called collective enterprises, groups of unemployed forming small businesses and sharing their earnings. An example was that outdoor hot-pot restaurant near the market in Chungking. And then there were the thousands of free marketeers, from peasants selling eggs to the old woman near the river with her six glasses of amber-colored tea. These were the signs of a new government abandoning ideology (which had dictated that the economy should move rapidly toward higher degrees of collectivization, not toward the proliferation of private peddlers) and taking new steps to deal with the colossal population. But meanwhile, what Chungking showed was the poor and marginal nature of life for the majority, for whom the principal obsession of the everyday routine remains, as it has remained for centuries in China, the task of obtaining a sufficient amount to eat.

Take, for example, the state of the markets in Chungking. On the afternoon of that memorable stroll with my Italian friend, I finally did find some fruit for sale. There were apples and tangerines piled in shallow wooden trays in the state shop. The apples were blemished with soft patches of rot; the tangerines were tiny and wrinkled. I remember thinking that in this enormous, overpopulated city, there must be another, larger fruit market; I assumed that this one was just a neighborhood shop. Yet, when I asked people in the crowd where the principal fruit market was, the answer came back: "This is it."

Throughout China in my years there I would confirm to myself the unsettling discovery that I made in Chungking about this very small and humble aspect of life. Nice, well-kept fresh fruit is a rarity; bruised, shriveled, wormy apples, peaches, and pears are common. And the same sort of condition generally applies to the markets for meat and vegetables as well. I visited the meat and vegetable market in Chungking shortly after looking at the fruit. It was near the city's main traffic circle and consisted of several dirt-floored lanes covered by an arched corrugated-metal roof. At that time, in the fall, the market was truly abysmal, unprosperous, empty, depressing, even shocking. There were people in large numbers but there was, almost literally, nothing for them to buy. A few dozen fish, crushed and unhealthy looking, were lined up on a dirty concrete counter. The cabbages, piled up in mounds near one of the entrances, were wilted and rotting. Other concrete counters displayed a few pathetic, scrawny chickens and ducks.

It was a strange and unexpected sight, the poverty of the Chungking market, coming as it did during a burst of self-congratulatory propaganda claiming that Sichuan had experienced sensational increases in agricultural and industrial production between 1978 and 1979 — 56 percent total. According to the newspapers and radio, Sichuan in 1976 had had to import over one billion catties of grain (about 550,000 tons) from other provinces just to feed itself. By 1979, these same official reports said, it had restored its status as granary for the rest of the country even as it had diversified its crops. The situation, in short, was excellent, just as it always was according to the dependable phrasemakers of the propaganda bureaus. Why, then, this empty shell of a market? Perhaps an afternoon in fall was a bad time to judge.

The market is important, more so perhaps than we in the West, accustomed to, indeed spoiled by, our perpetually well-stocked supermarkets, often realize. The basic concern of an ordinary person in China lies far more in such things as the availability of fresh bean curd or the fattiness of the pork than it does in the power struggle in Peking or Sino-Soviet rivalry. When two Chinese from different parts of the country meet, the first likely topic of conversation is the quality of food supplies in their respective home areas. And so, while the nature of food supplies in Harbin compared to Guilin does not provide many news stories for the journalist in China, I kept my eye on the state of the markets wherever I went. It was a test of that barrage of figures by which Chinese hosts overwhelm foreign visitors. A 56 percent increase in production means nothing if the fruit fails to reach the market or if the distribution system is so slow that it is battered, bruised, and rotten when it does. True, the markets, particularly the free markets, looked marginally better when I last left China than when I first got there. Nonetheless, they remained primitive, filthy, and sad, to an extent that has to be seen to be believed. More than once I have seen in a market a pile of blackened, fungoid tomatoes or of half rotten, wormy apples and have asked the attendant if anyone is actually willing to buy them. The question usually elicits a silent accusation of interfering in the internal affairs of China.

In my own various wanderings through Asia over the past decade, I have seen many markets, from Calcutta to Hong Kong to Taipei to Manila. They are always fascinating. In Hong Kong, for example, the market presents an array of staggering culinary variety. There are neat pyramids of fresh green vegetables, mustard greens, white cabbages, Chinese broccoli, eggplants, leeks, scallions, radishes, collard greens; there are trays of onions and garlics, lotus roots, and ginger; baskets overflow with several kinds of preserved eggs; flat trays are covered with gleaming white bean curd. There are shallow pans teeming with fish, with eels, even with turtles. Sometimes there are wire cages of snakes. Shelves are lined with scores of different condiments, from pickled cabbage to olive paste to shrimp-egg sauce to fermented bean curd. There are chickens, ducks, huge hunks of pork and beef, pigeons, and even on occasion tiny rice birds or domesticated quail. The Chinese have, as everybody knows, made almost everything edible and the market displays a rather grisly assortment of intestines, stomachs, kidneys, spinal columns, chicken feet (known metaphorically as "phoenix claws"), duck tongues, even pig testicles. For the superstitious worried about sexual potency there are sea horses, snake blood, deer antlers, even so-called tiger testicles, which I strongly suspect are really the private parts of unfortunate dogs, but which are nonetheless prized in some quarters for their aphrodisiacal qualities. And, there are the delicacies: live crayfish, purple prawns swimming in tanks, freshwater crabs wrapped cruelly in bands of straw. This Chinese smorgasbord is lively and vibrant. It is crowded with shoppers possibly even fussier than the French. Chickens are executed on bloody blocks and rapidly plucked and cleaned. Fish by the thousand fall victim to skillfully wielded choppers. Hawkers shout for attention. They squabble with customers over quality or price. A dozen competing odors fill the air. In short, the market is wonderful; it is immediate, central to life, filled with color, with sounds and smells; it is abundant, ingenious, absorbing.

Not in Chungking — or, at least, while there is liveliness and fascination, there is still nothing like the abundance of other Asian markets. In the summer of 1980 I went back to the main market in Chungking to compare it to its condition of the previous autumn. I jotted down my impressions:

> Reasonable-looking chickens and ducks but skinny and in very small quantities lying on cement counter. Horribly crushed, blackened tomatoes; dirty, battered onion, unbelievably bad corn — looks like the rats got to most of it before it reached here. A large heap of eggplant on earthen floor, have to pick through it carefully to find a few good ones. Not bad squash. Fish not fresh, frozen in large blocks and put on counters to thaw and crumble. Good bean curd, pork in adequate quantities but very fatty. No rationing for the pork but long lines. Great abundance of small black freshwater eels squirming in enamel pots and slaughtered with stabs of ice picks to the head (like Trotski). Overall impression: better, livelier than before but seedy, squalid. Why do they heap perishable vegetables up on the floor? Obvious supply and storage problems.

On the periphery of the state market in Chungking, as was becoming common all over China, there was a multitude of small-scale free-marketeering peasants who had their own supplies to sell — a wicker cage of live geese here, some eels there, shallow baskets of dried red peppers, piles of peanuts, a few tomatoes of better quality than the disgusting samples in the state market. The free market was the result of important policy changes made first in Sichuan and then during the course of 1978 and 1979 extended to the rest of the country. The new policy once again permitted, indeed encouraged, free markets, though, to guarantee that no one wax too wealthy on them, it limited peasants selling produce to what they could carry to market on one set of shoulder poles or on one bicycle. During that summer of 1980, I traveled by car some 150 miles south of Chengdu through vast stretches of farmland on the Sichuan plain. Every few miles, the sides of the roads would gradually fill up with farmers carrying their pairs of shoulder poles or wheeling bicycles piled high with produce or wicker baskets. They poured out of the fields in long single files. They trudged in from lateral paths and lanes. Eventually, as the car entered the next village, their destination would appear, an area between two buildings or pressed up against the rice fields where dozens of hawkers, their produce on the ground, competed to sell to a crush of buyers.

Traveling through the Sichuan countryside that time, and visiting the free market stalls in Chungking, I felt that an ancient pattern of life was restoring itself in China. Of course, most production still took place on the collective farms. But those peasants trudging down the road to the market, weighed down by shoulder poles, were probably doing what their ancestors had done centuries before, satisfying the needs of the rural population by selling the produce they couldn't eat themselves in some market close enough to walk to. That return to an older pattern was echoed in the central government by an overall decision to reverse the priorities that had governed Communist economics in China since 1949. Rather than concentrate on such grand industrial projects as steel mills and petrochemical works, the government decided to put first emphasis on agriculture — with light industry for consumer goods in second place and heavy industry third. Certainly they didn't intend it to mean this, but that inversion from the immediate past was a kind of restoration of the ancient economic pattern of a vast subsistence agricultural nation, where rural prosperity (and rural taxes) was the main objective of governments that, of course, were unaware of the blessings of steel mills. In that sense, Sichuan had come full circle to a renewed awareness of the fact that the economic transformation of the basic pattern of life would not be accomplished rapidly.

A look at that market in Chungking told why. Steel mills are meaningless if the state can deliver only blackened rotting tomatoes to the food stands. Chungking in the first thirty years of communism had been transformed from the major city in the southwest of China into a seedy, overgrown — and, paradoxically, somewhat industrialized — subsistence village. As China embarked on its much vaunted, pragmatic drive for the "Four Modernizations," the idea would be to transform the overgrown village back into a city.

6

Shu and Qin: Sichuan and China

CHUNGKING, MORNING OF DEPARTURE by boat nearly a thousand miles downstream to Wuhan. A 5:00 A.M. ride from the hotel to the wharf through the quiet dark streets of the city.

The vague forms of people along side of road — waiting for bus? Athletic young men in cotton shorts and sleeveless T-shirts jogging in chill, gloomy air. As always, the smell of coal smoke, penetrating, acrid.

At the dock. An immensely long staircase descending to the river. A few lights twinkling in the mist on the other side. Boats moored here and there, their electric lights casting vapors of yellow across the dusky water (this is the Jialing River, not the Yangtse). Already hundreds of people, thousands of people, all dark, barely visible forms, descend the steps, holding bags in one arm and tapping down the dark staircase with long poles held in the other. A murmuring of voices mixes with the shufflings of feet and arrhythmic tapping of a thousand poles on concrete.

We are brought to upper-deck second-class cabins, since, in a touching bit of modesty, there is nothing on the boat deemed first class. There is a contrapuntal blasting of various horns as ferries and freighters alike push through the muddy water. At the dock behind us is *East Is Red No. 33*, going all the way to Shanghai. We are *East Is Red No. 17* to Wuhan.

The sky brightens, revealing on the near bank some new concrete structures overlooking the long, broad river. Staircases appear, one leading down to the other ferry, which begins to ease out from the dock. A propaganda sign becomes visible above us — "Raise high the great banner of Mao Tse-tung Thought and advance victoriously." A chorus of throaty riverboat fog-horns rebounds over the water from one bank to the other. Loudspeakers on our boat come to life with a scratchy version of the revolutionary anthem

"Qian Jin" — "Advance." Ferry begins to move away from dock with slight trembling.

There is a great rattling of chains and winches. First, *East Is Red 33* drifts into center of river and turns downstream. Then our *East Is Red 17* swings out too, the bow sweeping 180 degrees through turbulent current to face downstream. Loudspeaker crackling with Chinese opera, cymbals and drums and shrill singing. Foghorn groans into still, heavy air. Warehouses, factories, staircases slip by. On the left, atop a brown hill, is a tall, yellow pagoda, marking the spot where we drift around left and enter the broad, mighty, muddy Yangtse.

The extraordinary interior region of China between Chungking and Wuhan, connected by the breathtaking Yangtse River Gorges, is more the China of the Western imagination than that of the Western experience. The towering cliffs, the pagodas, the small riverine villages, the site where the semilegendary King Liu Bei passed on the torch of leadership to the hero-strategist Zhuge Liang — these are part of the calendar-picture, Marco Polo image of the gorgeous East. Except for the last century and a half, foreign knowledge of China and actual experience of the place have come less from the vast interior than from the main coastal cities, like Canton, Shanghai, Tianjin. The more mercantile peoples of those areas, opened up by force to Western trade in the mid-nineteenth century, were the points of contact with the West. It was from these places that the vast majority of China's emigrants set out for New York and San Francisco, London, and Rio de Janeiro, thereby giving Westerners their impressions of China itself. But, in fact, the Chinese east had always comprised a kind of second China, a minority country in a vast land whose genuine focus was in the rural, noncommercial, subsistence interior. The hinterland was the "real" China, the vast stretches of hills and valleys that extended from the alluvial plains of the east through hundreds of miles of flat rice lands, rolling hills, oft-painted mountains, all the way west through such land-locked provinces as Hubei and Sichuan and up to the foothills of the Tibetan Himalayas.

Sichuan's history mirrors that of China itself. Indeed, it is fascinating how consistent are the nature and role played by the province as the larger nation passed through the centuries. When Sichuan was incorporated into the first, very brutish, short-lived Chinese empire, in the third century B.C., its main function was as a provider of rice to the northern capital at Changan, which is the contemporary city of Xian in Shaanxi Province. At the time Sichuan was already known as the *Tian fu zhi guo*, or storehouse of heaven. It had about four million people and between it and the capital at Changan some one thousand miles to the northeast, there must have been a mammoth overland traffic in agricultural goods. The road between Chengdu, which is now the capital of Sichuan, and Changan was then and remains now, twenty-three hundred years later, the only main road between the two points, though, of course, there is now also a railroad. I took that road a distance of thirty miles or so outside Chengdu on a misty morning once in early fall. There were a lot of army-green trucks creaking their way along in both directions but more hand-pulled carts loaded with stones or bricks or, sometimes, a pig or two, bound up in straw and being carted off to market. On one calm, small river, visible from the road, a man, outlined in rising vapors, sat in a narrow sampan with a pole and line in his hand and two fishing cormorants poised for action in the bow.

The road is a narrow two-lane affair, dusty, lined with trees, their trunks partially whitewashed. It plunges between ancient fields bordered by endless irrigation ditches. The soil is a dark, rich brown, suggesting the province's immemorial agricultural fertility. When a troupe of traveling Roman players arrived in Sichuan in A.D. 120 they found a cultivated plain already full of wheat, fruit, and vegetables and every bit as abundant as the Campania. It didn't seem to have changed all that much with the centuries. Tractors and other sorts of agricultural machinery were scarce. Teams of women now lifted water out of the irrigation ditches with long-handled buckets and scattered it over rows of vegetables. About twenty miles out of Chengdu the road passes through the so-called Three River Village (*San he cun*) with its one main street, earthen-floored homes, old men squatting in doorways smoking from thick, long, bamboo pipes. A stone archway over a stream at the north end of the village is called "appendicitis bridge," because it pinches the road and jams up the traffic. Appendicitis bridge was built in the Ming dynasty, which flourished five hundred years ago, a mere historical instant ago by Chinese standards. Before the Ming bridge, there must have been another bridge over which thousands of oxcarts hauled rice to Changan. In part the rice caravans were made more efficient by one of the chief measures imposed by that great, ruthless centralizer of power, the first emperor, Qin Shi Huang. In addition to such grandiose projects as building the Great Wall, Qin Shi Huang also standardized all axle lengths in his vast, newly united territory, so that all wheels would fall into the same ruts and the rice and other supplies could move smoothly to the capital.

Until its conquest by the armies of Qin, Sichuan was an independent kingdom called Shu, which according to legend had been founded by one King Can Cong some thirty-four thousand years earlier. It was an isolated area, bounded by impassable mountains on nearly all sides. The great river, the Yangtse, that passes through Chungking roars through rugged, narrow, spectacular gorges that were eminently defensible, and that separated Shu from the neighboring state of Chu, in current Hubei Province. In fact, it would have been geographically more logical for Sichuan to have ended up a separate country. It didn't, of course, and one legend explaining the region's absorption into China is a kind of local version of the Trojan Horse story. It seems that King Hui of Qin — the state that later unified all of China — wanted to embark on a conquest of Shu. But he was confronted with the problem of moving his armies through the rugged mountains and narrow defiles that separate present-day Sichuan from Shaanxi. So the clever king had five great stone cows carved by his artisans; behind each one he placed a generous lump of gold. The story spread that that was the usual dung of these extraordinary beasts, which aroused the avarice of the people of Shu. To transport the stone cattle, they widened the paths through the mountains into roads and in so doing created an invasion route for the armies of Qin. Shu, the land of heaven on earth, became a part of the empire.

For the next twenty-five hundred years, the region alternated between periods of near independence and other periods when it belonged to the powerful, centralized dynasties of China. One of the first great officials sent to govern the province by the central government was a certain Li Bing, a kind of precursor of China's current premier, Zhao Ziyang, who, like Li, was a governor of Sichuan. Li's most extraordinary accomplishment was an irrigation work, called Dujiangyan, north of Chengdu, which today, twenty-three hundred years later, in expanded form still irrigates the fertile Chengdu Plain. Li Bing's method for creating the irrigation system was simplicity itself. In the middle reaches of the unpredictable Min River, he built an abutment and a spillway, which divided the river into two parts, an outer river intended to carry off unused water and an inner river that was subdivided into numerous canals and ditches that did the actual watering of the fields. The entrance to the inner river was made intentionally narrow, so that when, in the spring, the melting snow in the mountains would increase the flow of water to flood proportions, the inner river backed up and spilled over into the outer river, which then carried the excess water harmlessly away.

While the idea for taming the Min River was wonderfully simple, the irrigation system itself required labor on a grand scale to dig the irrigation canals and ditches that would then spread out in capillary fashion over some 600,000 hectares of the Sichuan plain. It was in organizing the necessary labor that the central Chinese government excelled — and excels to this day. There is a tendency among contemporary visitors to China to be awed by the giant labor-intensive projects that the Communist government has undertaken. Even at Dujiangyan there is for the benefit of visitors an elaborate scale model built in a dramatically darkened room, complete with green mountains and moving colored lights that show how the Communist government has expanded on the system built millennia ago by Li Bing. In fact, what the large-scale projects show is not how much has changed in China, but how little. The country has always been able to get results by organizing large numbers of people to do backbreaking labor. It is the same today.

"When the world fell into chaos, Sichuan was chaotic," goes an old Chinese proverb. "After the world became calm, Sichuan was still chaotic." Self-sufficient in food, producer of silk, gold, and coal, the magnificent kingdom of Shu, isolated from the rest of China on the other side of the Yangtse Gorges, had to be integrated into the Chinese empire if the state were to be prosperous. At the same time, its very self-sufficiency and geographical isolation made it, sometimes for hundreds of years at a stretch, a particularly recalcitrant part of the centralized state. The ancient histories of China are filled with the movements of armies, the heroes and the battles by which the central government tried to keep Sichuan, or Shu, in the imperial fold.

It took two centuries of the appropriately named Warring States period for Sichuan to be united into the Qin empire in the first place, an epoch of almost constant civil warfare among kingdoms called Qi, Chu, Yan, Han, Zhao, Wei, and Qin, which were like the nineteenth-century German principalities except much larger. For nearly four centuries Sichuan — still known as Shu — was incorporated into the empire, first the short-lived Qin and then the very enduring Han, which lasted until the third century A.D. When the Han fell, China, and Shu, entered into another period of prolonged disunity that lasted for more than sixteen generations of Chinese, most of whose members did not live beyond the age of forty. At the beginning of this period came the Three Kingdoms, one of which was Shu, led by the legendary Zhuge Liang. The disorders came to an end, finally, with the rise of the dynasty that still represents one of the highest achievements of the human genius, which in many respects China itself has never again attained. This was the glorious Tang dynasty, which lasted nearly three hundred years.

During the Tang, Sichuan, like the rest of China, became part of a vast bureaucratic state that, from the standpoint of organization, bore a disconcerting resemblance to the even more vast bureaucratic state that is today called the People's Republic of China. The province was ruled from the national capital at Changan, by far the world's biggest city at the time. Again, the wagons, their axle lengths fixed by law, creaked from the rice collection centers of Shu toward the northeast, while the central government magistrates made their stately journeys in their palanquins in the other direction.

Peace in Sichuan always came during those periods of overall *pax sinensis* when the central government was strong enough to hold the province in its administrative grip. But the empire periodically weakened. States split asunder. And Sichuan fell into hair-raising disorder, usually as some local satrap made a grab for power, eliminated his local rivals, and tried to reestablish the ancient kingdom of Shu. After the fall of the Ming dynasty in the early seventeenth century, for example, one legendary and murderous character named Zhang Xianzhong managed to set himself up in Chengdu as emperor of an independent kingdom. Zhang called his dynasty Great Harmony but he tried to achieve this harmony in a strange way. Zhang had received a vision from the gods during a visit to his temple. He had been told — or so the legend went — that he would be heaven's tool for vengeance against a sinning, worthless mankind. Two decades later, he set up his empire and went off on a killing spree that has few historical equals. Soldiers who brought back one hundred pairs of adult male hands or two hundred pairs of female or children's hands were automatically promoted to sergeant. No Confucian, Zhang Xianzhong. His contempt for scholars was such that once he lured them into the east gate of his compound on the pretext that there were to be civil service examinations; he then had them murdered at the west gate. On another occasion, he ordered prospective officials to a "Hall of Tribute" for another sort of exam. He stretched a rope four feet above the ground and killed all those too tall to pass under it. In all, before he was done in by a Ming dynasty loyalist named Yang Zhang, Zhang Xianzhong murdered an estimated one million people, which was probably at that time about 10 percent of the population.

Fortunately, homicidal maniacs of Zhang's dimension were more the exception than the rule. But the province had episodes of chaos and disorder well into the Communist period. In the nineteenth century, it was the center of the worst scourge imported by European imperialists, opium. One estimate has it that in 1926, the population of Chungking spent as much money on the drug as it did on rice. Earlier, in the nineteenth century, an American missionary figured that in the spring, one-half of the province's best arable land was given over to poppy cultivation while some 70 percent of the urban population were habitual smokers. There may be some exaggeration in these figures, but early in the century other observers said that more than twenty-six million pounds of the stuff was produced in Sichuan and over twenty million pounds consumed. A British visitor to Sichuan in the 1920s described, near Chungking, the "fields of white and purple" that were equal in number to the fields of wheat and barley. "Towards evening," he went on, "the peasants may be seen moving in the poppy fields, each armed with a short wooden handle from the ends of which protrude three and sometimes four points of brass or copper blades. Seizing a capsule, the operator inserts the points of the blades near the top of the capsule, then draws them downward to the stem. From the incisions, a creamy juice exudes."

Whatever drugs did not accomplish in Sichuan during this dark period, warlord politics did. Reverting to a kind of Warring States instability during the early years of the twentieth century, the city of Chungking alone had no fewer than twenty-eight magistrates between 1912 and 1926 while, in general, the rest of the province was virtually unencumbered by any sort of effective central-government control. The region was carved up by numerous warlords who were constantly trying to eliminate each other. "The only regret of the people," remarks one Chinese historian, "was that so few of them died in the battles they fought."

For Sichuan, and for China as a whole, this period between 1911, when the Manchu dynasty was overthrown, and 1927, when the country was reunified by the Kuomintang (Nationalist party), was the great dividing line between premodern China and the contemporary Middle Kingdom. The epoch saw the acceptance of hundreds of diverse influences from the West, some of the notions of democracy and the importance of industrialization, and the final abandonment of the imperial form of government. All kinds of modern ideas were introduced, many of them from Japan and the West, including the liberation of women, the end of the dictatorial patriarchal family, the abolition of foot-binding, the adoption of Western-style systems of law, medicine, and science. All of this was symbolized by the so-called May Fourth Movement, a tumultuous reawakening that took place in the years 1917 to 1921. It began as a student movement of outrage against Japanese encroachments on China's sovereignty — and against the weak warlord government's acceptance of that encroachment — but it ended up as a thoroughgoing reevaluation of the entirety of Chinese society. After it, the search for renewed greatness would never again center on an attempt to reinvigorate the old Confucian-imperial system, but would consist of an attempt to create something new, to adapt the dynamism of the West to Chinese circumstances.

Modern literature in China arose from the May Fourth Movement, particularly with the stories of China's greatest twentieth-century writer, Lu Xun. In Tianjin, an idealistic, extremely gifted young man named Chou En-lai founded a study group called the Reawakening Society. Thousands of young people were stirred to action by a newspaper called *New Youth*, edited by Chen Duxiu, who later became the first chairman of the Chinese Communist party. And, not least, from out of the Hunan countryside came a very handsome, very intense young peasant (depicted in later paintings dressed in an elegant, old-fashioned scholar's robe) named Mao Tse-tung. Mao came to Peking during the May Fourth Movement and absorbed Marxism-Leninism and the thrilling idea of revolutionary change. In October 1921, he and an estimated eleven others had a secret meeting in the French Concession in Shanghai and formed, with the help of Soviet Russian advisers, the Communist party of China. Mao would have a chance to put his thrilling ideas to the test.

Sichuan, while remote, was hardly unaffected by these currents of change sweeping across the rest of the country. In his classic novel *Family*, the author Ba Jin depicts young people in Chengdu anxiously, if sometimes naively, reading the various publications that made their way from the coastal cities into the interior, filled with ideas of social liberation and the remaking of Chinese society. Among those most affected — not in fiction but in real life — was a slight but determined young man from a county seat in Sichuan who would go to study in France, join the Communist party, and eventually, more than fifty years later, emerge as the most powerful man in China. His name: Deng Xiaoping.

Meanwhile, Sichuan's remoteness became something of a blessing to the Nationalist government after the outbreak of World War II. In the years when communism remained very much an illegal, beleaguered, underground movement, the country was ruled by the Kuomintang under the firm hand of Generalissimo Chiang Kai-shek. Starting from a base area in Canton, Chiang had, between 1924 and 1927, given China a hopeful new start. In temporary alliance with the Communists, and with the help of those ubiquitous Soviet advisers, Chiang had launched a military expedition that reunified the country and, though he did not entirely eliminate the warlords, he did at least bring them into a loose confederation with the central government. With its capital in Nanking, the Kuomintang inaugurated a program of modernization that, while certainly flawed by the party's own mismanagement and corruption, had more success than its present-day image would indicate. But, in 1937, the Kuomintang's program was cut short by the full-scale Japanese invasion of China. That year, the chairman of the Nationalist Chinese government, Lin Shen, arrived in Chungking by gunboat from Nanking and declared that the capital of the country would be transferred there. The move was temporary. After the war and until the Communist victory in 1949, the Nationalists would move their capital back to Nanking. But for eight years, Chungking, a seedy if exotic provincial backwater, became one of the focal points of world history. Chiang Kai-shek moved his office there. The Communists, who were theoretically united with the Kuomintang to fight the Japanese, dispatched their best diplomat, Chou En-lai, to

Chungking. He lived just outside of town at a place called Red Crag — now one of the revolutionary holy places to which tourists and other visitors are taken to pay homage. Chungking was the site of the one and only meeting ever to take place between Nationalist leader Chiang Kai-shek and Communist leader Mao Tse-tung, the latter taking the first plane flight of his life from his base area in northwestern Yanan to Chungking as part of an ill-fated American effort to mediate a settlement between the Communists and the Nationalists.

In this sense, Chungking was one pole in what the Kuomintang's leaders correctly foresaw was the ultimate struggle in China, between them and the Communists, between Chiang and Mao. And here, while Chungking's isolation preserved it from occupation by the Japanese, it had a longer-term deleterious effect. The city became a symbol of all that was wrong with the Kuomintang and, by contrast, right with its Communist enemy. Chungking was too remote from the majority of China's peasant masses. It was corrupt and decadent, inefficient, overcrowded, steamy, tired, and decayed. It came, in short, to stand for what the Kuomintang itself had in many respects come to be, what with its coteries of reactionary, greedy generals competing with one another, not to fight the Japanese, but to line their own pockets.

The other pole was Mao's base area in remote Yanan in Shaanxi Province, the place where the Communists had fled in a shambles after Kuomintang assaults had forced them to give up their base areas in central China and embark on what legend would later proclaim the Long March. If Chungking symbolized the lackluster qualities of the *ancien régime*, dry, arid, Spartan Yanan reflected the vigorous revolutionary ideas of the rising Mao.

In Yanan, Mao was able to build the base from which he would launch his drive to ultimate triumph. A peasant himself from Hunan Province, Mao had been the first major Communist figure to see that power could be seized in China by organizing the countryside into, as he put it, "a force so extraordinarily swift and violent that no power, however great, will be able to suppress it." Earlier, through the mid-1920s, the Communists had tried to organize the revolution in classic Marxist fashion, among the industrial workers of Canton, Shanghai, Wuhan, and other cities. That effort ended in disaster in 1927 when Chiang and the Kuomintang crushed the urban worker movement and forced the Communist party underground. By default, the revolutionary movement gravitated to the countryside, to Mao, and eventually, by 1935, after the Long March, to Yanan.

There, while the Kuomintang festered in the somnolent heat of Chungking, Mao forged a devastating weapon for seizing power. He capitalized on the Japanese invasion to organize vast masses of China's peasants in a way, apparently, that had never occurred to the less imaginative Kuomintang. The farmers were attracted to the Communist banner by Mao's patriotic, anti-Japanese appeal and then cemented to the cause by a modest land reform that promised a better life to the vast majority of the impoverished rural people. When the Japanese invasion was finally ended by the American victory in the Pacific, Mao was ready for the final showdown. "Talk talk, fight fight" became the slogan, as Mao both negotiated, through American mediators in Chungking, and prepared for civil war. By 1946, the talks were at an end. A three-year "war of liberation" broke out, the result of which was an easy victory for Mao. The Kuomintang fled to Taiwan, the only province of China that to this day the Communists have not seized.

The Communists took Sichuan for good in 1949 and peace was restored — at least for a while. Like the rest of the country, Sichuan enjoyed seven years of quick recovery from the twin devastations of foreign aggression and civil war, until, in 1956, it, like China as a whole, entered into a long phase of intermittent political madness that put an end to the country's progress for more than two decades. The great divide was the Hundred Flowers campaign of 1956 and the drastic purge that followed it. In this well-known episode, Peking's top leaders first determined that a loosening of controls was needed and they thus called upon the people to unleash their criticisms, to let, as Mao put it, "a hundred flowers blossom." This characteristically capricious Maoist gesture resulted, however, in such a mighty chorus of dissent that Mao himself and the rest of the top leadership (including such current luminaries as Deng Xiaoping) cracked down fiercely. The year 1957 saw the full fury of Mao's tyranny as hundreds of thousands were shipped off for periods of what, drawing on communism's inexhaustible reserve of euphemisms, was called "reform through labor."

After that, drastic mistakes alternated with desperate efforts at recovery. In 1958, Mao launched the so-called Great Leap Forward, a headstrong, romantic attempt to overcome all the country's shortages, all its problems of underdevelopment and poverty, in a single burst of energy. This was the time of the rapid collectivization of agriculture, of backyard blast furnaces, of grossly inflated statistics, and eventually of stagnation and actual starvation for a still undisclosed number of people. Finally, of course, there was the Cultural Revolution, beginning in 1966, when Mao, who had been put on the shelf after the failure of the Great Leap, stormed back with a vengeance, purging most of the officials who had earlier seized power with him, closing the schools and universities, and sending emotionally charged youths, the "Red Guards," to attack practically the entire leadership in thousands of local areas.

So extreme was the Cultural Revolution that the entire event takes on a retrospective air of unbelievability — particularly when contrasted with the relative good sense, the innate anti-extremism of the Chinese today. Yet, a random sampling of only a few of its episodes attests to its status as one of the most irrational occurrences in modern history. Every single Chinese ambassador but one was recalled from his post and made to return home to face reeducation. Tens of thousands of scientists, teachers, government officials, writers, artists, and performers were sent to specially organized labor-reform camps known euphemistically as May 7 cadre schools. Those were the lucky ones. Many others spent years in jails, including minimum-security lockups known as *niu-peng*, or cow sheds. The rich world of Chinese art was reduced to six revolutionary ballets or operas, promoted by Mao's wife Jiang Qing, and about a dozen or so poems of Mao set to syrupy music. The personality cult around Mao reached such excessive proportions that every morning workers stood in front of a portrait of the Chairman and "asked instructions" for the day; then in the evening, they made a "report" on the day's activities to the same portrait. At the Peking Zoo there was a myna bird trained to cackle "Long live Chairman Mao." People were scrupulously careful not to use any portion of the daily newspaper with Mao's picture on it for any unseemly purpose, like wrapping food or throwing away garbage. That was an act of *lèse-majesté* that could land one in jail. Nobody knows how many people died during the Cultural Revolution, but the Chinese now say hundreds of thousands, maybe more.

Even after the most violent phase of the Cultural Revolution came to an end in 1969, Chinese politics remained afflicted by a series of power struggles that, while nearly comical in their abruptness and silliness, kept the entire nation from returning to the task of development. In 1971, according to the official document released later, Defense Minister Lin Biao attempted to assassinate Mao in a coup, then died in a plane crash while trying to escape to the Soviet Union. After the Lin Biao episode, power alternated between a relatively moderate group led by Premier Chou En-lai and a group of xenophobic radicals centering on Jiang Qing. The power struggle seemed to be promoted by Mao, who had an interest in keeping any of the factions from entirely dominating the others. Mao himself became more and more a reincarnation of the absolutist emperors of the past. He withdrew into the inner recesses of his residence in the guarded Zhongnanhai compound, issuing Delphic utterances that were then plastered on the front pages of all the newspapers. One of the last of these provided legitimacy to his successor as party chairman, the little known minister of public security, Hua Guofeng. "With you in charge, I am at ease," Mao is said to have assured Hua. Mao was never seen in public after May 1976 — that is, until he was installed in the glass-topped coffin in the mausoleum that now dominates Tiananmen Square in Peking. It was only with his death in September 1976 that, for most Chinese, the Cultural Revolution finally came to an end.

As it unfolded in Sichuan, the Cultural Revolution was bloody rampage pure and simple, bloodier, in fact, than in most of the rest of the country. Rival provincial factions went after each other with knives and battering rams, sulfuric acid, DDT, firearms borrowed or stolen from the army, and, in at least one instance, double-barreled antiaircraft guns. At one point 20,000 Red Guards were held in jail in Chengdu alone, 100,000 in the province as a whole. "Sichuan is swimming in blood," read one Red Guard slogan; "the Central Committee must act."

In fact, the Communist Party Central Committee in Peking, despite being riven by its own factions, did act. It replaced one leadership with another and then with still another in a desperate attempt to restore order. Still, thousands died. In one incident conservative workers and farmers combined to kill seventy to eighty radical students in Chengdu. In another, a hundred Red Guards were buried alive by angry farmers. On the Jialing River near Chungking, two factions faced off against each other in boats. One managed to ram the other and then sat calmly by as two hundred people drowned. "If you didn't live through it yourself," I was told by a stage director in 1979, "it is impossible for you to understand how the Cultural Revolution shook our lives."

In 1968, finally, a semblance of order was restored by the army. But for the better part of the next decade, factional quarrels continued in Peking and reverberated throughout the provinces. Now, the faction that is in power, like all other factions before it, has every interest in portraying past circumstances in the worst possible light. But even leaving some room for exaggeration, it does seem as though the province was, until 1976, at times near paralysis. As in other parts of the country, the schools were closed for at least five years. When they were reopened, admission was largely accomplished by having the right connections or by being politically enthusiastic, definitely not by being academically qualified. Agricultural productivity was low. Factory managers say they lost millions because of work stoppages resulting from factional battles. There were stories that beggars went beyond the borders of the province to seek alms. One Chinese intellectual swore to me that in the county seat of Wan Xian — where the Yangtse River ferry stops on its way to Wuhan — young girls were put on sale as concubines to river travelers. Certainly, until about 1978, few foreigners were allowed to go to Sichuan, a sign that conditions there were poor and unstable.

Given its centrality, its status as the heart of the country, it seems appropriate that after this terrible epoch Sichuan turned out to be the experimental ground for the new programs promoted by China's leaders to reverse the national decline. Shortly after the fall of the radical "Gang of Four," the province was entrusted to a skilled, energetic, provincial-level bureaucrat named Zhao Ziyang, now, of course, the country's premier, but then a man who had toiled away inconspicuously in China's local-level bureaucracy — until he was purged in 1966 with the beginning of the Cultural Revolution. Zhao was restored to grace in 1972 and at the end of 1975 became governor and party secretary of Sichuan. There he began to establish himself as the main advocate of the if-it-works-it's-good nonideological school of thought.

In the countryside, Zhao raised the amount of land given over to private plots from about 6 percent to 14 percent. He favored the free markets, which, by 1980, were flourishing all over the province. Rather than have masses of people farm all land collectively, he fostered a new "responsibility system" whereby small groups, or even families and individuals, signed a contract to farm a particular plot and then kept a portion of what they produced above a certain amount. In industry, Zhao wanted enterprises to succeed by making money. He provided incentives by letting factories keep some of their profits to use as they wanted, rather than mechanically turning all earnings over to the state. Thus, while many foreign visitors had once been impressed by the workers' contempt for material incentives, now, in Sichuan, great (indeed sometimes rather incredible) leaps forward in production were proudly attributed to the ability to make money without interference from the central government.

Visits to Sichuan in the late 1970s and 1980 were tours through the new economic paradise, to factories that claimed to be increasing profits by 60, 80, 100 percent a year, to production brigades in the rich emerald-green Chengdu Plain where commune members were combining sideline occupations with collective labor to make yearly incomes of more than a thousand dollars — a staggering amount in China. It was necessary to cling to a degree of skepticism in confrontation with the avalanche of statistics that swept over the visitor, to remember that the Chinese have always made it appear that things were going very well *now*, even though they were very bad a little while ago. And, of course, there was the awesome weight of the contrary evidence: the badly stocked market, the crowded, dilapidated housing, the vast throngs of bored youth on the streets. At the very least, the problems remained grave. Still, the significance of the statistics and the relative good sense of the economic program could not be ignored. It was necessary to keep an open mind to the possibility that if good sense prevailed, some of the mass of bored young people could be put to work.

Perhaps the most impressive thing was that some people were getting over the habit of lying. On one visit to Chengdu in the fall of 1980, I was riding in a taxi with an editor of the Sichuan daily newspaper, when the car passed by a giant white statue of Mao in front of the "Revolutionary Museum" in the town's center. "We are going to tear that thing down," the journalist said abruptly, and then proceeded to give me the entire, sad history of the totem to Mao. "Originally, in the mid-1960s, we were going to build a new sports center on the edge of town. But in the Cultural Revolution the money was shifted to build that thing instead, the statue and the museum. Before, it was a park. There was a building in it that was part of a third-century palace. It was torn down to make way for the statue. The people loved the park and were very angry, but nobody had the courage to raise a voice of protest."

There are many statues in China. In Sichuan, near the town of Leshan on the Min River, I have seen what is proclaimed to be the largest of them all, a 150-foot-high Buddha carved out of a sheer cliff. That Buddha was a product of the Tang-dynasty epoch of cultural greatness of well over a millennium ago. Clearly, Buddha is a less controversial figure than Mao, less evocative of bad memories. Yet it is ironic that the Leshan Buddha should last more than one thousand years while the image of Mao was dismantled a mere four years after the Chairman's death. All of these things — the economic program, the willingness to talk (within the confines of prudence, of course), the anti-Maoist iconoclasm — seemed to be parts of a return to innate Chinese good sense, even as the era of Maoism came more and more to stand out as a great aberration. Sichuan was on a better track. Nationwide, Chinese leaders were claiming a per capita income of one thousand dollars (at current value) by the year 2000 as their goal. Everybody was wondering: Could they make it?

Can they?

If, in days gone by, one of the standard clichés heard in Maoist China involved a disdain for personal gain, a new one now was to express confidence in the ultimate superiority of the Chinese way of doing things. Early in 1980, the newspapers began to encourage the people not to lose heart, not to become demoralized or disenchanted because of the hardships and failures of the decades past. "Maintain revolutionary steadfastness" became one of the slogans; a new and better leadership having been installed in place, it was the time to prove what the propaganda called "the superiority of socialism."

There was, I felt, a strong element of self-persuasion in this new theme, or, looked at another way, a poignant admission that, while socialism may have served China badly in the past, the country was stuck with socialism for the future. To have faith that it could be made to work better was the only recourse. One article in Peking's *Guangming Daily* cited a number of common forms of popular discouragement. "We have worked hard and led plain lives for several decades," went one sample quote, "but we are still very poor. We will never succeed." The official response to this understandable bit of skepticism was that there is, unfortunately, no alternative to still more "hard work and plain living," and, anyway, "compared with capitalism, socialism is still in its early stage. It has just been put into practice. Thus it is difficult to avoid failures and setbacks." We must, the paper went on, striking the Chinese media's usual hortatory tone, "still depend on our hardworking hands to strive for realizing its superiority."

That line, like so many lines in China, became an article of mandatory faith. In 1980 and 1981, China's newspapers recognized more and more openly that the tough times of the recent past had produced a certain anomie in Chinese society and, in standard fashion, these same newspapers tried to dispel that anomie with a few heavy doses of unflinching optimism. A major front-page editorial on the subject of patriotism even declared that love of country and love of the Communist party were indivisible. This was History triumphant. Because the Communist party was, by irrefutable scientific analysis, the vanguard force of History and bound to lead the Chinese people to the brightest possible future, it was *ipso facto* treasonous to oppose it. Arguments about such dubious phenomena as state planning or the Public Security Bureau or the absence of elected officials were not simply differences of opinion. It was impossible to love capitalism or Western-style democracy and the country at the same time.

Not surprisingly, then, conversations arranged under official auspices were inevitably exercises in this mandatory optimism. In Chungking, for example, I talked in an officially arranged meeting with a couple of one-time capitalist entrepreneurs, men who had owned factories in the past, possessed chauffeur-driven cars, liveried servants, had frequently traveled abroad, and who now, after long periods of suffering and persecution, were allowed to give advice to the local government on industry and commerce and foreign trade. I asked them if they weren't discouraged by China's poor record of the recent past, if they, as former capitalists, weren't convinced that the market system with its rewards and incentives, its flexibility and speed, would provide a better solution for China than a centrally planned system. The answer, inevitably, was: "In a few years, you will see the superiority of socialism."

In Chengdu in the fall of 1980, I met with a group of university students. This consisted again of one of those officially organized meetings during which I always suspect that what is said is not entirely what is believed. In any case, as with the former entrepreneurs, I pressed the question of the alleged superiority of socialism. "Your newspapers are always repeating that phrase," I said, "but these days when you want to learn about technology or management or even music, where do you look? To the capitalist countries! When you want to send students overseas, you send them to the United States, France, West Germany, Japan, not to Yugoslavia. Can you name a socialist country that has done better than an otherwise comparable capitalist country — South Korea versus North Korea, East Germany versus West Germany, Czechoslovakia versus Austria? No, in every case the capitalist country has done better. Therefore it is fair to ask, what makes you so confident of the superiority of socialism?"

The students crowded around a table in their classroom, clearly excited to have this contact with a foreigner. They were nice kids, bright, friendly, unaffected. But their answers were clichés of the mandatory kind: "Under socialism there is no exploitation. Under socialism you are guaranteed a job for life. In China you are not at the mercy of a boss who can fire you if he doesn't like your nose." Then, echoing the optimism of the former capitalists, the students declared: "Come back in a few years and you will see the superiority of socialism."

The students, like most people in China, were blissfully ignorant of the West, or, at least, their one-sided propaganda had made them aware of the problems of the West but not of such mitigating factors as unemployment compensation, labor unions with real power, food stamps and welfare to support the poor, and, of course, the free press. But, leaving aside their view of benighted capitalism and assuming that they were saying what they really believed rather than what the school authorities wanted them to say, the interesting question was not whether socialism was superior. The question was: how, after China's long succession of failures, were they able to believe that it was?

In this sense, the students' faith — and their concern for the country — goes to the central issue of modern Chinese history. For at least 150 years, China, that great, powerful, complacent, superior, condescending, self-sufficient, and immense empire, has pondered the spectacle of its own decline. And, throughout the nineteenth century, the country's thinkers simultaneously puzzled over a series of possible solutions that, taken together, encompass most of the received ideas of the last several centuries in both China and the West. Chinese intellectuals by the mid-nineteenth century were borrowing technologically from the West and building arsenals and steamship lines and sending students abroad. This last approach, now selectively revived under the Communists, was an extraordinary step, given that China's xenophobic attitudes toward the West were so strong that it was not until the late nineteenth century that the Middle

Kingdom deigned for the first time to send an ambassador to a foreign country. But the Chinese, in any case, always remained skeptical of a solution that came from abroad. Even in the nineteenth century, the governing slogan in this regard was: "Foreign learning for practical use; Chinese learning for the essence of things."

"The superior man is concerned about what is right," said Confucius some twenty-five hundred years ago. "The petty man worries about what is profitable." The moral-political genius of the Sage exemplifies two important things about China's long search for renewal: first, that it must have a Chinese spirit, including a component of ethical quality; second, that ethics and politics are linked together in a way foreign to the West. Rule in China has for centuries been in part by state terror and by rewards and punishments, but it was always, in theory at least, mainly by the moral example set by the emperor and his officials. There is little room in this for private or personal ethics to be divorced from public morality. Government — or, put into a more contemporary context, politics — is responsible for the moral order. Thus, when Chen Duxiu, one of the most probing of China's early twentieth century intellectuals, agonized about the deplorable state of the Chinese people, bemoaning the "pit of chilly indifference, darkness, and filth into which we have fallen," he looked not so much to personal moral rearmament as the solution but to a new form of political organization. Chen railed against the Chinese for their slothfulness and their insouciance, their passivity and complacency, their uncleanliness and their uncombativeness. He called for them to become restless, dynamic, iconoclastic, and in that way find a path to the twin benefits of wealth and power that China had already lacked for a century. He made his comment about the "pit of chilly indifference" in 1920. In the next year, he irrevocably cast his die. Chen joined the fledgling Chinese Communist party and became its first chairman until, already a criminal in the eyes of the Kuomintang, he was branded a "rightist opportunist" by the Communists, who disowned him in one of their earliest struggles for power.

It was a long way from Chen Duxiu to the former capitalists in Chungking and the eager, fresh-faced students of Sichuan University, but it is amazing how similar their concerns were. For Chen, in 1920, and the students, in 1980, China's was a history of sometimes hopeful but in the end failed experiments. Under the tutelage of the Kuomintang — which tried to combine Confucian morality with Western learning in a rather puerile state philosophy embodied in the so-called New Life Movement — the Chinese made far more progress than history has generally acknowledged. Universities were created. Factories were built. Small rural reform programs were started. In the ten years of the "Nanking decade," between 1927 and 1937, China experienced one of its fastest periods of economic growth ever. But the Kuomintang program was vitiated from within by its own corruption and venality and by its failure to establish firm control over China's warlord-dominated territory. Then, when the Japanese began their attempted conquest of China in 1937, the KMT's response was docile and uncreative. While waiting for the Americans to win the war against the Japanese, it lost its own more crucial battle with the Communists for the hearts of the Chinese people.

When Mao ascended the reviewing stand in Peking's Tiananmen Square and proclaimed the People's Republic of China on October 1, 1949, the Communist party faced the most favorable situation of any Chinese government in over a hundred years. The country's external enemies had been defeated. The warlords had been finally wiped out during the Japanese war. The party enjoyed widespread prestige and enthusiastic backing by the large majority of the Chinese people. For the first time in more than a hundred years, a Chinese government could rule under conditions of internal peace and political unity. "China," Mao said that day in Tiananmen Square, "will never again be an insulted nation." It never again was, and that is not an insignificant accomplishment. But, by the Chinese' own reckoning, "success" (the word used by the Peking *Guangming Daily*) eluded it. When those students and those onetime capitalists in Sichuan displayed their confidence that it would finally be achieved, they were adding their voices to a long chorus that extended back in time beyond the likes of Chen Duxiu, beyond the Kuomintang, beyond even the forward-looking nineteenth-century imperial officials, all the way back to the initial responses to the first shocking contacts with the unmistakable material superiority of the West. Echoing down the long corridors of that history were millions of voices clamoring for a way to restore Chinese greatness, demanding, insisting that it could be done. It was the same in 1980 in Sichuan, in the heart of China and a province officially designated as a model for the rest of the country to follow. What an extraordinary irony that the fundamental issue for China had changed so little.

And here, perhaps, is one explanation for the Western fascination with China and the benevolent impulse among so many looking at China from afar to find reasons for its success: the very continuity of the nation's search for self-renewal. In the 1930s, China was an object of both Western charity and missionary zeal. Chinese greatness was an ardent Western hope. It was unrealized under the Kuomintang and during the first thirty years of Communist rule. Now, with China once again turning west, it seemed as though things had come full circle. For the first time in Communist history, the country was inviting our participation in the great historical endeavor of bringing the benefits of prosperity to the most cultivated and ancient people on earth. The challenge had returned.

But, of course, there was one big difference. Chinese experimentalism in the past could be attached to any one of several models. Governments were interested in power but they were either unwilling — or, more often, unable — to insist that all the citizens of the country subordinate their thoughts and their efforts to that government's particular outlook. The Kuomintang was an authoritarian state, but it was not so authoritarian that it could prevent its people from attaching themselves to alternatives — like the Communist party itself. Moreover, earlier Chinese governments had wanted what the Communists wanted: wealth and power. But they did not insist that their ambition was Reason itself, as embodied in History. The Communists, by contrast, are more serious, far more dogmatic. What's more, they go so far as to insist that a lack of faith in the party is a negation of the very element that binds together all those historical voices calling for China to renew itself: patriotism. Given the might of the party, it can, unlike other authoritarian governments, enforce this heavy burden on virtually every individual in society. Thus, the alternatives have been reduced to what the party decides, and it is a party that, by its own strange admission, has not decided well in the past.

And thus, back to the students at Sichuan University. After my formal, supervised meeting, I managed to talk to two or three of them outside the classroom, strolling about the campus. Outside they were refreshingly different. It is not that they were dissidents or rebels but that they had realistic worries: about the lack of choice in the curriculum or about the fact that after graduation they would be assigned by the employment bureaucracy to a job, without themselves being able to express a preference. They showed impatience and boredom with classes in Marxism-Leninism. One student told me that in the competition to be chosen to go abroad to study, flattery of the university leaders had risen to outrageous proportions.

My meeting with these students took place on my third trip to Sichuan, after I had become a resident correspondent in Peking. It happened that the editors of *Time* wanted me to go back to talk to them again and collect enough information for a story, and so I began to go through the procedures for a fourth visit to Sichuan. Since I had already been to the university, I called the foreign-affairs office there directly and spoke to a certain Zhang (the name has been changed). Zhang told me that I would be welcome to return and see any of the students I wanted. I told him that I would be there in the middle of the following week and, to that end, applied for a travel permit to the Information Department of the Foreign Ministry, making the fatal mistake of informing them of the purpose of my intended trip. A few days later, my "handler" at the Information Department, a certain Mr. Li (this name has not been changed), called to tell me that he was very sorry but the students were on a "field trip" and thus could not see me.

Skeptical, I called the university foreign-affairs office and asked to speak to Zhang. That person, it seemed, was no longer there. And, moreover, the person I did speak to confirmed that the students were indeed on a field trip. All of them? I asked. Well, most of them, came the reply, and the others were working very hard preparing for their exams. I waited a week and called again. Zhang again was not there. The students were still on a field trip. I tried yet again, another week later.

"Your students," I began, "are they still on that field trip?"

"Are you from *Time* magazine?"

"Yes."

"I'm afraid the students are not yet back."

"Aren't there any students that I could talk to?" I asked, in what I knew had to be my last try.

"The ones that are here are very busy," the man who was not Zhang announced at the other end of the line. He was unfailingly polite, unflinchingly professional. "It's not really very convenient for you to see them."

I thought about what Chen Duxiu wrote six decades ago about the questing, roving Promethean spirit that, in his view, had enabled the West to surpass the great Chinese empire. And I asked myself about those students in Sichuan who had dutifully proclaimed the superiority of socialism. Did they believe it? Did they know that I, who had been so warmly received on my visit to the university, was being prevented from talking to them again? Did they know enough about their own history to see the connections between themselves and eager, patriotic young Chinese of the past? And while, no doubt, they had heard of Chen Duxiu, did they ever have a chance to read what he himself had said about breaking the shackles of traditionalism and forging a new path for the future?

As Simon Leys pointed out in *Chinese Shadows*, the Communist party has never in its entire period of rule allowed a history of itself to be written for public consumption. I have no doubt that Leys is right when he attributes this to what would certainly be the awkward and numerous liberties with the historical record that any party chronicler would have to take to ensure that heroes remained heroes and villains stayed villains and the party itself could retain its place as the embodiment of History.

7

On the Sacred Mountain

IT IS COOL the morning after a rain in the town of Leshan, 250 miles south of Sichuan's provincial capital, Chengdu. The town's proudest feature: the towering (and rather ugly) Buddha, carved out of stone on the banks of the Min River. But far more interesting than the Buddha are the glimpses of town and country life possible on a visit to a place that is truly provincial China. In the river, barges float downstream toward the Yangtse, one hundred miles to the southeast. Ramshackle factories line both of its banks, a cement works, a boat repair yard, a chemical plant expectorating a foul effusion of gray-white pollution into the water, which then speckles the downstream eddies and currents with foam and bubbles.

The riverbanks are the same seedy collection of sheds and warehouses and jetties that can be seen in many riverine ports around the world. But away from the river, rural China reasserts itself. On the road leading north out of Leshan, wiry men in tattered blue pull flatbed carts in the shade of the plane trees that line the road. A strap fits over the shoulder; the forearms drape over the protruding handles of the cart; the body tilts forward at an extreme angle so that all its weight can be exerted against the weight behind. They pull cement slabs or eggplants, sand or bricks or fabulous piles of hay and straw, bags of rice, slaughtered pigs or live pigs, cages of chickens and ducks, or piles of black stamped-coal bricks. The observation has often been made that the sight of wiry, sinuous men straining against the shoulder straps of heavily loaded carts corresponds exactly to one of the propaganda clichés most frequently used by the

Communists to show the horrors of the old society. Never mind. The simple fact is that, given its massive amounts of labor power and its scarcities of technology and money, China cannot afford to abandon this method of hauling goods. I notice one fellow, tilted forward halfway to the ground as he drags several slabs of concrete. Above him in bold, black characters across a dilapidated brick building is a slogan: "Mechanization is the only road for agriculture."

On the outskirts of Leshan, rice fields extend up to the squat laterite hills that are themselves painstakingly terraced and planted with corn, vegetables, and mulberry trees. There is not a soul to be seen in the fields this wet morning. There is little to be done there at this time of year except to let the crops mature until the labor of sowing can be followed by the equally hard labor of reaping. It has been that way for thousands of years and, the promise of mechanization notwithstanding, it will probably continue that way for a long time to come.

This ride out of Leshan took place on my second trip to Sichuan, in the summer of 1980, after I had already taken up residence in Peking. My purpose was to see as much of the Chinese countryside as possible. In the company of guides, I visited production brigades on the Chengdu Plain and on the slopes of Mount Emei and was impressed by the difference. In the Chengdu Plain, collective peasant incomes often rose above 1000 yuan (about 650 dollars) a year. I remember one home, in the midst of a clump of persimmon and bamboo on the Golden Horse Commune, twenty miles west of Chengdu, where the family of one Hu Yuanqing had been living for four generations. It was a three-sided thatch-roofed affair surrounding a courtyard. There was a grape trestle, and a few chickens; pigs could be heard grunting nearby. Hu wore a wine-red sleeveless T-shirt and black cotton trousers rolled up above his knees. He owned a bicycle and a watch and had 300 yuan in the bank. Inside the house where he lived with his wife and child and eight collateral family members, there was a four-poster wooden bed, an earthen floor, a small transistor radio, a pile of potatoes, lots of cobwebs, a straw mattress, double happiness signs on red paper (red is the color of prosperity), a mirror, a porcelain vase, a thermos, a wicker basket, and, on a battered wooden dresser, a framed red certificate commending Hu for having achieved "wealth through diligent labor."

Questions that would be rude in the West are considered appropriate in China, where, in any case, private lives are often subjected to intense public scrutiny. So it's natural to ask Hu what his yearly income is to deserve such commendation. Together, he and his wife make five hundred yuan from the collective and another four hundred yuan raising rabbits, pigs, and chickens privately. That is a clear indication of the importance of the renewed encouragement of activity geared to the free market. Nearly half of Hu's income comes from that minor, noncollective part of his agricultural efforts. I asked Hu what he would do if he were suddenly to come into a lot of money. "I would make some improvements on the house," he said, "and buy some high-quality commodities, like a color television set."

Hu said that he was twenty-eight. He had one small daughter and agreed that, given the population control policy, he could not and should not have a second child. The house was fifty years old. It smelled of earth and mildew inside but it had plenty of picturesque charm. "It's cool in winter," Hu said, "but it easily catches fire." It turned out, though, that Hu could not build a new house in the same place as the old one because the collective was trying to clear away the sites of the thatch-roofed homes to make way for new planting. Instead, long blocks of concrete housing divided into two-story apartments had been built in what was intended to be a new village center. "If I want to build a new house," Hu said, "I have to build it according to the plan, so it would have to be an apartment. Every commune member must conform to the plan."

The new houses were charmless, barracklike structures complete with cement balconies on the second floor and pigsties for private pigs in the back. To put waste to good use, there were nearly odorless methane gas pits behind the pigsties. There was running water and electricity. The houses were sterile but dry and fireproof. They were part of a master ten-year plan depicted on a large color painting displayed in the center of the production brigade. It showed a neat quadrangle of concrete dormitories where eventually everybody would live. They surrounded a pool complete with a pavilion and a jagged causeway leading to it. There was an industrial area showing a cement factory, a silk-processing plant, a pig farm, and a storehouse. The fields, uncluttered by houses like Hu's, were divided into two zones, one for grain and the other for cash crops, mostly vegetables for sale to Chengdu. There was a meetinghouse, an elementary school, a clinic, a small pond surrounded by a white picket fence, and in the distance the brigade boundary, marked by a stream.

The painting was a visual self-conception, an image of the perfect rural life. And the brigades' leaders had organized everything so that it could be realized. Even births — indeed, especially births — were determined by the plan. During the preceding year, there had been six deaths, nine births, and four abortions (in a total brigade population of twelve hundred). Since the new stress on regulating the population, the brigade had determined the number of babies that should be produced each year and it allocated them, like ration tickets, to the couples who had no children. "They stand on line," the brigade official who showed me around admitted frankly. "We talk to all the families and decide who should have babies first. Women who get pregnant without permission must have abortions." The year before, there had been a woman with one child, a girl, who insisted on having another, hoping for a boy. She was fined three hundred yuan and told there would be no grain ration for the baby. Several meetings were held in the brigade to "criticize her," the brigade leader explained. "One of our purposes was to teach her and her husband. But we mainly wanted to give a lesson to the other people." I asked, hoping for the unfortunate woman, if at least she had succeeded in acquiring a boy. I am happy to announce that she did.

The Chengdu Plain is the kind of well-favored place likely to benefit from the agricultural experiments of the central government. The most important of these consisted in the reduced importance of "work points," the measure of labor that each person contributed to the collective, which could be converted into grain or cash. Instead, groups, or even individual families, were being assigned plots of land to farm as best they could, with the very important right to keep everything they grew beyond a fixed quota. Naturally, this program was presented in the propaganda as a victory for the true socialist line. It was, in fact, a great leap backward from the theories of socialist agriculture.

After visiting the brigade in the Chengdu Plain, I told my local guides that I also wanted to see a brigade that was, well, not so close to the city and thus more truly rural, perhaps a bit more representative, even less prosperous. And so we visited a brigade in a commune called Dragon Pond not far from Leshan in a region of rocky-soiled hills in the shadow of the sacred Buddhist mountain, Emei. I dutifully wrote down the statistics provided during the "brief introduction": 17 brigades, 156 teams, 4,054 households, 18,000 mou of cultivated land, a work force of 7,700, 4,000 buffaloes and oxen, 12,000 pigs, 400 radios (no television sets), a total grain yield of 10,660,000 catties, and so on. But among the statistics that meant something was the fact that 2 of the 17 brigades had no electricity at all, that until 1977 the commune could not provide enough grain to feed itself, that for most of the 1970s the birthrate was an alarmingly high 35.5 per thousand — so that, between 1971 and 1976, total population had gone up from 16,000 to 20,000. The commune's per capita income in 1979 was 66 yuan ($44), more than half of which was the value of the grain ration. That meant that the yearly cash income of the average commune member was about $20. Visually, moreover, the brigade looked poor, Appalachian; it suggested the bare subsistence rural economy of a country where for 20 years the average rural income had increased at the snail's pace of 1 yuan (about 65 cents) per person per year. Beginning in the valleys and trudging single file up the steep, rocky hills were peasants carrying wooden night-soil buckets on their backs to fertilize the fields. There were no roads to the upper levels of the production brigades, no way to carry fertilizer, seed, or tools into the hills, except by immemorial human labor.

Still, if the statistics are to be believed, the Dragon Pond Commune had improved its standard of living markedly since 1977 — which means, of course, that during most of the period of near religious belief among foreign friends in the great victories of Chinese socialism, the area must have groaned under the burden of grinding poverty. I believed, moreover, that things in general had improved on China's farms. In Peking in the beginning of 1981, I met a young man who was in his tenth year as a middle-level agricultural official from central China. We were introduced informally by a common friend and talked for two hours while strolling through the hilly paths of the Summer Palace. The official was smart, irreverent, tough-minded, nonideological, and without illusions about China's peasants. He described them as shrewd, calculating, and extremely conservative. He talked about the prevalence of superstition, the continued practice of such age-old customs as bride prices, geomancy, astrology, fortune-telling, disregard of female babies, and wife-beating — in other words, all of the habits and predilections that socialism was supposed to destroy. He told me the story of one woman who hanged herself after being teased sexually by some men of the village, so afraid was she that her husband would exact retribution from her because of the shame she had suffered.

But what was most interesting in what the agricultural specialist said was that the main "contradiction" (to use the standard terminology for a conflict or dispute) was not between the pragmatic leaders and the more radical ones. It was, he said, between the peasants themselves and the local officials. The central government, he explained, had pushed through the new agricultural program because all the purer socialist alternatives had been tried and had failed, because after twenty-five years of collective farming, Chinese peasants lived in disheartening poverty. There was no question, he added, that the policies of individual initiative and of the responsibility system were working and that the top leadership in Peking wanted to retain them. But the losers were the party officials at the local level who before had been able to live like "feudal lords" (his term) by raking funds off the top and basking in the status conferred by their positions. "Why," he said, "would they want to change things when they were able to lord it over the people as things were?"

Now, however, there was almost no politics at the village level. The party had lost prestige. More and more of the production was moving into the free economy and the peasants had more money. Work points were worth less and, moreover, they were handed out only for real work so that the party secretaries and the accountants were finding it necessary to go to the fields in order to maintain their living standards. The army was having trouble recruiting peasant sons because conditions on the farms had improved and the value of having sons stay at home to provide more labor power for the family had increased. Many local political leaders thus were unhappy and the peasants knew it. The peasants, given all the twists and turns, the parades and speeches, of the past, had a hard time believing that things would not change again. There were even preemptive moves by the farmers to garner as many rewards as they could while the good times lasted, such as cutting down trees for lumber before they had reached maturity out of fear that the trees would be recollectivized if they waited. The peasants had a new expression for their point of view, the man told me: give us two, three more years, so that we can feather our nests. Then you can return to your political struggles.

None of this, of course, can be observed by the foreign visitor to Chinese farms in Sichuan or anyplace else. In all of the various production brigades that I have visited over the years, never once was there any hint of the complexities, political or social, that I knew had to exist in rural China. In fact, they exist in any society, but consider the more than ordinary tumult that the hundreds of millions of Chinese peasants have endured during the thirty years of Communist rule. At the beginning of the revolution, they went through the often violent and, no doubt for many, exhilarating process of liquidating the landlords. They were losers or beneficiaries of land reform. They were divided up into categories that themselves overturned the traditional patterns of status and prestige: there were poor peasants and lower-middle peasants as well as middle peasants, rich peasants (which probably meant that they had owned a water buffalo, and perhaps had three sturdy sons and a hired laborer to stand with them knee-deep in the rice paddies), and, of course, the new condemned of the earth, the landlords. Hard upon the land reform came small-scale agricultural cooperatives, then large-scale cooperatives, then the leap headlong into full-scale collectivization. All of this took place in the space of less than ten years.

After that, the policy veered from rigid leftist to moderate rightist and back and forth again. There were private plots and free markets / there were private plots but no free markets / private plots were discouraged / private plots were approved again / free markets flourished. Trying to earn money to buy things was bad / it was essential to try to get rich. Studying the works of Chairman Mao was the key to higher production / the main element in increasing production was higher pay for more work. Liu Shaoqi was the revered head of state / Liu Shaoqi was a renegade, a traitor, a scab. Chairman Mao was China's red son / Comrade Mao made mistakes. From year to year, the central government visited upon the peasants its various experiments in social engineering. They were told to "teach" the intellectuals who came down from the city. The Red Guards came by the thousands to make revolution. The farmers built dormitories for the educated youth who descended en masse in the wake of the Cultural Revolution. They had mess halls / they abandoned the mess halls. They had loudspeakers blasting propaganda over their fields and over the graves of their ancestors from 6:00 A.M. until evening / the loudspeakers fell silent. For ten years they were told to emulate the model production brigade, Dazhai / they were informed that Dazhai was a fraud engineered by liars with statistics. Could anyone reasonably expect that these traditionalist farmers whose basic pattern of life had changed very little for centuries would not be confused? Was it possible for them not to be skeptical? It would have been amazing after all those years, in fact, if the peasants had not cast a jaundiced eye over the latest proclamations of the party, had not distrusted the party's appointed (never elected) supervisors of their lives. That was only plain common sense. What I wanted to know was, what were they able to cling to, to maintain some sort of inner stability?

My two-hour clandestine conversation with the agricultural official in Peking gave one indication. Another came in Sichuan when I least expected it: climbing the sacred Buddhist mountain of Emei. I did that on my second trip to Sichuan as a kind of touristic diversion from my main task of visiting collective farms. But I discovered during the course of the experience that it was a good way to catch hold of what seemed to be some of the verities of rural life.

Emei is covered with temples and with tens of thousands of Buddhist pilgrims visiting them. At the base of the mountain, which sweeps upward from the plains to an elevation of ten thousand feet, is the sprawling Bao Guan Monastery. When you visit the collective farms of China, you talk to tough-looking party secretaries or commune vice-directors. You see lean, hard, "advanced" peasants who talk about yields per mou, the importance of better seeds, and the advantages of socialism. In the Bao Guan Monastery the hundreds of Buddhist pilgrims preparing for the ascent of Emei mountain also came from production brigades. But they seemed to belong to a different world, the world referred to by the officials as "the old society." The courtyards of the monastery swarmed with pilgrims, aged, sturdy, weathered, dressed in black, carrying baskets on their backs. An old monk named Pu Chao said that nearly two thousand of them passed through the temple each day on the first stage of their ascent to the summit. Among them were groups of men with wispy beards and photogenic faces lined with age and experience. But far more than half were women, like the eighty-year-old Yang Guinian, who said she had come from her native village to climb the mountain every year for seven years — ever since propitiating the gods of Emei was released from its Cultural Revolutionary ban. I asked her why she climbed Emei. "Because," she said with literal-minded precision, "there is no sacred mountain in my county."

The climb was breathtaking, inspiring, replete with a spiritual component that is absent from the places where foreigners can normally go. On the slopes of Emei, at the crests of steep gorges that plunge for thousands of verdant feet downward to the rice fields below, was a richness of custom and belief that had survived ten years of strenuous, bewildering effort to stamp out "superstition" and replace it with the dry and inconsistent orthodoxy of Marxism-Leninism–Mao Tse-tung Thought. "During the Cultural Revolution, I suffered greatly because I was a Buddhist," said one old woman with a basket strapped to her back. "My house was taken over by somebody else. The images of the Buddha that I had were taken away." China's countryside has always been materially poor, but the thousands of legends and stories, ghosts and demons, magically empowered monkeys and goddesses of mercy and fertility, the semihistorical heroes and villains that populate Chinese myth — these were elements of an interior diversity and richness that compensated for material scarcity. Mao Tse-tung once said that the Chinese people were "poor and blank" and that that was good because poor people want to make revolution and "on a blank sheet of paper the most beautiful words can be written." It was a disparagement, an insult to the imagination, to have supposed that the Chinese people had ever been blank. And the devotion shown on Mount Emei disclosed that the arid "science" preferred by Mao had not eliminated the spiritual world that many Chinese continued to seek elsewhere.

Emei in June teemed with life. An unbroken stream of pilgrims made their slow, patient way to the summit, some of them carried in wooden harnesses on the backs of local commune youths for a few pennies a kilometer. There were ancient women with staffs and tiny bound feet making painful but relentless progress up the mountain slopes. At the top was a sprawling temple and barracks, built in the 1930s, to accommodate the fifteen hundred to two thousand people who arrived for lodgings each night. There was a vast, dim restaurant filled with wooden tables. At the highest point of the summit were the stone ruins of a temple that was burned, not, I was assured, by the Cultural Revolutionaries but in an accident in 1972. Yet there was one political desecration in the form of a giant steel-frame radio antenna built several years before to broadcast the precious sayings of Chairman Mao to the millions down on the plains.

In the roofless temple, people prostrated themselves before the western wall and burned incense and lucky money to send to their ancestors. The prayers were naive and direct: "I am sorry, Lord Buddha, but since I have to work hard, I only have time to come and see you once in a year. Please give me good luck and good health and I'll come back to see you again next year." In the evening, with a cool mist sweeping over the top of the mountain, several hundred people sat on the ground and took turns singing atonal Buddhist hymns, like: "We pilgrims come from afar and we see the Lord Buddha riding on the white elephant and Guanyin [the goddess of mercy] sitting on the lotus flower and the four gods guarding the temple."

I talked to one woman, about forty, who was tying a paper prayer to a piece of string near the ruined temple. She was gap-toothed, brown skinned, dressed in peasant black. She was putting small stones in her pocket, since, she explained, last year her pigs had died and this year she would carry something down from the sacred mountain to prevent it from happening again. I sought clues to her standard of living. She was from Leshan County. She had a husband and five children. They were able to eat meat once every ten days or two weeks but there was enough rice for everybody these days. Her family income for the year was 200 yuan (about $130).

I spent a sleepless night on a hard bunk in the labyrinthine dormitory of the old temple, listening to the wind and to the groanings of the ancient wood and to the murmurings and snorings of the pilgrims. I saw the Lord Buddha riding on a white elephant and the four gods guarding the temple and the old woman with bound feet toiling her way up the side of the mountain. It was far from the China of propaganda and red flags. Was it the heart of China? Yes. And, of course, no. But it was of the essence of this agrarian giant, a deeper part of the mystery of the China beyond the guidebook, a symbol of the things that quietly endure even as Theory, Revolution, and History rush headlong to the fore.

II

THE
UNDERGROUND
GUIDE TO PEKING

8

Dancing and Discovering

JUST AFTER ARRIVING to live in Peking in April 1980, I learned that a dance would be held at one of the city's universities. A small matter, a dance party. But what would be small matters of personal life anyplace else become questions of unrelenting public scrutiny and intense controversy in China. They are barometers for the nature of political and social life. The dance would, I hoped, add a bit of the color of personal intimacy to the abstract political blacks and whites of Peking.

For ten years during the Cultural Revolution, social dancing was regarded with nearly the same opprobrium in China as nonmarital sex or other offenses against public morality. In fact, dancing was forbidden on the grounds that it was decadent and bourgeois (never mind that the old revolutionaries like Mao Tse-tung and Chou En-lai used to have regular Saturday evening dances in Yanan). Even after the Cultural Revolution and the return to relative good sense, dancing was regarded alternately with a kind of reluctant tolerance and sheer puritanical killjoyism. Late in 1978 it was tolerated, but by the end of the next year it had fallen out of favor again and turned into a kind of underground activity, "tacitly allowed," as one student whispered to me, but still regarded officially as somehow corrupting, morally slack, subversive of work, revolution, and — this is important — of obedience.

The trouble with dances, one lower-ranking official solemnly explained to me, was that "hooligans" often seized on them as opportunities to make trouble. An irate self-appointed guardian of public morals complained to the newspapers that on Sunday afternoons, young people were gathering at the Beihai Park in Peking, where to the music of harmonica and guitar they "shook their bodies obscenely while performing a lewd wagging of the buttocks."

In Chungking in the fall of 1979, I had seen young people dancing at night (not at all lewdly) in the park high above the Yangtse River. When I returned in the summer of 1980, a taxi driver told me that sometime in the spring, government notices had been pasted up around town forbidding that activity. At Sichuan University in Chengdu, there was a brief period, again late in 1979, when dancing was allowed, but by the following spring it was proscribed on the grounds that it interfered with studies.

"The problem," said one student who tended to sympathize with the ban, "was that some of the boys and girls danced all night." This student was part of a group of English practicers who lay in wait outside the Jinjiang Hotel in Chengdu each night for Western tourists on postprandial strolls. We walked down one of the city's broad avenues, shouldering past great throngs of Chinese.

"Don't you think that the students are old enough to decide for themselves whether they should dance or not?" I asked.

"Not if it interferes with their studies," he replied.

In Canton in the late 1970s and early 1980s, private dance parties were often organized as ways for young men and women to meet, but these same parties were often broken up by police. Even before moving to China, I had met one escapee to Hong Kong who played the violin at these dances and was twice arrested during police raids. The young man was supposed to be working in the countryside on Hainan Island but actually maintained an underground existence in Canton, where he made a living by teaching the violin to children, especially the sons and daughters of government officials who could afford to pay. When police interrupted a private party, he said, they routinely separated those who were legal residents of Canton from those, like the young violinist, who lived in the city clandestinely, with neither registration card nor ration tickets. The latter would be locked up for a few days and then shipped off to the commune where they were supposed to live. Once a month a special boat departed from Canton to Hainan to return those, the dancers and others, who had been discovered by the Public Security Bureau living illegally in the city.

And so, a dance party had a kind of speakeasy or opium den quality, an aspect of sinfulness that made it at least moderately rebellious as an activity. Dancing was, moreover, something that the foreigners did, and that made it, in the eyes of many, more daring still. Ironically, in Peking, where there is so little to do at night or on weekends — particularly for nightlife-inclined Westerners — there were dance parties galore. They rotated among the Western embassies, the American, the Australian, the Swiss (which had the best parties), all of which had sound systems and the latest disco music on tape. I, who had never been to a disco in New York, did more dancing in Peking than I had ever done before in my life.

I remember in particular one Bastille Day when the French had a grand alfresco soiree in the spacious front courtyard of their embassy. It was, in the Chinese environment, as though some fantastic Malinowskian primitives had descended on Peking one warm summer night, and started wild, exotic gyrations to the absolute astonishment of the restrained and drab local folk. Grim Chinese army guards kept watch just outside the embassy's gates — the purpose of these guards is theoretically to provide security to the foreign diplomatic establishments, but in reality it is to screen the Chinese who might want to enter the compounds. Lined up on the street outside the gates were a few hundred Chinese, standing expressionlessly, watching into the early hours of the morning with who knows what thoughts racing through their minds. Inside the compound on the sacred soil of France, champagne bottles popped, wine and whiskey flowed freely, American imperialist music pulsed in waves over the ground and rose up into the still, warm Peking night; hundreds of people, sexy little French schoolgirls and their boyfriends, diplomats, journalists, visiting business delegation members, the so-called foreign experts, all shook their bodies obscenely and performed lewd waggings of the buttocks until dawn had nearly broken.

I left the Bastille Day celebration in the early morning hours, walking past the ever unsmiling army guards in their baggy greens, glancing at the ranks of neighborhood people who remained to gawk at the strange goings-on, and drove through the deserted, lifeless streets of Peking into the dark vastness of Tiananmen Square, which had been eerily empty since about nine o'clock on that night as on every other.

The Chinese authorities had by the late 1970s accommodated themselves to the foreigners' quest for nighttime recreation and even to profiting from it. There were two state-owned enterprises in Peking — the International Club and the Nationalities' Palace — which had regular evening dances for entry fees of two dollars and seven dollars respectively. There were drinks and taped disco music and, at the Nationalities' Palace, such other amusements as bowling (you had to set up your own pins), billiards, and even Mah-jongg, an ancient game that in all the vastness of China was permitted only in this small enclave of foreigners and overseas Chinese and was banned everyplace else. The goal of the authorities was to quarantine the foreigners' dances from the rest of the population, to contain them like microbes in a laboratory. And usually, the quarantine worked. Except for the ticket and drink sellers and the plainclothes members of the Public Security police who leaned against pillars and walls and never smiled, there were virtually no Chinese. But, following the political mood, some Pekingese from time to time would seep in for a few weeks and then again disappear, apparently observing some signals that were largely invisible to us foreigners. The fact that occasionally a few Chinese youths took the risk to come to the tightly guarded confines of the Nationalities' Palace suggested that not all Chinese people accepted the moral strictures of the state as readily as did the earnest student from Chengdu. And here is the point of this disquisition on discotheques in China. Dancing, of course, is not a measure of a society. But some Chinese want to dance, and the fact that they are prohibited is a reflection, not only of the prudery of Chinese communism, but also of its morally absolutist character, its suspicion of the sensual and spontaneous urges of its people.

In this sense, dancing is not really a minor issue. During one of those periods of relative tolerance in Peking, early in 1981, I often met the same group of young Chinese people at the Nationalities' Palace Saturday soirees. They were in their mid-twenties to mid-thirties, well educated and politically well enough connected to dare make appearances at the discotheque. Some of them also loved to dance and they did it with an unpracticed enthusiasm that was quite similar to my own. I used in particular to dance with one young woman who became the object of a romance of a very innocent, old-fashioned, yet attractively illicit kind that was restricted entirely to these chance encounters at the Nationalities' Palace. She was one of those people who were born happy. She was pretty and insouciant, entirely irreverent, and given to didactic pronouncements on the fact that China was different from America, that while "you are free and can do what you want, we cannot afford to be so casual or to get carried away." These speeches, always delivered in my ear over the throbbing crescendos of *Saturday Night Fever*, I took as warnings to keep my impulses in check. Nonetheless, once, just once, when we were doing a rare slow number, she let her head fall against mine and I, a bachelor in Peking — not a good place to be a bachelor — and filled with affection for this nice and charming girl, planted a kiss on her cheek. She smiled, as if to reassure me that my act of impetuosity had not given offense. But then she said that the plainclothes policeman was watching us and perhaps I shouldn't do it again.

The young people at the Nationalities' Palace were uniformly cynical and a bit on the smart-alecky side, savvy, quick on the draw, prone to an insider's jargon that half the time I could not comprehend. But if they reminded me sometimes of young New Yorkers, what easily distinguished them was their overriding seriousness about the one thing that virtually everybody takes seriously in China — politics. And, like practically all generations of educated youthful Chinese since the Opium War, they were perpetually inquisitive about the nature of their society and what was wrong with it. I used, late at night, to drive some of these people home after the dances, and on one of those nocturnal excursions through Peking's empty streets one of my friends provided me with the link between dancing and the Big Issues that I had been seeking. This was a woman in her early thirties who had unabashedly shot question after question at me about why I was not yet married and whether I wanted to be.

"And why," I said, trying to take advantage of the mood of frankness, "do you never bring your husband with you to dance?"

"He's not interested," she replied.

"What is he interested in?"

"He's only interested in studying, in reading the *People's Daily*, and in trying to understand the political situation," she said. Then, after a silence, she went on, evidently still thinking about her dull husband, "You foreigners love to play, don't you?"

"Yes, I suppose we do."

"But you yourself work all the time," she said to me somewhat inconsistently in what I defensively took as a kind of accusation.

"What do you expect me to do in Peking?" I replied. "There's nothing to do but work here, unless you think taking a walk through the Summer Palace on Sunday afternoon is a good way to play."

"The Chinese people don't know how to play," she went on, in apparent agreement. She fell into silence as I drove at high speed through one of Peking's broad, deserted avenues, thinking about the dread lifelessness of the city at night. "They don't know how to work either," the woman went on, suddenly providing me with a kind of Confucian epigram that contained the key to the significance of dancing. "The difference between us is that the Chinese don't know how to work because they don't know how to play; while in the West, it is precisely because you do know how to play that you also know how to work."

The time I went to the Saturday night dance at the university was much earlier than this, well before I had become privy to Chinese self-scrutiny. This dance was to be held inside a Ping-Pong room. I was able to go through the invitation of the student relative of an overseas Chinese friend of mine.

Together with the latter of these contacts, I set out by taxi for the university shortly after dinner. We met the relative at the gates of the Peking Zoo, which had been arranged beforehand as a point of rendezvous, whence we drove together to the university. It was dark and raining. We parked, not on the grounds of the university itself, but across the street inside a walled entryway so as not to attract attention.

Our student ran to the hall where the dance would be held. My friend and I waited in the car, gradually enveloped in the crepuscular gloom, listening to the rain drum on the metal roof. Nearby was one of those obsolescent Mao slogans in bold black characters on a field of crimson calling for great unity among the peoples of the world. After fifteen minutes, the relative came back saying that the students had gathered, but "Chinese students are very timid. It will be some time before the dancing begins."

So, we waited. We had the driver take us inside the university, where we parked on a muddy, puddle-strewn lane between two drab dormitory buildings. The student, who was cautious but unflappable and confident, coached me on how to behave once inside. He did not want me to reveal my identity as a journalist. I would be a foreign expert, perhaps a businessman, or an English teacher visiting Peking from some other city, anything — but not someone who would appear to be seeking information. We would go in when the party had picked up some steam and the unexpected entry of a foreigner would not cast such a pall of embarrassment over the affair that the dancing would never get started. When, finally, we got out of the car and walked quickly through the drizzle to the dance itself, our student friend had first to be recognized by someone inside and a padlocked chain removed from the door before we could make our way past the crowd of people who lingered outside. If the door is not locked, someone explained, too many outsiders would want to get in, including, the explanation continued ominously, those ever present threats to peace and order, the "hooligans."

Affected by all the preparatory slinking about, the waiting in the car, the restricted entry to the dance, it was impossible to avoid the expectation that some exotic, mysterious, clandestine rite awaited us, that we were about to be made privy to the erotic ultrasecret that lay at the core of Chinese puritanism.

That was not the case, of course. At the last minute, we again had to wait, in an auditorium adjacent to the dance hall, while our student guide made a final check of the situation. And then, when we finally entered the hall, we found, not a debauche, not even any lewd wagging of the buttocks, but a rather sedate group of a hundred or so young Chinese dancing rather conservatively to tinny taped music dominated by 1930s-like big band sounds, spiced by an occasional bit of *Saturday Night Fever.*

Like almost everything else in China, the hall was dim and dingy. It had the usual gray cement floor, the stained whitewashed walls, the smell of dankness and mildew. A few hand-drawn and clearly obsolete Mao slogans were up on the walls. The boys and girls were wearing the usual blue cotton clothing, or an occasional muted sweater. They danced well, surprisingly well, gliding in graceful tangos, waltzes, and fox-trots across the floor with such assurance that it was clear they had been practicing at home, very likely under the instructions of their parents who had danced together during an earlier era before Communist puritanism cast dancing into a kind of moral purgatory.

One dominant aspect of this university dance was that the students, in their early to mid twenties, obeyed the conservative conventions of China. The dance was social. No doubt it was used as a way for boys and girls to get a look at available romantic counterparts. But it was entirely asexual. There was no bump and grind, no cheek to cheek, no belly to belly; there was no clutching or clinching or grabbing or squeezing, not even any couples sitting alone holding hands, no furtive glances or retirement to the shadows for private talks — as there is outside in every park at night. The concentration was entirely on the dancing, on getting the steps correct, on doing it well. A few boys even tangoed or fox-trotted together for what seemed entirely pedagogical purposes. Having seen this university dance party, I could have assured any worried parent or commissar that nothing immoral was taking place.

As for me, I lurked in the shadows like a phantom, sticking to the dim periphery among folded-up Ping-Pong tables near the outmoded Mao slogans, having been earlier persuaded by my cautious student guide that untoward consequences might result if I made myself conspicuous. In fact, I needn't have worried. Gradually, the place became used to me, like an eye adjusting to light, and some curious students even talked to me, while I vaguely and with an increasingly guilty conscience told them that I was the representative in Peking of an American chemical company. Some of these students were impressive — bright, eager, personable, earnest, confident. I left the dance after an hour or so of watching, but as the padlock was being removed for me to leave, some of the students pledged to meet me again.

And so they did, one Friday afternoon at a so-called masses restaurant not far from the Peking Hotel. At this second meeting I came clean about my identity, explaining rather sheepishly that, in fact, the chemical company was an invention, that I was a journalist. The students were tolerant of my lie. They said they understood the reason for it. But nonetheless, after we had talked for a couple of hours about various things, from the U.S. presidential election to the failed attempt to rescue the American hostages in Iran (this was early May, 1980) to Chinese humor and whether the *People's Daily* lied (sometimes, they said, but much less than it used to), the students made the polite but firm demand that with hardly an exception every private Chinese makes either before, during, or after a conversation with a foreigner, especially a journalist. Please don't, they said, reveal our names; and if you write something about the dance, they added, please don't tell anybody at which university it was held.

I attended the university dance party only a few days after arriving to open up the *Time* magazine bureau in Peking, and as one of my earliest slices of real Chinese life, it remained during the ensuing months one of the most emblematic as well. After all, one of my main purposes, both journalistic and personal, was to penetrate beyond the suspiciously glossy propaganda images of China to the varied and elusive unofficial realities that lay beyond them. The dance party was a kind of start, as was my conversation a few days later with the students. But, it was also a lesson in the barriers that needed to be overcome. My near clandestine attendance at the student soiree also underlined my own foreignness, my status as an outsider in a society that did not allow the strangers in its midst ever to blend entirely into the crowd.

I had arrived in China as a resident, rather than as the short-term visitor I had been on five previous trips to the country. And my earliest discovery consisted of what most of the foreign residents already knew: that the practical problems of settling in and the political problems of mixing with the local citizenry make China a uniquely difficult and challenging place to discover.

Some fundamental practical problems came even before the task of getting to a student ball, and though practical, they are all suggestive of the kind of society that has emerged during China's three decades and more of communism. There was, for example, no housing available in the for-foreigners-only compounds, so I set up both an office and living quarters in a large, seedy, but friendly, hotel called the Qianmen, or Front Gate, located in the southern part of the city. As I settled in, I quickly learned, as all resident foreigners do, of the controls and restrictions on life. The rules are simple and straightforward. Anytime you want to leave the country you must apply, first to the Foreign Ministry, then to the Public Security Bureau, for an exit permit and, since I always wanted to come back, a reentry permit. Travel, while far easier than in earlier days, was still tightly regulated; permission, again both from the Foreign Ministry and the Public Security Bureau, was needed for any trip outside Peking, which itself is surrounded by a fifteen-mile radius beyond which foreigners are not allowed to go. But by far the single most important factor in my life as a reporter in China was the barriers put up by the Peking authorities between me as a foreigner and the ordinary citizens of the country. These restrictions could be surmounted in part — witness the university dance party. Nonetheless, the unrelenting efforts of the authorities, particularly the Public Security Bureau, to monitor all contacts between me and nonofficial Chinese was a constant source of anxiety and frustration.

In the Chinese language — which is by its pictographic nature both symbolistic and metaphoric — the words for a large gall bladder (*da danzi*) mean to be daring, to have the courage of one's convictions. To have a small gall bladder (*xiao danzi*) means the opposite. The English language, of course, uses another component of the viscera — the guts — to mean roughly the same thing. In any case, one's willingness to be friends with a foreigner in China is a good measure of one's gall bladder. And, like everywhere else in the world, there is a near infinite variety of sizes. During my stay in China, some few people became genuine friends, in the sense that they were willing to be frank with me about their lives, their thoughts, their aspirations. It is on these few people that my most revealing insights into China depended. There were others who were plainly mercenary in their relations with foreigners, expecting and sometimes even unabashedly demanding the favors that they believed were in the power of foreigners to bestow — foreign currency exchange coupons, an introduction to a foreign consul who might give a visa, the purchase of cigarettes or tape recorders at the Friendship Store, the spacious hard-currency emporium for foreigners where the best Chinese merchandise and some imported goods were on sale. But by far the vast majority were like those very likable students from the university dance party — curious, hesitant, polite, even at times enthusiastic, but never unaware of the line that divides them from the others, from the foreigners.

Like so much in China, an individual's ability to cross that line depends on what cannot be seen. Another Chinese expression, for example, is *hou-tai*, meaning literally "behind the stage," a term that indicates the support and protection a person might enjoy from people who hold power. For that reason, the best news sources in China were often the children of upper-level Communist party officials — because they had access to information via their parents while their party connections offered them some protection from persecution by the police for having foreign contacts. But, as one ranking army official's daughter once told me, "your *hou-tai* only reaches to a certain level." In general, there is an enormous gap between the Chinese and the foreigners that requires courage — a sizable gall bladder — to bridge. Thus, the fears and hesitations of ordinary people, the rules and regulations of the bureaucracy, the entanglements of political custom — all are part of the complex practical anthropology that any resident foreigner, whether journalist, diplomat, or businessman, must learn in China.

After I had been in the country for several months, I had occasion to talk to a group of journalists, and, on the grounds that we were engaged in a "frank exchange of ideas," began to complain that few local people were willing to carry on a normal friendly relationship with me, that all associations with the hospitable and gracious people of China were filtered through the distorting lens of political control and suspicion. The meeting came to an end without much comment on that aspect of things. But then, as I was walking out of the reception room, one of the Chinese there, a tall, well-dressed man who had been quiet through the entire discussion, discreetly whispered in absolutely perfect English what I took to be an embarrassed apology on behalf of those people who had succumbed to political fear. "You should realize," he said, "that any Chinese who has regular contacts with a foreigner is very closely monitored. And you should know that your telephone is bugged and so is your room. They might," he added, without explaining who "they" were, "even search your room when you are away from Peking." Having said that, my until then quiet friend shook my hand and walked away.

Why did he decide to give me that dire account of real life in China, I wondered. In fact, the information was superfluous. Only the naïf would think that his phone was not tapped or that his Chinese friends were not subject to scrutiny. Everyone made allowances for those very good possibilities, everyone adopted certain rituals of prudent behavior in maintaining contact with Chinese friends. Generally, for example, I waited for them to call me — particularly since few of them had phones in their homes where I could call them. When they did call, they tended not to identify themselves by name, relying on me to recognize them by their voices — a practice that, particularly in the early stages, caused a few awkward misidentifications. And even later, as the circle of my friendships widened, I occasionally went through the awkward ritual of holding phone conversations ("Hello, I am the person you saw last week" was the start of one I remember) with people whom I never identified at all.

Deciding on a place to meet was a constant problem, the occasional solution to which brought great, if sometimes spiteful, satisfaction. Not very many people were willing to have a foreigner, especially a reporter, to their homes very often, and in many cases, not at all. The only watering hole in China's capital city of five million people is the lobby of the Peking Hotel, which swarms with plainclothes security agents and where Chinese have to register their names, and show their identity cards to gain entry. The restaurants, the few that there are, are noisy, crowded, and unprivate. A journalist cannot carry on an interview or hold a conversation with a source jammed together at a table with numerous others while hordes waiting for seats press in on him from behind.

I knew one man whom I occasionally could visit in his home but more often had to meet someplace on the street, so that while we became well acquainted, we had an almost entirely ambulatory friendship. We got to know each other by walking, rarely by having a meal or a drink together, and never with him capable of genuine relaxation. There was always the feeling that we were engaging in some minor crime. We used to get together in the same atmosphere wherein teenagers in the United States might gather to smoke marijuana. Once, only once, the very first time we got together, he came to see me in my suite at the Qianmen Hotel. On that one occasion he conveniently forgot his identification card and registered at the reception desk under a false name, a false workplace, and a false address, pulling off his act with the remarkable sangfroid more common to cold-champagne-and-cuff-links special agents than to ordinary, real people. Once we had gone up in the elevator and to my room, he explained to me that he had once registered to see a foreigner at the Peking Hotel, and within forty-eight hours, agents of the Public Security Bureau had appeared to check up on him at his work unit. "If it hadn't been for one cadre who was very good to me," my friend said, "I would never have known that the police had come. The cadre wanted to warn me that I should be careful." Then in a more succinct version of what the journalist had already told me, he added: "China is still a police state."

In the spring and summer and early fall, the ambulatory friendship is at least climatically feasible. But when the dread, cold, windy Peking winter sets in, many friendships become not only ambulatory but refrigeratory as well. The question of where to go for a talk becomes awesome. Some people are bold enough to go to warmed-up places of refuge for foreigners, like the International Club or even the lobby café of the Peking Hotel, but not many, and certainly not often.

In the dead of one winter, I accidentally met a young woman who seemed to be willing to tell me of her life's experience. But she lived with her family, who, she said, would have strongly disapproved of her having a foreign friend. She was understandably unwilling to come to my room or even to the dining room of the hotel because she was already on the Public Security Bureau's list for some other noncriminal misdemeanor and couldn't risk another unfavorable entry in her file. Once in a great while we went to the International Club, but she was always nervous that some Public Security stool pigeon would take note of her frequent appearances in the unsavory company of a foreign reporter. And so, we used most often to meet outside near a particular bus stop and then walk through the icy windswept streets of Peking. I heard about her experiences during the Cultural Revolution while jostling crowds in Wangfujing and Qianmenda streets. We went over her life in the countryside as a sent-down educated youth while wandering slowly up and down the aisles of department stores. She told me, as I stamped my feet to keep warm outside the Temple of Heaven, of her two years working in a provincial cotton-spinning mill. It was while walking through the teeming free market in the Chaoyang district that we first talked about Chinese attitudes toward love and sex and child rearing and she confessed to me the unhappiness of her love life.

Once the weather was just too cold for still another walk so we risked the café at the Peking Hotel. I remember trying to be deeply immersed in conversation with her as we walked to the main door so the security guard there would not disturb us and demand that she register before entering. But he saw her. She was unmistakably indigenous with her pigtails and her yellowing plastic glasses and her enormous blue coat. He nodded at her and said curtly, "Go in and register." We ignored his instructions and just made our way directly to a table in the café lobby. Everything seemed all right. Then that same security agent stalked through the lobby examining each table, his eyes seeming to linger malevolently on ours.

"I think he's noticed me," said my friend.

"Don't worry," I said, already quaking with fear for her myself, "he won't do anything with all these foreigners around." But our conversation became nervous, disjointed, as my friend and I kept looking out for the reappearance of the cops. Resisting registration, drinking coffee with a male foreigner without permission, premeditated entry into a restricted hotel lobby — I could imagine the charges. "We'll go through the door of the back wing of the hotel," I said. "That way we'll pass a different set of guards."

Why? Is the regime's terror of uncontrolled contacts the simple reflex of a totalitarian state, the impulse toward conservative authoritarianism of the security apparatus? Or is it entirely Chinese, deriving from the powerful traditions of the Middle Kingdom of centuries past when China, proud and xenophobic, viewed itself as the sole land of civilization surrounded by dangerous barbarians?

The gentle answer, the culturally relativistic and more apologetic answer, is to blame the tradition, to bear in mind that for millennia the Chinese, with considerable justice, saw all the rest of the world as crude, unlettered, miserable, unphilosophical, violent, strangely complexioned, immoral, gorilla limbed, and malodorous. When the Europeans first wanted to open China to trade, the Middle Kingdom resisted. "Magnificently our great emperor soothes and pacifies China and the foreign countries, regarding all with the same kindness," wrote an imperial official named Lin Zexu in a famous mid-nineteenth-century letter to Queen

Victoria. "Of all the things which China exports to foreign countries, there is not a single one which is not beneficial. On the other hand, articles coming from the outside to China can only be used as toys. We can take them or get along without them."

For decades in the late eighteenth and early nineteenth centuries the foreigners were confined to small riverbank enclaves in Canton, where they were required to work through special middlemen, known to later history as compradors, rather than deal directly with imperial officials. It was only by fighting a series of very aggressive imperialist wars, beginning with the Opium War of 1839–1842, that the British, the French, the Americans, and others got the right to travel freely in the interior of China, to station diplomats in the capital city, eventually to carve out spheres of influence in the major cities. Given their attitudes and their unhappy experiences during the imperialist era, how else could one expect the Chinese to feel about the foreign presence in their once again sovereign country? They were bound to have a strong "we and they" mentality, to be a bit suspicious, to isolate the foreigners in their own special areas and to scrutinize the contacts they had with ordinary Chinese.

Yes, but that is not the entire reason. Indeed, the longer I lived in Peking, the more I felt that the historical wariness of foreigners was a lesser factor than another, more pervasive impulse, also with deep roots in history — to control not just the foreigners but everybody. In centuries past, Chinese governments established a system of mutual surveillance and control that a Westerner, imbued with ideas of privacy and liberty, can contemplate only with dismay. The principle was simple but effective. Populations were divided into groups of one hundred and then further subdivided into groups of ten, each with a head who bore responsibility for any wrong done by members of his group.

Since 1949 this system of mutual surveillance has been replaced by the vast, shadowy bureaucracy of the Ministry of Public Security and the bureaus it maintains in every city, town, and village. While the philosophy is compatible with China's tradition, the methods employed come directly from the country's early mentors in total control — the Russians. Peking may indeed have shed its good relations with Moscow and its status as the world's most devoted pupil of Stalinism; nonetheless, the dead weight of Soviet methods and styles still presses heavily and conspicuously upon Chinese society. It can be seen in Peking's grandiose, clumsy monumental architecture and in the rows of lifeless, ugly apartment blocks that seem to have been built to prove an incompatibility between the utilitarian and the imaginative. It is visible in the elaborate centralized organization of the Communist party, in the immense black limousines of the powerful, in the China Travel Service (modeled on Russia's Intourist), in the propaganda apparatus, in the well-organized associations of writers, artists, doctors, dramatists, and so on, in the walled-off, isolated foreign residential quarters, in the travel restrictions, and, of course, in China's counterpart to the KGB, the Public Security Bureau.

There is no right to privacy in this system. It is alien to its modes, to its motivating spirit. Every factory, every enterprise, school, performing arts troupe, professional association, neighborhood, or government section contains a security department (often known as the personnel department) that supervises the lives of the members of that unit, approving or disapproving travel abroad, marriage, divorce, or a change of jobs. Every person is followed around by a dossier, which that person has no right to see, containing he knows not what information about him. One important, unannounced step taken after the disorder of the Cultural Revolution was to throw out all materials in the dossiers that dated to that ten-year period — on the grounds that there was so much slander being tossed around then that it would be impossible to tell genuine material from false.

Some foreigners in Peking who sent their children to Chinese schools were disturbed to discover that teachers encouraged pupils to inform on one another — rewarding what in any elementary school in the West would be regarded as a brownie, a tattletale, a teacher's pet, a fink. The public humiliations, the written self-criticisms, the endless meetings to discuss personal behavior, all of these practices of the Chinese Communists are presented as examples of the new democracy, as supervision by the masses. In fact, they are refinements of the mutual surveillance systems that are part of the heritage of the feudal past, combined with the control methods pioneered by the Russians.

The control mentality has numerous, often petty manifestations. Diplomats stationed in Chinese embassies abroad are not allowed to receive mail from relatives in China except through the diplomatic pouch, which in many embassies comes only once a month, evidently — or so some diplomats have whispered to me — so it can be read by the security people. These same Chinese posted abroad are prohibited from leaving their embassy compound, even for a brief stroll, without being accompanied by at least one other Chinese. I have met diplomats stationed abroad for years who never once ventured outside by themselves. Back home, ordinary people are not allowed to have overnight guests in their homes unless they register them first with the neighborhood committee. Nor are social or sexual matters left to consenting adults to decide for themselves. I once got into a rare discussion of relations between the sexes with, of all people, a female Travel Service guide.

"What would you do," I asked her, "if your best girl friend were having an affair with a married man?"

"I'd try to persuade her to stop," she replied.

"And if she didn't listen to you?"

The female Travel Service guide, who was in fact lively and irreverent about most matters, did not hesitate. "I'd report her to the superior authorities," she said.

Not everybody would have the same answer, of course. Many would help to keep the secret. Many are angry and resentful over the way their lives are examined. But what the sytem of mutual responsibility reveals is that the fears and hesitations that the Chinese feel toward foreigners are echoes of a more general concern they have about all people. The average Chinese worries that if he speaks too frankly, his words may well be reported to the superior authorities. Indeed, in a strange way, the foreigner is in a unique position in China. Difficult as it is to break through to any inner circle, once a non-Chinese has done so, he may find that his friends confide in him more readily than they do in their ordinary friends or neighbors. The foreigner is an outsider. He cannot, as the Chinese say, "make reports" to the party secretary. But the possibility that others will leads to a high degree of generalized distrust and suspicion. Most people keep their opinions to themselves. They have little to gain and a lot to lose and find it better to stick to the few safe, prefabricated phrases, particularly when dealing with people they don't know very well. Apart from their spouses and family, most Chinese tend to have very few true friends, very few people to whom they are willing to entrust the secrets of their heart.

9

Restoring Chineseness

DESPITE THE TRICKY SHOALS of personal caution and political fear that I and all foreign reporters had to navigate in Peking, the atmosphere, by virtually all accounts, was far better in the late 1970s and early 1980s than it had been before. It is difficult to pin this down. The political mood, the degree of political interference in the lives of the Chinese, went through numerous subtle alterations even during the time that I lived in Peking. And, in any case, what would be moderation and relaxation of controls in China would, even in such authoritarian regimes as South Korea and Taiwan, be an iron grip over the minds and the lives of the citizenry. One feature of the Peking psychology consists of a constant wariness that, while matters might seem more relaxed now, there is always the chance of a new tightening just around the corner, particularly as the dictatorial hard-liners and the moderates within the top party leadership vie with one another for power and position. A stress in the party newspaper on giving free rein to the initiatives of the masses might change the next month to a hastily renewed stress on political study every Saturday afternoon or on renewed warnings against leaking "state secrets" to unauthorized persons. Yet, matters never reverted to the absolutism that characterized the Chinese political mood in the last years of Mao Tse-tung. While the party's grip on the lives of its people remained tight by any standard, there was some room, among the Chinese, to make personal choices in the way they would conduct their lives and, among the foreigners, to learn what they thought and what they felt.

One of my first friends in Peking was a scientist who worked in a suburban laboratory and whose piano had been taken from his home by Red Guards during the Cultural Revolution. The instrument was not for him; it was for his daughter, then about eleven years old, who showed considerable musical talent. The scientist doted on her, his only child, and he had gotten the piano some years before in order to let her cultivate her skill. Then, in 1966, when the Cultural Revolution picked up steam, his modest two-bedroom apartment was invaded and ransacked by young hotheads who, spurred on by Chairman Mao, believed that they were making revolution. The scientist, his wife and daughter were forced to move out of their apartment and into a much smaller dwelling where, for the first few weeks, they had to sleep on the floor. And, the piano was confiscated. The daughter, said the Red Guards, was using it to play "bourgeois music" like that of Beethoven and Chopin. Besides, they declared, it was unfair for one family to enjoy such an instrument; it should go someplace where "the Masses" could use it too.

In 1978 the scientist got the piano back. He went to the factory from which the Red Guards had been dispatched in the first place and was told that the piano had been shipped to another province. Later he was informed by local Peking authorities that he should go to a certain warehouse. There, he discovered a large room full of pianos, all of which had been confiscated, taken from Peking and then returned. Many were alike, and after twelve years the scientist was not sure which one belonged to him. "Just pick out a piano and take it back," the warehouse attendant told him.

One cold winter evening, when I visited this friend in his tiny apartment for the first time, his daughter, now a grown-up woman in her early twenties, played the piano for me. It was an old battered upright. Ivory was missing from the keys. It stood against the wall between the bed and the sofa. The daughter played a bit of Chopin and, despite the piano's long disappearance, she played it well, though she had long ago given up any idea of a career in music and had taken a regular job in a factory. As she played, her mother and father stood silent and attentive. The piano was sadly out of tune; its tone was shallow and metallic; but, as the rest of us listened, the slightly off-key Chopin filled the room with flowers of sound, with the music of a kind of restoration.

In fact, one way to look at Peking, and at China as a whole, as the decade of the 1980s began was as a somewhat off-key, slightly out-of-tune restoration. For some fifteen years, China had been swept by the madness of Mao's extremist politics and by the power struggles that surrounded his death in 1976. Now it was in the midst of a multifaceted atavism that was itself struggling with the remaining influences of Mao and the dislocations of socialism. The city was plagued with shortages, long lines, bureaucratic red tape, and, of course, the omniscient mechanisms of control. But other facets of life, both good and bad, had made their return. The veteran bureaucrats who had been purged during the Cultural Revolution were back in control of the government and they were managing to keep their factional quarrels from bursting open. The efforts to get rid of special privileges, which remained an incessant theme in the press, were obviously failing. Peking was garlanded with the enormous black limousines of the powerful. Their big homes in back of the Forbidden City displayed huge red gates, garages, and armed guards. No longer required to mouth political slogans, youths were cynical. They got their news from the Voice of America and yearned, schemed, and plotted to find some way of studying abroad. Few of those who succeeded in making private arrangements abroad planned to return to China.

Polls of student opinion were taken at many schools and universities and the results were so embarrassing that they were held as state secrets. On a trip to Shanghai, I learned the results of one poll taken at Fudan University, one of the country's best institutions of higher learning. It showed that only 30 percent of the students believed in communism, that a vast majority of them had grave doubts about the ability of the government leaders' program to effect economic modernization, that an even greater majority thought that another Cultural Revolution was either likely or inevitable. When the results of the poll slipped out to the foreign press, students at Fudan were instructed by the university authorities not to deal with foreign reporters unless under official auspices.

The most conspicuous, and often the most touching, aspects of post-Mao restoration came in the domain of personal life, where a whole series of interests, worries, and pleasures made a comeback. On my first trip to China in 1972, for example, it had been absolutely impossible to coax out of anyone the admission that the Chinese people paid attention to personal appearance, much less to sexual attractiveness. But in 1979, the national airline was holding beauty contests to choose air hostesses. True, the scarcities of cloth and the unstylishness of the off-the-rack wear in the stores continued to impose a rather drab look on the Chinese, even by comparison with other poor Asian countries. Still, there was more color, more panache, than during the politically rigid Cultural Revolution a few years before. Beauty parlors were filled up with rank after rank of women, sitting under driers to have their hair set in curls. A performer I know went into the hospital for a month of plastic surgery to make herself prettier. Young bucks started sporting longer hair, bell-bottom trousers, and sunglasses with the label stuck onto the bottom of the lens — a pathetic form of snobbery designed to attract attention to the fact that they had been imported from abroad.

In Peking, the tone of life was a blend of ongoing Communist-style politics and the desire on the part of the average person to carve out a sphere of untroubled privacy. The city was far less political than it had been in other years, although, to be sure, the inexperienced or first-time visitor to China might have found Peking still nearly inundated by revolutionary rhetoric. The press shouted its usual hortatory slogans, and metaphors of struggle and war. The newspapers were, more ominously, filled with dire warnings about "certain comrades" who had made mistakes and refused to recognize them — a terminology suggesting that factional quarrels were still going on inside the leading groups. Something called "ultraleftism" was continuously attacked as the ideological mistake that lay at the heart of China's recent misfortunes until, in the fall of 1981, the chief target of attack became something called "bourgeois liberalism," presumably the opposite mistake from "ultraleftism." Of course, in any society lacking a free or independent press, the themes that come to public attention can easily be dominated by the holders of power. And, in this sense, the casual visitor to Peking would get the impression of a country swimming in a sea of highly political jargon. The chief aim of the propaganda is to convey the impression that the entire country is of one heart and mind about any given subject; the reader gets an impression of tens of millions out there somewhere unanimously striving to build socialism by following the latest party directive.

Still, while all this might have seemed obsessive to the uninitiated foreigner, to most Chinese, the late 1970s brought a respite. Allowed for the first time in years not to participate in political study, in parades, in sessions of criticism and self-criticism, most simply tried to go about their business, while consigning the propaganda to the status of unattended background music. Politics became a more residual than central activity, something to which occasional lip service had to be paid during those periods when worried political leaders decided a new dose of ideological study was needed. In fact, for most, politics created little genuine interest except as gossip and as the reason for very vivid bad memories.

One constant reminder of the horrors of the immediate past was the steady return to Peking of thousands, perhaps tens of thousands, of intellectuals, musicians, novelists, playwrights, actors, professors, scientists, technicians, and others who had been interned for periods of up to twenty years in some sort of prison, labor camp, or reform farm. These were the people who, when the Communists took power in 1949, had chosen to remain in the country, not as active party members, but simply to pursue their life's work. Peking had always been a center of intellectual life. Old scholars used to tell me that the city once had been the best in China for three things that were related to one another: scholarship, bookstores, and brothels. Of the last of these, all but the most secret had now been wiped out. There were far fewer bookshops and those that remained had a far narrower range of books. But the old scholars had returned. They moved back into the low houses, built around courtyards, where they had lived before; they received visitors, they talked about old friends, especially those who had not survived the purges; they restored to Peking at least a small measure of its status as China's center for quiet, gentlemanly conversation and civilized hospitality.

In the fall of 1980, I arranged a visit to one of China's most renowned actors, a man whose name is known to virtually any Chinese more than twenty years old. The actor received me in a small study that gave onto a charming, if shabby, courtyard. There, surrounded by old furniture and antiques that had somehow survived the ravages of the Cultural Revolution, the actor talked through the afternoon — about the repertory of plays, about other actors, about the time in the late 1960s when he had been forced to spend three years on what were called May 7 cadre schools, that is, farms for manual labor and ideological study. The actor recalled how, decades before, he had gotten started in the theater as a kind of street-side barker. His job had been first to attract people to buy tickets for a performance. Then, inside, he announced each scene by writing its name on the ground in fine, white sand. The actor demonstrated this nearly lost art on the floor of his study, pouring sand from an old crock into his palm and letting it fall between his fingers to form graceful, old-style characters on the floor. Had I visited the actor a couple of years earlier, it would have been in the company of a guide from the Foreign Ministry. The actor would have talked of his love for Chairman Mao, his hatred of the Gang of Four, his yearnings to achieve the Four Modernizations. But this private visit was a time for only the most passing references to Chairman Mao (known almost universally as "the old man"), for reminiscences, both pleasant and painful, for writing old-style characters with sand. For once, it seemed that politics existed only outside the courtyard; it did not intrude within its precincts.

This does not mean that the horrific experiences of the Cultural Revolution and the struggles for power that followed it did not weigh on Chinese minds. Few Chinese intellectuals enjoyed the luxury of many of their counterparts in the West who, from a safe distance, idealized and romanticized the last Maoist campaigns as valiant attempts to destroy the growing inequalities of Chinese society. Millions of Chinese tended to see the Cultural Revolution, in particular, as the final and ultimate expression of the megalomaniacal and irrational components of Maoism. They regarded it as the degeneration into absurdity and horror of the Chinese nation itself, as a final accelerated stage in the country's long fall from greatness. And so, in the years after Mao's death, if the mood still contained a high degree of quiet skepticism and contempt for the well-publicized ideals of communism, there was nonetheless widespread acquiescence in the political situation that emerged.

The most welcome event was the fall from power, one month after Mao's death, of the extremist leaders — known to the world now as the Gang of Four — who had prosecuted the Cultural Revolution and competed for power with other leading groups in the months leading up to Mao's death. Also welcome as a change for the better was the rise to supremacy of one of Mao's and the Gang of Four's chief victims, Vice-premier Deng Xiaoping. Deng, who represented the pragmatic school of thought of his sponsor, Chou En-lai, was viewed, if not with actual admiration, at least with some relief. He was shrewd and tough, a master of political manipulation; he was also predictable, sound, and of a decidedly practical turn of mind. Perhaps most important of all, he had been purged twice himself, once in 1966, once in 1976, and then resurrected. He enjoyed the popularity of one who has succeeded against great odds and then had the good grace not to gloat in public.

At the same time, after the fall of the so-called Gang of Four, Deng got considerable popular support for his effort to discredit the radical faction that had brought about the Cultural Revolution. This included his masterful elimination of the man who, in theory, should have been the most powerful in the country, Premier and Party Chairman Hua Guofeng. Bland and dull, Hua had risen to those exalted posts during the power struggle when compromise, rather than competent candidates, was needed. But Hua was a Maoist, increasingly an isolated one as Deng gradually weeded out the others; Hua did not fit with Deng's plans to bring into power a corps of younger specialists, men of equal parts knowledge and politics, who could lead China into the twenty-first century. Slowly, then, Hua lost power and prestige. He became the butt of jokes. He was induced in 1980 to resign as premier, becoming the first top Chinese Communist leader ever to resign voluntarily from a major post. He was probably promised that he would be compensated for his loss by being allowed to remain on as a figurehead party chairman. But by early summer, 1981, Hua had lost that post as well to Deng's handpicked successor, Hu Yaobang.

All these goings-on at the top in Peking attracted the curious stares of the man in the street. Courtyard gossip played commonly on the theme of Deng's maneuvers, Hua's fall, and the compromises that Deng had to make in order to get his way. But for once, these political matters had to compete with personal concerns. When, in the winter of 1980, the Gang of Four went on a spectacular show trial, the event elicited enormous initial attention, especially among people who had been victims of the Cultural Revolution. The trial, televised in nightly, edited segments, drew large audiences, fascinated by the spectacle of the widow of Mao sitting defiantly, unrepentently in the dock. But soon, a Chinese habit of mind as old as the centuries seemed to reassert itself. It was the notion that "Heaven is high and the emperor is far away." Many people became bored with the televised trial. "We are tired of all that stuff," one intellectual told me. "We have other things to do. Besides," he added, with a resigned shrug of the shoulders and an upward lift of the eyes, "it's their affair, not ours."

All of this had an impact on the foreigner living in Peking and trying to discover China. The restoration of Chineseness presented a great opportunity. For the first time in years, there was more to the life of the foreigner in Peking than single-minded attention to what was called China watching, that is, deciphering the shifts and turns of the political situation, of who was rising and who falling. Slowly, serendipitous, sporadic discoveries of the true nature of things in China's capital were becoming possible. I began to compile a description of what I was able to learn of the city, both historical and present, political and personal. This was my underground guide to Peking.

Look at a map of China and you will see how very far north Peking is compared both to the rest of the country and to other places in Asia. It is north of Tokyo, north of Pyongyang, almost as far north as Vladivostok. The dominant image of China abroad is of a southern, semitropical civilization composed of bamboo copses and flooded rice paddies. But Peking's location on the map serves as a reminder of the fact that China is in large part a northern society, cold, brown, forbidding. Chinese civilization originated in the great bend of the Yellow River in territory that is sere, implacable, awesome in the scope of its desolateness. Through the centuries, it spread southward, until it absorbed and conquered the softer, mellower, but also mosquito- and fever-infested territory below the Yangtse River. Probably, the north produced a stronger breed, one whose blood was mixed in both war and intermarriage with the fierce, indestructible nomadic "barbarians" even farther north — the Mongols, the Huns, the Kazaks, the Uighurs.

Today too, China is visually demarcated into the original northern zone and the absorbed, conquered regions of the south. If you take the train, for example, from Canton to Peking you will pass, in thirty-nine hours, through a kind of geographical archaeology of China. For the first few hours, between Canton and Changsha, the landscape will be hospitable and green, filled with whitewashed kiln-brick villages surrounded by luxuriant clumps of slender bamboo, spreading banyans, jacarandas, and thick banana trees. One index of the train's slow movement north is the delicacies that can be bought at various station platforms — bananas in Canton, tea-soaked eggs in Changsha, pigs' feet in Hubei, and soy-sauce chicken in Shijiazhuang, four hours south of Peking.

But it is the visual change that is the most striking. Somewhere north of the Yangtse, above the triple city of Wuhan, the lush, wet rice lands of the south give way to the dry landscape of the north, where the fields are sown primarily with winter wheat, sorghum, and millet. As the train moves through northern Hubei and into southern Henan, the villages turn from white to brown. The bamboo disappears and is replaced by plane trees or locusts. Sunbaked mud becomes the principal building material. Walls are no longer made mostly of red brick but of tamped earth, layering upon layering of loess soil, one tapped down upon the other. The dominant color changes from a glistening green to a desiccated yellowish brown. Even the sky is often filled with clouds of tiny, yellowish particles. Eight months of the year the people wear suits of heavy, quilted clothing that make them look stouter, broader, more robust than their counterparts farther south. The villages have an aspect of changeless China, where life is reduced to an eternally spare, hard routine of survival, where the diet is unvarying — rough, thick glutinous noodles, boiled and served in starchy water, and sweet potatoes.

The Yellow River, that immense shifting expanse of walled-in water, silt, and mud, is the central artery of the north. The train crosses it near the city of Zhengzhou in Henan Province and plunges northeast toward Peking, which means, literally, northern capital, and which is quintessentially that. The summer in Peking is brief but hot. There are short, mild autumns and springs and endlessly long, bitterly cold winters. More than the brutally frigid temperatures, however, what make the Peking climate one of the most unendurable in the world are the wind and the dust that sweep down from Inner Mongolia and transform the atmosphere into a blinding, stinging monster. There is no urban sight more desolate in the world than that of Peking on a windy day in late March during one of its sandstorms. Long lines of people, looking a bit like cat burglars with their heads wrapped in gauzy scarves, endure for hours at the market to buy heads of half-frozen, half-rotten cabbage — the only vegetable readily available on the market from November through April. In the road leading out to the suburbs, bicyclists hunch over their handlebars, their heads also swathed in gauze, as they make their way with painstaking slowness against the buffeting wind down one of the city's broad, gray avenues. The great monuments, engulfed in swirling billows of gray-brown sand, are almost invisible.

Very near the present Peking there was once a certain city called Qi, the capital of the ancient state of Yan, one of the many such small principalities swallowed up by the unifying emperor, Qin Shi Huang, when he established the first great Chinese dynasty twenty-three hundred years ago. For centuries, Qi remained one of the standard walled mud-brick villages that are still flung out at extraordinarily regular intervals across the entire North China Plain. The basic pattern consisted of a protective surrounding wall, enclosing twisted rows of *ping-fang*, or ordinary one-story houses built around interior courtyards and shielded from the outside by high exterior walls. Even today, Peking remains a city of walls and *ping-fang*. Just a few meters from one of the main commercial streets, you find yourself in narrow alleys, lined by mud-brown walls and small crowded houses that have all the atmosphere, the sounds, and even the smells of old rural villages — not of capital cities. Americans who lived in Peking in the 1930s have paid nostalgic visits to their former homes and have found them still there but entirely stripped of their grace and charm. Courtyards have been filled with primitive shanties. Moon gates that connected the courtyards have been torn away. Most of the intricate wooden latticework on the windows has been stripped off. A house that might in the old days have accommodated a Chinese or foreign family of four, with three or four servants, will now house seven or eight families and thirty or more people — with one room assigned to each family.

In the Tang dynasty, Peking was called Yuzhou and was a district capital. Yuzhou was destroyed by the northern barbarians, who turned it into a new city, which, reflecting their own geographical bias, they called Nanking, or Southern Capital (not to be confused with present-day Nanking). It remained under the control of various non-Chinese northerners — including the great Mongol Kublai Khan, whose imperial splendors were described by Marco Polo in the thirteenth century — until, finally, the native Ming dynasty drove them out in 1368. The Ming displayed the Chinese sense of geography by renaming the city Peking (Northern Capital) in 1421.

Except for the brief period in this century when the Kuomintang took the capital to Nanking (another southern capital) and during the war to Chungking, Peking has remained the center of Chinese political life ever since, a total of five and a half centuries. As such, it was the physical expression of the Chinese self-conception. In its center was the vast, orange-tiled Forbidden City, surrounded by high walls and a moat and, until it was turned into a museum by the Kuomintang (not by the Communists, as is often claimed on their behalf), it was strictly off limits to all common people. Farther out from the imperial center itself was the city's outer rampart, which, alas, was destroyed in one of China's postrevolutionary periods of zealotry. It was broad enough at the top to accommodate patrols on horseback and was connected by a series of nine grandiose gates, only one of which has been left standing. Inside this outer wall were compounds for such permanently tributary states as Korea and Vietnam. South of the Forbidden City, where the Museum of the History of the Revolution now stands, were the branches of the imperial government — the boards of war, or rites, of revenue, and so on.

As the seat of government, Peking was the focus of attention for both ambition and intrigue. Every three years, scholars from the entire realm converged on the city to take the imperial exams in the hope of becoming officials. The Hall of Examinations consisted of long, grim rows of cubicles, eighty-five hundred in all, each five feet square and ten feet high, and containing a stool, a table, and writing materials. The candidates were sealed inside for three days and two nights, keeping themselves awake by jabbing their thighs with awls and by tying their queues to the ceiling so that their heads would be jerked abruptly upright whenever they nodded downward in sleep. Those few who passed the national-level exams became part of the great imperial bureaucracy, the scholar-official class, which was, at least when the system was functioning according to plan, as adept at painting and poetry and the ethical science of Confucianism as at the art of government. There was a strong echo of this in postrevolutionary China when, in such purist periods as the Cultural Revolution, officials got ahead, not because they knew about economic development or technology, but because they showed themselves to be well versed in the tenets of Maoism. Mastery of the ideology was in both instances more important than technical knowledge.

Peking was, by many accounts, a lively place, far more so than now. Marco Polo said that the multitude of inhabitants was "greater than the mind can comprehend." There were, he reported, twenty-five thousand prostitutes in the suburbs to minister to the "vast concourse of merchants and other strangers who are continually arriving and departing" — this added to the extraordinary array of different types at the imperial court itself. During the great Ming dynasty, for example, there were as many as twelve thousand concubines in the harem and seventy thousand eunuchs to take care of the inner portions of the palace. Later chroniclers, even including several from the 1920s and 1930s, talk about a host of charms and excitements in Peking. There were cricket fights in numerous places, cockfights in a large arena three thousand feet around and thirty feet deep; there were temple fairs with puppets, mountebanks, and pantomime shows. One popular entertainment was *xiang sheng*, a stand-up comic dialogue that was often, in Chinese terms, yellow, or pornographic. There were tea pavilions and bathhouses (which offered a bath, a massage, tea, steamed buns, and good, relaxed conversation). There were the so-called flower houses, which were upper-class brothels with such euphonious names as Garden of Beautiful Fairies, Garden of the Fragrant Clouds, Garden of the Transplanted Flowers. Street vendors were out by the thousand, each with his own chant or cry. One foreign scholar in the 1930s compiled a record of all of the delicacies that could be bought outside on the city's lanes and alleys. He found sixty different types, with sixty different types of sellers crying out their chants. In the Tian Qiao area — which is now a somber, dull, charmless residential quarter not far from the Qianmen Hotel — there were acrobats, conjurers, and magicians. And, of course, there was that craze of the Pekingese, the opera, which, according to various chroniclers, seems to have had a festival atmosphere somewhere between that of an Elizabethan play and that of an American baseball game. The writer Lin Yutang even described a peculiar form of Peking eccentric who wandered the streets singing and acting the part of one or another of the celebrated operatic dramatis personae.

Today, after ten years during which it was virtually obliterated, the opera has returned. It is shown on television and performed in the few dingy, dank theaters that remain in Peking. The shows come complete with extravagant costumes and strutting generals, acrobatic monkey kings, drunken court jesters, mincing princesses, and resolute heroes, who, to the deafening accompaniment of cymbals and drums, do battle and sing arias before once again rapt audiences. (The latter seem to consist overwhelmingly of old, grizzled men unaccompanied by their wives.) Other elements of life in Peking have also made a comeback. There are a few bathhouses. There are occasional, determinedly nonpornographic performances of comic dialogue; there are street vendors selling ice sticks, though they fall far short of the old vendors with their sixty delicacies and sixty chants. But Peking is quiet and dull and entirely lacking in that spontaneity that can come only from individual creativity. The city is not exactly a ghost. It can best be described in the negative "un" form — as unlively, uncolorful, uninspired, unbeautiful. It is a city that has declined enormously since its splendid imperial past and is struggling to restore itself to mediocrity.

Yet, the slow, hesitant, partial, out-of-tune restoration of Chineseness brought with it a rampant return to certain age-old patterns that even the Cultural Revolution was unable to wipe out. The China of history books had always been a place where an informal, quasi-legal system of networks, favors, gifts, exchanges, and private understandings not only paralleled the rectitudinous official Confucian society but actually enabled it to function. In the Peking of the early 1980s, this casual, shadowy world reasserted itself, and even received negative attention in the press.

Perhaps most common was the elaborate exchange of favors by which people obtain scarce goods or services or advance their careers. This is called "going through the back door," the name originating in the practice whereby high-ranking officials got their children admitted into universities by using their political influence and connections to pave the way to the institution's rear gate. But backdoorism came soon to mean getting almost anything through personal connections — from exit permits for travel abroad to industrial goods coupons for bicycles or sewing machines, to the allocation of new apartments, to tickets for the latest play or ballet, even to a job as a waitress in one of Peking's hotels.

This sometimes depends on a specific exchange, as in the case of the man who was able to get medical care at Peking's best hospital because he could provide one of the doctors there with publications from abroad. More often, backdoorism depends on a more subtle general ability to establish relations with people in authority and thus reap advantages in a number of ways. This is known generally as *guan-xi* in China, a term that describes a state of being generally well connected. There is a successful popular singer, for example, who got her start when she was noticed by a top-ranking official from the same province. The official wanted someone who sang the local folk melodies he loved to travel with a performing arts troupe abroad. After that, her career advanced rapidly. She even went through a serious personal scandal, involving a husband who deserted her, a lover married to somebody else, and an illegitimate baby — the kinds of moral peccadillos that would have destroyed someone without *guan-xi*. But the singer escaped censure by going "through the back door."

The key elements in backdoorism are the scarcity of things and the fact that access to them is privileged. These characteristics have been common throughout Chinese history so it is not surprising that backdoorism permeates Chinese society today in the same way that a certain acceptable margin of corruption did during imperial days. In centuries past it was called "squeeze," this private area of activity whereby officials received payment for settling a dispute in somebody's favor or a rich merchant handed out red envelopes filled with money to get his son named a court official. Backdoorism is its postrevolutionary manifestation. Like the special privileges of the top bureaucrats, it represents a tropism in Chinese society; it is a restoration of a past way of doing things.

There are many other manifestations of this practical social and economic lubricant, of these ways by which individuals bypass the strict rules of socialist society for the sake of personal gain. I knew, for example, the son of a very high-ranking military officer. He used to lunch with me from time to time. I was in search of information; he, of foreign-made cigarettes. Thus, every so often, he would give me, say, fifty yuan (thirty-five dollars) and I would go to the Friendship Store and, with the equivalent amount of foreign-exchange certificates, would buy him a few cartons of Players or Benson and Hedges, which, I presume, he passed along to friends, receiving favors from them in return.

Similarly, foreign businessmen began reporting on the resurgence of still another common feature of the prerevolutionary society: corruption. Suddenly in the late 1970s and early 1980s, officials in the state trading corporations, in factories, in the government exporting divisions, began accepting color TVs, cassette players, sponsorships for their children to study abroad, in exchange for highly desired contracts. The quest for money and material goods — those eternal *bêtes noires* of Maoist puritanism — quickly became obvious, and in many cases obsessive. When local trading corporations in 1980 gained the right to make their own sales to foreign companies, the central state trading corporations were sometimes discovered to have been overcharging during the time when they enjoyed a monopoly on dealings with foreigners.

To make profits was around that same time pronounced a legitimate and praiseworthy function of any unit of production, and a new system of bonuses ensured that at least a small portion of those profits would go into the hands of the workers of that unit — this after a long period of "ultra-leftism," which had decreed the desire for profits a relic of bourgeois selfishness and unproletarian greed. There was, for example, a terrible shortage of the better-quality cigarettes. The reason: local tobacco-growing communes, rather than shipping their produce to the regular cigarette factories, began to set up their own workshops. There, without the proper technology or capital investment, they manufactured cheap, low-quality cigarettes, which they then put onto the market themselves.

This, of course, remained different from the squeeze, the corruption, the profit seeking of prerevolutionary China. In its latter-day manifestation, it became incorporated into the system of state capitalism and in this sense, perhaps, the receipts were often more justly distributed than they had been before. At the same time, it humanized the Chinese; it made them appear as they really were: susceptible to the same sorts of temptations and greeds that afflict the rest of us. And yet, given the self-righteous professions of the propaganda about the superiority of socialism, given the standard claim that greed and corruption are encouraged by a materialism in the capitalist system that is absent in postrevolutionary China, the return of squeeze carried with it a particularly hypocritical odor. Moreover, while, in general, the restoration of Chineseness, in both its best and worst aspects, was reassuring to many, it was taking place only after a long experience of socialist experiments that would never allow China to be exactly the same. Indeed, in Peking, the heritage of Mao and the nature of communism produced a host of special problems that had not existed before and that would have to be solved by the country's new pragmatic leaders if they were to succeed in their ambitious program of modernization.

10

Monuments
and the Meaning of Maoism

A SUGGESTION of the most serious problem — that of the Maoist legacy — can be had by a look at some of the magnificent and not so magnificent monuments of Peking. Begin at the Great Wall. Everybody goes
there now. By late morning the traffic is so heavy that it is backed up two
or three miles, a parade of tourist buses, army trucks, limousines carrying
important visitors, farm tractors hauling cargoes of live sheep, groaning
and shuddering as they strain over steep hills. At the head of the long de-
file marking the Ba Ta Ling pass, the natural boundary between the
North China Plain and Inner Mongolia, stands what has become the chief
touristic symbol of China. It is, say the American astronauts, the only
man-made object that can be discerned from space. While many portions
have been dismantled by local people eager for building stone, it still
stretches an awesome length as it follows the curves and rises of China's
inner Asia frontier, from the eastern shore to a point in Gansu Province
nearly four thousand miles to the west.

Everybody knows that the Great Wall was built in the third century
B.C. by China's first emperor for the purpose of warding off the northern
barbarians, who tended to carry out raids into the sedentary Chinese civilization to the south. In that sense, it is symbolic of the Chinese view of
their place in the world. You sense that on the wall itself, as you stand
atop one of the guard towers, face into the cold wind of, say, November,
and look north over the barren, intimidating hills leading to Mongolia.
You can sense the wall still as an outpost, as the frontier of civilization.
Peking itself, two hours by car to the south, may be forbidding in its own
way, but it is a welcome relief after the stark vistas of the other side of the
pass.

But there are other, more contemporary meanings. On one of my trips to the wall (I had to go there whenever I had guests in Peking), the full irony of the thing struck me with the force of an icy blast from Inner Mongolia. The histories say that a million people died building the wall. Yet despite the staggering sacrifice, the wall did not succeed as a defensive rampart. When the empire was strong, the barbarians were kept at bay by dint of its superior military power and its own expeditions of subjugation into the nomads' territory. When the empire was weak, the wall could hardly prevent the barbarians from their raids and conquests. Yet, even though it didn't work, dynasty after dynasty repaired and rebuilt it. In that sense the wall emblematizes a habit of mind as characteristic of the China of the late Chairman Mao as of the emperor of Qin (with whom Mao defiantly compared himself).

You can see it on the massive, iron-gray stones of the wall, which did not keep the barbarian invaders away. You can see it in the elaborately worked, soaring terraces of the model agricultural production brigade, Dazhai, which in 1980 was exposed as having grossly falsified its production figures. You can see it in the drill rigs of the industrial model, Daqing, where, despite a vast investment of labor and money, oil production failed to go up in the last few years of its existence. It is the Chinese — and the Maoist — instinct to solve problems by throwing staggering amounts of backbreaking labor into them; it is the historic Chinese tendency to perform great tasks by mobilizing the resource that it has always had in greater abundance than any other country, its vast population. And this reveals something of profound importance about the nature — and the limitations — of the Chinese revolution.

The men who brought communism to China in 1949 were, unlike those in Russia in 1917, not urban intellectuals. They were, for the most part, rough-hewn, semi-educated peasants, who, while possessed of the modern idea of political organization, tended, once power was theirs, to fall back on the same age-old way of doing things as their imperial predecessors had. This habit of mind, moreover, was fortified by the major feature of the revolutionary war itself: that it was accomplished by a vast uprising of China's peasant masses. The Communist leaders of China who arrived from the wilderness into Peking in 1949 thought very much in terms of solving problems by mobilizing huge numbers of people, of accomplishing tasks in the same guerrilla-war fashion that had won them the country in the first place. This is the essence of the Maoist spirit by which China was ruled, or misruled, for the first twenty-nine years of the Communist exercise of power. It is the spirit of the Great Wall.

Certainly, there is no question of how Mao saw himself in relation to the builder of that great monument, China's first emperor, Qin Shi Huang. In 1975, Mao was under attack for being autocratic, like the emperor of Qin, who for centuries has been one of China's greatest historical villains. Mao's defiant reply was that Qin Shi Huang was not a villain but a great hero, and what's more, that whereas Qin Shi Huang had buried only 460 scholars, he, Mao, had killed thousands of them. That, to Mao, was reason for boasting. Later, in the wake of the Cultural Revolution, Mao promoted a veritable campaign to restore Qin Shi Huang's historical reputation. As the great unifier of China and the oppressor of the feudal aristocracy, he was proclaimed a great hero, a great predecessor for Mao himself.

Mao's identification with Qin Shi Huang is conspicuous back in Peking too, in the form of still another monument, which, in 1977, took its place alongside the grand imperial structures that still survive — the Forbidden City, the Bell Tower, the Temple of Heaven, the Marble Barge, and the beautiful Qianmen, or Front Gate. Directly behind the Front Gate, occupying a large section of Tiananmen Square, the spiritual center of Peking, is the mausoleum of Mao. I passed it almost daily, noticing how unfavorably it compares architecturally to the Front Gate beside it and thinking that it is more than just a monument to the father of Chinese communism. It, too, is in the tradition of the Great Wall. It is a symbol of Mao's way of making revolution.

After Mao's death in September 1976, the decision was made almost immediately to entomb his preserved remains — following that ghoulish Communist practice applied already to Lenin and Ho Chi Minh — in a glass coffin, so that future generations could view the body of the man who had changed the course of history. Mao, it was decided, would be enshrined in far grander state than any emperor before him, grander even than Qin Shi Huang himself with his gigantic tumulus near Xian complete with a now excavated underground army of life-size terra-cotta soldiers. And so, in typical Chinese Communist fashion, the Peking government organized what they call a *da hui zhan*, a guerrilla war term that loosely translates as a "battle in which all forces are mobilized." The materials were assembled, the design quickly drawn up, and, most important, vast amounts of labor were pulled off other projects and thrown into the construction. It was finished in less than nine months. And the official boast became, not that it was a beautiful monument, not that it was a suitable memorial for the Great Helmsman, but that it was built so quickly in a great outpouring of mass energy and enthusiasm.

Given the haste of its construction, the mausoleum is not an absolute monstrosity in architectural terms. I have not seen a single building in China constructed since 1949 that is distinguished; given the Communists' predilection for massive, pretentious, epic-heroic, and often garish buildings, the mausoleum can even be considered a pleasant surprise. Nonetheless, compare it to the inspired Front Gate next to it. The gate rises gracefully upward in five separate tiers, three curved roofs, and two balconies. It is a somber oxblood red and imperial green and is a perfect amalgam of strength and grace. More important, it shows how, as in Renaissance Florence, the strands of power and art came together perfectly in China. The men who founded the great dynasties and became emperors were violent warriors, but the running of the state was taken over by the confident Confucian elite, the literate, cultivated scholars who were as good at painting and poetry, and building gates, as they were at governing.

By contrast, the mausoleum is a petit-bourgeois confection, a Levittown Parthenon, consisting of an unimaginative cream-colored, columned rectangle with an insipid burnt orange band around the upper floor that, I suppose, represents a frieze. I have tried to imagine the committee meetings to design the mausoleum that would have taken place in the wake of Mao's death. There would have been a couple of architects and engineers, representatives of the Peking municipal government and the Communist party Central Committee and several of those peasant soldiers who held real power in China. Charged with creating something grand and inspiring, the committee would have had to reject the old feudal-imperial style as unfitting for a proletarian hero. China, at the time, was in a rabidly antitraditionalist, anti-elitist mood, which was itself part of the Maoist heritage left over from the Cultural Revolution. The designers of the mausoleum needed to create something that would appeal to "the masses," to create something in a genuinely "popular" style. Fortunately, they did not come up with one of those immense concrete towers surmounted by illuminated red glass flames like, for example, the Revolutionary Museum in Canton. They did better than that. Still, having rejected the elitist tradition, they really had nothing to put in its place. Western modernism, with its stench of capitalism, would have been out of the question. And so, with neither tradition nor modernity to serve as a model, the design committee had no alternative but to fall back on yet another variation on the theme of Stalinist architecture, producing something massive but without grace, new but not modern, sanctimonious but not awe-inspiring. The mausoleum is, to borrow the Chinese expression, *mama-huhu*, meaning neither horse nor tiger.

There is irony aplenty in the presence of the tacky mausoleum in the middle of Tiananmen Square. But the greatest irony lies in the fact that even as it was being constructed, China itself began with astonishing speed to turn away from what Mao represented. Subtly, and then not so subtly, Mao, after 1978, was criticized. His mistakes were proclaimed;

then in 1979 and 1980 respectively, his greatest enemies, former defense minister Peng Dehuai and former head of state Liu Shaoqi, were posthumously awarded great honors. I arrived in Peking to open the *Time* bureau in the middle of the 1980 Qing Ming festival, when the Chinese honor the dead. Long rows of school children in Tiananmen Square led up to the Martyr's Monument, where they placed wreaths to the memory of Liu, the man vilified by Mao, with typical rhetorical overkill, as a "renegade, a traitor, and a scab." For twelve years Liu's name had been synonymous with villainy in China. Scorn and abuse had been heaped on him with all the combined forces of China's propaganda machine. Now, suddenly all was changed. Liu was a socialist hero again. What's more, there were no wreaths to Mao. A giant photograph of him hanging above the entrance to the nearby Museum of the History of the Revolution watched over the ceremonies in honor of Liu. Then, one night a few months later, the photograph of Mao came down, as did those of Marx, Engels, Lenin, and Stalin nearby, leaving just one Mao picture in the square at the entrance to the Forbidden City.

Of course, the mausoleum, just a stone's throw away, also remains. And so too does the problem of Mao. Not only the problem of what to do to his reputation, but how to deal with all those in power, all those peasant warriors, who cling to his memory and to notions of his greatness. And then, there is the problem of the Great Wall mentality. How to shed Mao's inclination to launch *da hui zhan*, his inclination to assault all problems as though they were enemies on a battlefield; in other words, how to modernize?

Mao was that ultimate rarity in ultraconservative Chinese society, an extreme iconoclast, a startlingly original thinker, and a man of abrupt and often impetuous action. An old Chinese scholar once remarked to me, in as perfect a statement of the traditional Chinese character as there could be, "I am a Chinese and therefore I cannot be an extremist." What he meant, I think, is that it is a profound part of the Chinese nature to act, as Confucius did, according to a doctrine of the mean, a middle way between opposite extremes. Traditionally, the Chinese eschewed struggle. He believed in a natural hierarchy. He was patient, and wise enough to resign himself to the imperfections that he found in his fellow man.

The brilliant peasant whose remains are now half decomposed in Tiananmen Square was decidedly none of these things. He was a peasant intellectual, largely self-taught, who came to maturity in the 1910s, a time when Chinese students and intellectuals were engaged in the rampant experimentalism and renewal of the May Fourth Movement. Mao was idealistic, tireless, committed, and, apparently, imbued with the conviction that he had been singled out by the fates for a great destiny. That conviction may have been self-fulfilling, for history has rarely seen a purer example of a man who succeeded through the unyielding application of personal will.

Mao's strategy during his long quest for power was always based on a logic and pragmatism so commonsensical that they seem, in retrospect, obvious. Unlike the Kuomintang generals, he saw the importance of public relations. During his various guerrilla campaigns, for example, he devised a few rules of conduct for the army — from not raping the women to returning all borrowed objects — that gradually ended the peasantry's well-founded terror of any armed group. His early land-reform campaigns were also models of good sense. They were antiradical. The goal was to direct the "class struggle" against only a few bad landlords in each village so that, in the redistribution of the land to the tiller, the Communist party made the maximum number of allies while antagonizing the minimum number of enemies. Indeed, through the seizure of power in 1949, Mao's policies were extraordinary in their flexibility, their moderation, their freedom from predetermined ideological notions. It was his creative pragmatism that, along with such other factors as the Japanese invasion, enabled him to emerge victorious in the Chinese civil war.

Except for one other thing: for his entire career, Mao, earthbound peasant that he was, remained profoundly suspicious of China's intellectuals. He needed Chinese with skills and education, teachers, writers, artists, scientists. But he never overcame a contempt for them as impractical eggheads always prone to serve themselves rather than the revolution. This anti-intellectualism was ironic in a man who thought that he was something of an intellectual himself, if largely a self-taught one. But a petty consistency was not the hobgoblin of Mao's mind. He once described himself as part monkey and part tiger, part reflective, patient analyst and part impatient, intolerant, and megalomaniacal man of action.

Mao's anti-intellectualism erupted in the early 1940s with the first of the "rectification" campaigns that were to take place from time to time for the rest of his political tutelage of China. Cruel and often vindictive, the Mao of that first episode developed some of the dehumanizing tactics that were to be used in subsequent purges of intellectuals: the mass struggle session, the campaign by innuendo, the beatings and isolations, the humiliation of public self-criticisms, and, finally, the complete disgrace of any and all who refused to toe the official line.

I talked to a middle-aged man from an intellectual background who, during his youth, had been an activist in some of the early campaigns in the 1950s — the so-called Three Anti and Five Anti campaigns. "I was too young and impetuous to realize it at the time," he said, "but later I understood how terrible the tactics that we used were. We slandered people, we frightened everybody so much that they were willing to attack any scapegoat we came up with. There were beatings and murders even in those early campaigns. In each place we were given a quota. Three to five percent of the people had to be branded counterrevolutionaries no matter what the actual situation was. So, there were some places that had no real targets but we attacked three to five percent of the people anyway. There were some places where there were a lot of people against the revolution, but not all of them were attacked."

It is hard to overestimate how heavily Mao's peasant anti-intellectualism, his drive for purity, weighed on the Chinese nation, how destructive it has been of what was once among the greatest cultures in the world. The catastrophic failure to adopt a population-control program may well have stemmed from Mao's political faith in gigantic mobilizations of labor. That is also the common thread that links together such other policy disasters as the various ideological campaigns of the 1950s, including the Great Leap Forward, as well as the Cultural Revolution. One crucial result of these episodes of recklessness and excess is a society in which sheer terror was the common everyday experience of millions of people. The fear of making mistakes was so great and so persistent that in the 1980s one constant refrain in the propaganda consisted of reassurances that things had truly changed forever, that it was both safe and indeed necessary for those in positions of power to take initiatives without worrying about retribution. The Maoist campaigns had impelled millions of Chinese to remain as uninvolved as possible in the great tasks of nation building, to retreat into a world where their main object was to keep personal disaster at arm's length, where they tried to say only the few phrases deemed orthodox by the Maoist tyrants and to remain as inconspicuous as possible. For example, with hardly an exception, none of the grand old men of Chinese literature, whose stories between the 1920s and the 1940s had created a new awakening in the country, wrote a single major work after 1949.

One of the most damaging parts of Mao's heritage is the army of peasant bureaucrats he brought to power with him in 1949 and again during the Cultural Revolution, that enormous band of semiskilled politicians deeply imbued with the Great Helmsman's sense that all bad things can be swept away by a well-organized outpouring of goodwilled energy. As one Chinese journalist explained to me: "There are thousands, millions of peasants out there, unsophisticated people who don't understand the outside world. They liked Mao because of his extreme xenophobia. They believed all those simplistic slogans about imperialism and they are very reluctant to turn away from them. These are the people who took up arms and fought the Kuomintang and the imperialists in the revolutionary war. They see everything the way they saw things during the civil war, in terms of large amounts of force. There will be a struggle in the future between them and the pragmatists who are running the country now. The peasants are still there."

Maoism as the state philosophy seemed to come to an end in October 1976 when the great Helmsman's wife Jiang Qing and the rest of the so-called Gang of Four were arrested, paving the way for the return of the moderates. But other aspects of Maoism remained. In the wake of the arrests, China's leaders impetuously announced a series of sweeping national goals — to upgrade industry, agriculture, defense, science and technology — known collectively as the Four Modernizations. The early targets were so unrealistic that they were followed by nearly two years of confusion, vacillation, and uncertainty until they were finally abandoned. The early, eventually discarded, targets were pure, reflexive Maoism. So too were a number of other disastrous economic decisions. Hundreds of millions of dollars were sunk into foreign imported-steel mills — one in Wuhan and the other in Shanghai — that were so badly planned as to be almost worthless. The plant in Wuhan has an inadequate supply of iron ore; to run it at full capacity would take so much electricity that most of the rest of the province would have to go without power. The even more notorious plant near Shanghai — the so-called Baoshan Iron and Steel Works — has inadequate port facilities, and is on land so soft that the construction piles did not hold. Originally the Chinese planned to spend nearly five billion dollars on imported equipment, but they would have needed another nine to fourteen billion in local costs like roads and electrical power. The total cost of that one project would thus have been equal to more than 20 percent of the entire national budget for 1981 (sixty-one billion dollars). Nationwide, the press admitted, there was twenty million tons of steel already sitting in warehouses that could not be used because it was produced blindly without any consideration of what the end users might want or need. (The amount was also included in the nation's production figures to show how fast industrial abilities are rising.) Finally, in 1981, the Chinese announced that they were canceling all but the relatively modest first stage of the Baoshan plant, even though hundreds of millions had already been spent on imported equipment.

By the early 1980s, it was clear that the forces of moderation were trying to put the revolutionary monumentalism of Mao into the past. As Hua Guofeng was gradually stripped of power, one of the most common charges made against him was his headstrong idealism in economic matters symbolized by a call he once made to "build ten Daqings," a reference to China's model oil field in Heilongjiang Province. Beneath Hua, a group of officials known collectively as the "oil clique" were also eased out of power. They had predicted that by the mid-1980s the country's total production of crude would be about two hundred million tons a year. They spent billions of dollars importing sophisticated petrochemical refineries from Japan and West Germany to convert this oil bonanza into exportable products. But the oil wasn't there; new, saner predictions put production by the mid-1980s at under one hundred million tons. Not a single new Daqing had been created even as the original Daqing's production was going down. In a final acknowledgment of the disasters of impetuous Mao-style economics, Peking had to cancel many of the contracts it had signed for imported petrochemical plants, even though China had already paid for hundreds of millions of dollars' worth of work and equipment.

This loss too was part of the heritage of Mao. The handsome visionary youth from Hunan was one of history's most successful figures, particularly if success is measured by the distance one must travel to get from obscurity to fame, from insignificance to power. But in the end what became China's own official reassessment of Mao placed the party chairman more or less where he belonged in history. Mao reunited China, made it independent, and elevated it again to worldwide significance. But during much of the twenty-seven years of his near imperial rule, he moved closer and closer to the mentality of those who built the magnificently useless Great Wall. The mausoleum in which Mao's earthly remains are exhibited is a constant reminder of that costly bad habit.

Early in the summer of 1981, the Chinese Communist party officially admitted that Mao had brought catastrophe to the people of China. This extraordinary statement came in the form of the party's final resolution on the contributions and mistakes of its former Great Leader, published as part of a meeting of the Central Committee. "Comrade Mao Tse-tung was a great Marxist and a great proletarian revolutionary, strategist, and theorist," the assessment declared. And then it went on to belie that claim by proclaiming Mao chiefly responsible for a host of disastrous errors: slanderously attacking thousands of intellectuals during the 1957 antirightist campaign, fostering his own cult of the personality, and, especially, launching the Cultural Revolution in 1966. Mao, said the party's official declaration, "confused right and wrong; . . . he gradually divorced himself from practice and from the masses, acted more and more arbitrarily and subjectively, and increasingly put himself above the Central Committee of the party." His mistakes were "comprehensive in magnitude and protracted in duration"; they "plunged the nation into turmoil." The assessment of Mao asserted what most Chinese already knew: that the heavy concentration on "class struggle," on the mass campaigns, on movements and parades, on constant rectification, ideology, and politics, had subverted the revolution. The assessment was an attempt by the post-Mao leadership to regain prestige by disassociating itself from the leader everybody had once been required to worship. From now on, China's new party leaders seemed to be saying, there would be communism without Maoism. The party would now devote itself to what it termed the "scientific principles of Mao Tse-tung Thought" — rather, that is, than Mao's unfortunate mistakes — and would embark on just what China needed, a "period of peaceful development."

The reappraisal of Mao was a long time in coming. It was issued nearly five years after his death; the thirty-five-thousand-word document required at least one year of drafting and debate before it was pronounced official; its promulgation was accompanied by the dismissal of Mao's handpicked successor as party chairman, Hua Guofeng. In these ways, the reassessment itself was an emblem of how long it takes to accomplish anything of significance in China; it showed that all major decisions — and many not so major ones — are accompanied by a tough jockeying for power and position among the topmost leaders. The document also contained all of the stilted abstractions and shards of prefabricated jargon that are themselves an unfortunate part of the Maoist legacy. It was replete with "erroneous leftist theses" and "right deviationist trends"; it talked of the "universal principles of Marxism-Leninism": of "counter-revolutionary cliques," and "opportunists, careerists, and conspirators," and "democratic centralism." It also contained the mandatory references to "the masses," to "criticism and struggle," as well as to the "oppressed nations of the world" and the "progress of mankind," and the rest of the pseudoscientific vocabulary of imprecision and vagueness that is communism's contribution to world literature.

This is not to say that the reevaluation of Mao was not an important event. While less bold and certainly less abrupt than Khrushchev's criticism of Stalin in 1956, the Mao reassessment was a promise to do things differently, more sanely, in the future, and in this sense it was a Communist milestone. And yet, it was troubling. It was a judgment of Mao that partook of many of the themes of Maoism itself. Most important, its very definitiveness precluded future free inquiry on the man whose actions and beliefs had affected every person in China. Its effort to determine by some near mathematical formula Mao's contributions and shortcomings stems from the notion that communism is "science," that there are "correct" policies and there are "mistakes," both of which can be measured against some clear historical standard. The assessment itself would quickly enter into the canon; it would become a part of the "scientific truth" and remain as such until some future leadership determined that the "truth" once again needed to be revised.

Why could the party, anxious to restore its tarnished image, not have thrown the question of Mao open to public debate? Why could it not have disclosed the whole truth? Because to do so would have brought far more than the acts of a single individual into question. A free debate on Mao would naturally lead to the conclusion that it was the intolerance and dictatorial nature of the Communist system itself that was at fault, not Mao alone. To avoid that, the debate, like everything else, had to be controlled, stage-managed, dictated by the upper levels of the leadership. The leadership hoped to convey the impression that Maoism was mistaken only because of its excesses, because of its reckless campaigns. That is to some extent true. But Maoism was also the same imperative to control that determined how the Mao reassessment would be drafted, that is indeed at the heart of communism. In that sense, its release called attention, not so much to how far the post-Mao Communists had distanced themselves from their great predecessor, but to how much distance they still had to travel to separate themselves from Maoism itself.

11

Power and Privilege

FROM ONE VERY CONSPICUOUS Peking monument to an inconspicuous, secret, but very important, one, you have to walk only ten minutes. It is a revealing stroll. Start, as I have done, from the back entrance to the Forbidden City — the conspicuous monument — where the buses and taxis stand in rows awaiting the tourists and other visitors who troop through it every day. Across the street to the north is the park known as Jingshan, surmounted by a Chinese-style gazebo. The quickest way to the secret monument would be straight north over the hill. But I choose to take the roundabout, level way, walking down Jingshan East Street, keeping the high, chipped, and faded imperial-red wall of the park on the left. Jingshan East Street plunges between twin rows of sedate plane trees. On its right side is a long row of low-slung houses, concealed from the street by another wall, this one of stained whitewash, irregularly broken by open entryways or by doors of old, heavy wood. Arched, black-tiled roofs peer over the wall, steep slanted ones with small dormer windows, some with faded painted trim. There are the tops of wooden latticed windows, a few small chimneys that are connected inside the houses to iron potbellied stoves.

The tops of *huai shu*, Chinese scholar trees, are also visible, disclosing that within there are courtyards, some with wisteria in the spring. And there is a *hutung* or two, the small lanes that wind among the compounds in truly labyrinthine fashion like the mazes lovingly constructed by Tang dynasty princes. But what most impresses about this quarter of town is its homogeneity, its lack of pretense, its absence of features, its studied and by no means charmless drabness. There is no sense here at all of the magnificence of the Forbidden City, which lies only a few paces back.

At the north end of Jingshan East Street is a large crossroads where you turn west, keeping the oxblood-colored wall and the ancient wooden towers of Jingshan on the left. Across the street is another whitewashed wall, this one also concealing the nature of the residential quarter within, except here a Tudor-style house surmounted by an iron weather vane projects above the wall, a reminder of the days when wealthy Europeans built houses in Peking. From the very center of the park, Dianmen Street, the precise north-south axis of Peking, extends northward, between two near monumental five-story buildings, mirror images of each other. These are unfortunate Sino-European hybrids of the kind that were often built in the republican and early Communist eras in which a conventional Western-style edifice was topped off by a Chinese-style roof. In this case, the buildings are unidentified, unmarked, their front doors barred shut, a sign that they are occupied by either the military or the security service. Passersby say they don't know what the buildings are. There are soldiers posted outside them. In any case, they are close to our destination. Just beyond the monumental hybrid on the west side of Dianmen is a factory called the Peking Calculator Equipment Company, evidently placed in this ancient, residential quarter by some strange zoning irregularity. A modest *hutung*, called Grain Storehouse Lane, runs west past the factory and into another of those neighborhoods of low whitewashed houses and black-tiled roofs that seem entirely without unusual features or distinctions. Yet, while it is hardly visible from the street, or even from considerably farther into the lane, camouflaged within is our inconspicuous monument, the residential quarters of China's most powerful political figure, Deng Xiaoping.

Like so much else about them, the dwelling places of China's top leaders are secrets (if sometimes not very well kept ones), as are such other things as their telephone numbers, the location of their offices, the number and identities of their children, all but the bare skeletons of their personal histories, their whereabouts at all times when they are not making their rare public appearances, even occasionally the particular job they are supposed to be performing. Some of the highest leaders, like Mao and, before his disgrace in the Cultural Revolution, Liu Shaoqi, lived inside the Zhongnanhai compound, a guarded, walled-off, entirely isolated area whose adjacency to the imperial palace suggests a startling irony. The Communists, as I have noted, have made much propaganda over the fact that the ancient seat of the imperial Chinese government was sealed off to all but the highest government officials and princes of the realm. But, the Zhongnanhai compound is a spiritual replica of the palace; it is a latter-day Forbidden City, sealed off to the old hundred surnames, except at times to groups of schoolchildren paraded in to view Mao's old study. (And, of course, to the foreign heads of state who were granted audiences with Mao, much as the old tribute-bearing missions on the rims of China used to be ushered within the Forbidden City into the imperial presence.)

There is a bridge behind Zhongnanhai over a lovely lake that extends from the government compound north into the Beihai Park. While Mao was alive, it was forbidden for cyclists or pedestrians to stop in their progress over the bridge, presumably because of the very partial view it affords of the exclusive precincts just to the south. While that regulation has been annulled, even today the two sides of the lake are divided by the bridge into entirely separate worlds. On the north side, in the Beihai Park, the lake is thronged with that monochromatic crowd that jams into most of Peking's few recreational spaces, either rowing boats or ice-skating, depending on the season. By contrast, the southern portion, lying outside the secure walls of Zhongnanhai, is nearly empty — except in winter for the occasional ice skater or two, evidently people privileged enough to gain entry to the off-limits half of the lake.

Architecturally, the Forbidden City of the Communist regime is not to be confused with the glorious one of the emperors. Those few foreigners who, accompanying some head of state on a visit to Chairman Mao, have been inside its precincts, say that it is unsplendid. The functional offices of the State Council, China's cabinet, are located there as are the gray, rectangular, utilitarian, unattractive brick buildings of other parts of the bureaucracy, the upper stories of which are higher than the surrounding walls and thus visible from the outside. Nonetheless, the Zhongnanhai restricted zone and the absolute seclusion of China's top leaders from the public eye seem far more than simple matters of security or privacy. They are resonant of the imperial style. They serve to mark the leaders off from the other members of society, whose lives are exposed in every detail to the personnel departments of their workplaces or their neighborhood committees or to curious agents of the Public Security Bureau. Precisely because of their exclusivity, the top leaders are also the subject of a major share of the common gossip of Peking. And since the children and grandchildren of party cadres are among the principal gossipers, it is sometimes possible to discover some of their secrets — like where they live.

If you visit Deng Xiaoping's house, however, you will most likely not be invited in for tea. Unlike both public and private Americans or Europeans, Chinese leaders simply do not entertain at home. Thus when, during the celebrated postnormalization visit of 1979, Zbigniew Brzezinski had Deng Xiaoping over to his house for a home-cooked roast beef dinner, he had no reason to think that his hospitality would be reciprocated at Deng's place if he visited China again. So, one's visit to the powerful vice-premier's house must be unannounced. Moreover, it will not be very welcome.

There are two entrances, a rear one giving on a small alley on the north side and a front one on Grain Storehouse Lane. Both consist of massive, rusting steel grates. On the afternoon when I went to look at the place, there was a troop of about sixteen P.L.A. soldiers parading outside the front gate. Approaching the back, I could see barbed wire atop the walls surrounding the house, which is itself a two-story structure of ordinary gray brick, with a small patch of lawn and some shrubbery visible through the entry gate. As I got closer, I could see the cover of a peephole slide open and then shut. And as I wandered through the tiny, ordinary lanes beside and behind the house, I noticed numerous men in the roomy greatcoats of the army flit like phantoms across a lane from one entryway to another. The area seemed nearly deserted but for these swiftly darting shadows. Yet, I had the definite crawly sensation on the back of my neck of being scrutinized at every instant during my stroll through the neighborhood.

Much has been written about the new Communist classes, the new czars or the new mandarins, who, like the more equal pigs in Orwell's *Animal Farm*, take the place of the czars and mandarins they have overthrown, enjoying mistresses and limousines, foreign travel and exclusive villas, all far beyond the reach of the common people. It should be remembered, however, that some of the things that set leaders apart are not marks of hypocritical privilege, even in a socialist society where a kind of egalitarian democracy remains a theoretical goal. In a society as poor as China's where things are difficult to get and where the routine of ordinary life is filled with inconvenience, one could hardly expect those charged with the security of the state to do without cars and better housing, housemaids, personal secretaries, and special supply shops. Not very far from Deng's residence, for example, is a square building with curtained windows where the top leaders can send members of their staff to buy meat, vegetables, and fruits that are not commonly available on the market. Just down from the Foreign Ministry, an inconspicuous red-painted wooden shop is a special bookstore where high-ranking party and government officials can pick up the works that are produced in limited editions for their eyes only — especially translations of foreign books like Hedrick Smith's *Russians* or, ironically, Milovan Djilas's *New Class*. I once went over to the bookstore, having been supplied with the address by the son of a ranking official, and, as I expected, was politely but firmly refused even a quick glance inside.

It should not be supposed that access to these conveniences extends very far down the strict hierarchy of China's officials. Chauffeured limousines, for example, are reserved only for those at the rank of vice-minister or higher (meaning probably a couple of hundred officials in Peking) and for regimental commanders in the army. Indeed, at least in theory, there is nothing accidental in who gets what in China's system. There are twenty-four grades of what are called "state cadres" in the governmental hierarchy, each corresponding to a certain salary and a certain set of prerogatives. Above rank nine (the lower the number, the higher the grade in China's system), for example, an official can have a maid paid for by the state. Certain levels signify certain sizes of apartments and whether there will be a bath or not and whether or not the cadre's bureau or ministry will dispatch a car to take him to and from work.

One extraordinary aspect of this system is that it seems intentionally to have been modeled on the structure of the imperial bureaucracy. In fact, the similarity is no doubt unintentional: it would be denied by the Communists of today. But, like the Communist bureaucracy, that under the emperors was also broken down into an elaborate series of grades and ranks — sixteen in all during the Qing dynasty, led by the Grand Secretary of the Grand Secretariat, a kind of prime minister. Like the contemporary grades, the imperial ranks carried with them elaborate, and often ceremonial, distinctions, from the length and color of the sash that held together one's silk robes to one's seating at imperial banquets. Perhaps even more eerily similar to later Communist practice was the terror, the career ups and downs, or, to put it into a modern context, the purges and restorations to grace that were part of the pattern of official life in centuries past. Deng Xiaoping fell out of favor twice and bounced back twice. So did many of his imperial predecessors. One study by Adam Liu of the early Qing bureaucracy shows that of sixty-seven Grant Secretaries who served at one time or another in the court, only eighteen had never once been demoted or dismissed throughout their service. So severe was the capricious terror of the Ming dynasty that, in the words of historian Charles Hucker, "officials of the capital always bade their wives and children farewell on leaving for court audience each morning and if evening came without disaster, they congratulated one another on surviving another day." Lower down in the hierarchy, as Liu has written, officials were constantly subject to official examination by a Bureau of Metropolitan Inspection — today this work is done by the Party Central Discipline Inspection Commission — which graded each official regularly on such criteria as faithfulness and administrative competence as well as on such possible offenses as greediness, cruelty, carelessness, or senility.

The imperial middle class of government officials has its counterpart in the vast middle levels of the contemporary Chinese bureaucracy, the huge civil service of the revolution. And here, my impression is that drabness and routine and a daily struggle with the necessities of life are far more the rule than special provisions or access to Red Flag limousines.

I have been in a few homes of the Chinese revolutionary civil service, including the homes of the so-called *sanshiba ganbu* — the 1938 cadres. These are the men and women who joined the Communist party near the beginning of the full-scale invasion of China by Japan, a personal commitment that still confers on them an ineffable prestige for being an "old revolutionary." One such man whom I visited for tea was a "section chief" in one of the cultural bureaus. His tiny apartment was in the bowels of a dark and immense structure dating from the early 1950s. The long, dingy corridor was cluttered with bottled-gas containers and single-burner stoves, since, especially in the summer, most people preferred not to cook their meals inside their apartments. The walls were covered with yellowed sheets of newspapers to protect them from grease. Bicycles, not limousines, were parked outside. The apartment consisted of one plain, sizable room with an alcove. It had the luxury of a wooden floor (virtually all of the new buildings for mid-level cadres are cement above, below, and all around). There was a collection of old pieces of furniture, a table, an armoire, a bed, a calendar on the wall, a glass-enclosed case with a few books and what looked like photo albums. Three generations lived there, the old revolutionary himself, his wife, his divorced daughter, and his grandson. The home did not constitute an enormous material reward for his forty-five years of devoted service to the Communist party.

In the western quarter of Peking there are ranks of apartment blocks also intended for state cadres. These are new, having been carved in the last few years from what was an area of plain *ping-fang* and agricultural land. I was invited to dinner at the home of a grade-twelve cadre, who worked in one of the scientific bureaus, doing exactly what, I could not determine. He was a small, deferential, decidedly rural type with horrific teeth and an even more horrific country-bumpkin accent, who had also joined the Communist party in his teens and had fought during the anti-Japanese, anti-Kuomintang campaigns with the legendary Fourth Route Army. His wife too was an old revolutionary cadre. I brought along a bottle of white Bordeaux and they politely, but with undisguisable distaste, sipped it (instead of the sweet red stuff they would have preferred) at dinner. The high-rise apartment was cramped, cement, gray, purely utilitarian, devoid of any beauty or grace. Dinner was of very fatty pork cold cuts, preserved bean curd, dry, sliced, boiled store-bought beef, stir-fried cabbage, and mounds of heavy dumplings, all of which was piled on my plate by my seven Chinese hosts crowded with me around a rickety wooden table about the right size for bridge.

The conversation was startling. One of the younger people — the son-in-law — wanted, like millions of Chinese, to go to the United States. But he was afraid that if he wrote a letter to the American embassy in Peking, it would be intercepted by the Chinese Public Security Bureau. He asked me to deliver the letter for him (I did). As the conversation went on, the younger generation expressed more and more their displeasure with their lack of choice, the restrictions on their lives, while the old revolutionary father remained quiet, a bit melancholy I thought, like an old immigrant grandparent who just cannot keep up with what the young people are saying these days. He devoted himself to piling my plate high and, from time to time, asking me questions like did we have Chinese food in America and how much would one pay for an apartment like his. As we adjourned from the dining alcove to the other room for tea, the young people continued to grumble about their lives even as they helped the old folks show me the revolutionary photo album. I saw scratched, badly focused black-and-white snapshots of the revolutionary father in his Fourth Route Army uniform and of the mother thirty or forty years earlier. But the prizes in the collection were photographs of members of the revolutionary pantheon. There was a young, dashing Chou En-lai. There was Mao in Yanan with his second wife, He Zizhen (I had never seen any photographs like that one), and Mao again, this time with Jiang Qing, standing by the side of a pond supposedly inside Zhongnanhai (I asked if the old revolutionaries had ever seen Zhongnanhai themselves and they said that they had not). I left after an hour amid warm handshakes and promises that we would see one another again and, on my part, a strong sense of the existence of a kind of lower middle class of old cadres, pensioners of the revolution, who saw the top politicians in the light of movie stars and who did not think very deeply about the consequences of their life's work.

Of course, there are more fabulous rewards for the stars, for the few who scramble to the top in China. There are the Mercedes Benz or the huge black China-made Red Flag limousines, those obscene brontosauruses of the road so big that they emerge from Peking's narrow lanes like toothpaste squeezed out of a tube. Every place has its complement of these cars. I remember one interview I had in Lhasa, Tibet, with the head of the foreign-affairs office, not a very high official even by Tibetan standards. We talked about the rights of the Tibetan minorities and the urgent need to raise their very low living standards. And then, when the interview was over, the head of the foreign-affairs office — a Tibetan himself named Ja Ba — slid into the backseat of a sleek, black Mercedes 280 SL, and sped off into primitive, dilapidated Lhasa, where most people don't even have mules.

Back in Peking, the highest-ranking officials live in large spreads like Deng Xiaoping's, complete, I am told, with TV's and tape recorders and rosewood furniture, though I suspect that even in the domiciles of the powerful, the toilets often leak. The home of a member of the Politburo or top-ranking general is identifiable by the large, red-painted solid wood gate giving onto the street that can swing open to let in the limousine, and, in some cases, by army sentries posted outside. The most distinctive characteristic of this Communist-mandarin class is summed up in a commonly heard Peking expression: "If you have power, you have everything." While in the West, privileges usually go to the wealthy, in China money means almost nothing. It is a grasp on the levers of power that produces whatever comforts and opportunities the country has to offer.

Many of these are clearly material, like the big homes and the limousines, and the maids, and the vacation cottages in the seaside resort of Beidaihe. But perhaps the most important of them are of the intangible sort that money cannot buy even in the non-Communist world. (Many of them are birthrights in the West.) It is no accident, for example, that when studying in the United States became the fashion, the children of the very top leaders were among the first to go. Many of them use assumed names to disguise their connections to the power elite so it is impossible to know them all, but among those who left for American universities in 1979 and 1980 were the children (sometimes two children) of at least four members of the Politburo — Deng Xiaoping, Huang Hua, Song Renxiong, and Yu Qiuli — and numerous other high-ranking officials; this while thousands of the unconnected were stigmatized at their workplaces because of their interest in leaving the motherland, or, in some cases I knew of, refused passports by the Public Security Bureau with no reason or explanation provided.

In this sense, the greatest intangible benefit of power in China is, quite simply, freedom. The powerful official can read what he wants, go where he wants, stay at the state's expense at the best hotels, see the movies of his choice, including the foreign films that are banned for the masses. Mao's wife Jiang Qing had a private collection of Greta Garbo films that she used to show to her guests and retainers in the various villas across China that she occupied. Cadres above the grade of nine are also privy to that other key to status and prestige in China — information. In a society where most aware ordinary people depend for their news on the BBC or the Voice of America, there is also a group of "internal" publications that, unlike the publicly available newspapers, provide information about what is really taking place both at home and abroad. These various internal publications are ranked like the cadres themselves, with some of them distributed widely and some to only the elite among the elite. The contents of, say, *Internal Reference* — one of the more secret of them —might include an upbeat article on the replacement of incompetent cadres in Heilongjiang, another telling the tragic story of a misused intellectual who committed suicide, still another about young Shanghainese sent to remote Xinjiang who were holding a hunger strike to dramatize their desire to be allowed to return home. The elite are informed and thus one of the little games played by those close to them is to show better access than others to privileged information.

There is no proof, but the children of ranking officials also insist that many of the top leaders make use of their freedom to flout the country's strict puritanism in matters of sex. In his later years, for example, Mao himself was often in the company of a young woman named Zhang Yufen, who started out as an attendant on the Chairman's special train. Nobody, of course, ever caught the Chairman in flagrante, but certainly the fact that he abandoned two women and married three indicates a need on his part for some variety in his female companionship. It is also conspicuous that, in cases when the identity of the old revolutionaries' wives becomes known, they often turn out to be a generation or so younger than their husbands. Chinese friends explained to me that when the guerrilla hero-warriors entered triumphantly into Peking in 1949, many of them quickly got rid of the peasant women they had married during their years in the wilderness in favor of new, sophisticated, urban brides. At the lower levels of the bureaucracy, there are, say many Chinese, similar sexual privileges, particularly for the commune and brigade party secretaries who are virtual dictators in local areas. For years, for example, the millions of young people sent down to labor in the countryside tried their best to get permission to return to the cities. One way for women, I have been told more than once, was to make themselves sexually available to the local leader. During the Cultural Revolution, too, there were many cases where women were able to get party memberships by using more or less the same methods. One friend who worked in a cotton-spinning mill in Henan during the early 1970s told me how, suddenly, a half-dozen young, female spindle operators were admitted into the party. One of those workers, my friend said, was widely respected. But the others seemed never to have manifested the slightest interest in politics or any knowledge at all of Marxism, Leninism, or the Thoughts of Chairman Mao. Nobody at the cotton-spinning factory ever proved anything but most people believed that the privileges of party membership had been exchanged for the joys of sex.

For years the official propaganda machinery has railed angrily, if rather vaguely and with a general absence of specifics, against what it calls "special privileges," a sure sign that the emoluments of power continue to be widely enjoyed. In fact, given that the Chinese are as human as the rest of us, there should be no surprise that officials use their power to secure better lives for themselves. What disturbs many unprivileged Chinese, of course, is the hypocrisy of it. "Live in a straw hut but keep your eyes on the world" is a standard hortatory slogan, meaning roughly to live simply but work for the triumph of the progressive forces. A couple of my Chinese friends in Peking, members of a bureau within the Ministry of Culture, told me: "There are ten party members in our group. Two of them are women who got into the party by sleeping with the leader. Three others have left to study abroad; one will soon leave to go to Hong Kong; and two more have applied to go. The members of the party are supposed to be the most advanced, to set an example for the rest of us. But, if they are all trying to get out of our socialist motherland, what do they expect the rest of us to want to do?"

In a one-party state where power, not wealth, is everything, the political bureaucracy naturally becomes the chief avenue for upward mobility. The peasant or worker or intellectual joins the Communist party — whose forty million members constitute about 4 percent of the population — in order to gain those things that people in other societies want: recognition, status, power, and what in other societies would come with wealth — cars, travel, and better housing. And yet, while the cynical quest for advantage is hypocritical in an allegedly revolutionary-socialist society, it may not be the gravest affliction of the Chinese bureaucracy. It does not fully describe the unique sort of social-political animal that, molded during the years of revolutionary war, was brought to power with the Communist victory in 1949. These are men motivated, not by the desire for privilege, but rather by a self-important, unreflective, extreme puritanism that poses a grave problem in its own right.

I am sure, in fact, that most Chinese leaders are dedicated Communists, schooled and tempered in years of what the press calls "revolutionary struggle," devoted to the principles of communism, and obedient to the idealistic dictates of the party. There are hundreds, thousands of old revolutionaries who are ready to sacrifice themselves, their comfort, their personal desires, for "the revolution," who live to work, who recoil at the very idea of "special privileges," and who practice a relentless and even enthusiastic self-abnegation. That might make it sound as though China were blessed with some of the best leaders in the world. In fact, I believe that these leaders are not a solution for China. They are the problem.

I got to know rather well — not personally but through the meticulous description of a relative — one such old revolutionary who, I believe, is representative of thousands of others. This man — let us call him Song — joined the party's underground organization in Shanghai in

1935, when he was eighteen, having spent his life until then in the bosom of an educated, middle-class family. From then on, Song's entire life, his whole being, was shaped by the great authoritarian family of the party and by the revolution. He served with single-minded zeal in a number of different posts, first during the anti-Japanese resistance, then in the revolutionary war against the Kuomintang, then as a high province-level official, provided with a nice house, a car, a chauffeur, in two different localities, before being transferred in the early 1960s to the head of the personnel department of a bureau in the Seventh Ministry of Machine building, which is the highly secret ministry in charge of arms production.

It was the party that introduced Song to his wife, a cadre of roughly equal rank and devotion. During the long struggle for power, the party provided everything for the couple so they would not be disturbed in the historic tasks set for them to perform. Everything: a succession of available wet nurses for their infants, day care, sleep-in kindergartens and primary schools so that they needed to be parents only on Sundays. It provided housing, a cook and a maid; a car and a driver were at their disposal. And, in return, they were at the disposal of the party. Song and his wife had virtually no possessions of their own. They led the way in denying themselves personal satisfactions or comforts, vacations, or radios, or even bicycles. When the party demanded that the husband transfer to Peking, even though it would mean a relative loss of the status he enjoyed in the province, he went without complaint, always ready to do the work of "the revolution." And, through it all, Song not only sacrificed himself, not only purged himself of selfishness, he also stood ready to be a living model of revolutionary values by adopting an objective, nonfeudal standpoint vis-à-vis his family. One instance: he had a bright and hardworking son who had studied foreign languages and wanted to devote himself to China's relations with the outside world. The son, who had had various generational quarrels with the father, applied to the school attached to the Ministry of Foreign Trade in the hope of eventually becoming an interpreter or an official dealing with imports and exports. When Song learned of his son's intentions, he wrote a letter to the Ministry of Foreign Trade in which he declared that the younger Song was not fit for foreign-affairs work and thus should not be admitted into the school.

There is, of course, something terrifying, inhuman, blind, about this kind of dedication, this willingness, indeed eagerness, to make superior sacrifices. In one of his essays, George Orwell linked it to the dictatorial habit of mind, writing: "If you have embraced a creed which appears to be free from the ordinary dirtiness of politics — a creed from which you yourself cannot expect to draw any material advantage — surely that proves that you are in the right. And the more you are in the right, the more natural that everyone else should be bullied into thinking likewise."*

Orwell was talking about Count Leo Tolstoy but, like so much else he wrote about the totalitarian impulse, he might well have been talking about Chinese communism and, in this case, about our revolutionary cadre so full of the spirit of self-abnegation that it transformed itself into its opposite, into a kind of megalomaniacal self-righteousness. For decades, after all, this man has been told that he is the embodiment of History itself, of the forces of Progress, that he is a kind of monk in the service of the Higher Purpose of the Revolution, that while he lives in a straw hut, his eye is cast on the world. There were thousands of such men and women schooled in the discipline of the Marxist-Leninist party (the most effective form of organization for seizing political power ever devised by humankind), persuaded that to obey its dictates without question, to labor patiently in the vineyards of the revolution, was the sole way of achieving its sacred purposes. They came to regard themselves as a special breed. In fact, with their wet nurses and boarding schools, their homes and their cars, their freedom from ordinary, routine chores and concerns, they constituted a kind of Communist aristocracy. And now, more than thirty years after the seizure of power, they still staff the middle and upper echelons of the huge state bureaucracy, where they are often a stubborn, ultraconservative, moralistic, self-protective force that, while superspecialized in politics, is at best semi-educated in the ways of the modern, cosmopolitan world.

I do not claim to understand Song or his confreres completely. I cannot, for example, understand how any person with a brain could have endured the shifts and extraordinary about-faces made by the Communist party during its years in power, its abrupt transformations of black into white, of heroes into villains, its reversals and re-reversals of itself, its coups and countercoups, and all the other unpredictabilities and uncertainties that have characterized its rule, without having at least some of his faith shaken, without entertaining just the slightest suspicion that he may have been fanatically dedicated to an erroneous cause. Some of the old revolutionaries do experience despair. But not Song. Perhaps in his case, the only possible answer lies in fanaticism itself.

Whatever the explanation, I do know something about how our Comrade Song spends his day, and that reflects considerable concern with keeping a finger on the elusive political pulse of China as well as a concern

---

* George Orwell, "Tolstoy, Lear and the Fool," in *Collected Essays, Journalism and Letters* (New York: Harcourt, Brace, 1968), vol. 4, pp. 301–302.

that all he has worked for all his life is in peril of subversion by a lack of diligence in the younger generation. Song reads a lot. He consumes the *People's Daily* and the other national newspapers as well as the various "internal" publications that he is privileged to see — often calling his similarly privileged wife in to read this or that article but scrupulously keeping all of the confidential material out of the reach of his children. Song follows every political nuance. He dwells in his thoughts and in his conversation at great length over who is up and who is down and who will be promoted to what — reminding me of the comment made to me by an irreverent party member that "in China, everybody is a China watcher." But Song not only watches. Like the "friends of China," he also defends, making arguments to all who will listen of the correctness of any policy of the party — forgetting conveniently that he just as ardently defended the opposite policy when it was in force. This is accompanied, moreover, by a relentlessly didactic attitude toward his children, whom he always lectures on the verities of socialism, though this does not always produce happy results. More than once, family dinners have been ruined when father Song stalked away from the table after one of his children reminded him of his past inconsistencies. Once he got so angry that he overturned the table altogether, spilling plates, bowls, meat, vegetables, and rice on the floor of the apartment in his anger and irritation. But Song, now in his early sixties, remains above all a loyal servant of the party. If you asked him what his purpose in life was, he would reply simply: to serve the revolution.

In Peking, I had a friend who took great secret pleasure in mocking the personal styles of the high bureaucrats. In particular, he loved to imitate the peculiar way of speaking that virtually any Chinese can easily identify with the *ganbu*, the cadres. The tone of this style of speech is preemptively oracular; the wisdom that is being dispensed comes enveloped, protected, encased in assumptions of infallibility and access to superior, scientific truth. Characteristic of it also is a kind of lingering emphasis at the end of each phrase, which is supposed to convey to the listener sincerity, earnestness, and good sense. All of this is imitable and reflective of these somewhat caricatural leaders' self-images. But what makes it even more fascinating is the fact that, due to their rural origins, the accents of the vast majority of high-ranking Chinese are a good deal less standard than those of most first-year foreign students of Chinese. In 1980, we in the foreign press were allowed to attend certain sessions of the meeting of China's National People's Congress, the thirty-five-hundred-member rubber-stamp parliament. One of the sessions consisted of a speech by then party chairman Hua Guofeng, a man whose Shaanxi accent is particularly remote from what might be called the emperor's Mandarin. Most of the foreign reporters brought their Chinese interpreters along for help in listening to the speech. But as they plied them with questions about what Hua was saying, it soon became apparent from the interpreters' collectively reddened faces and nonreplies that they could understand Hua hardly better than the foreigners.

For the last three years, the dead weight of China's bureaucracy has become ever more an officially recognized curse upon the nation. The *People's Daily* (which is staffed by some of the brightest and most liberal Communists in the country, railed incessantly against "bureaucratism," by which it seemed to mean a sluggish conservatism, literal-minded devotion to regulations, a self-protective timidity, and a fear of taking initiatives and making decisions. These had, the paper said, to be eliminated. Moreover, the aging revolutionary leadership had to make way for younger, brighter people, who were more highly trained in the specializations needed to run a centralized state of one billion people. But bureaucracy, and its instinctive resistance to change, is endemic in almost all countries, not only China. The difference in China is the size of the governing class, the fact that so much depends on it, and that, given the circumstances of its creation, it is soaked in delusions of its own infallibility and rightness.

12

A Day in the Life

IN THE SPHERE of everyday necessities, virtually everybody in China is a kind of accountant. As the above list shows, the purchase of the basic commodities is hedged about with a plethora of rules, percentages, and small strips of paper ration tickets — always decorated, ironically, with scenes of rich fields of grain or bristling refineries — marked PEKING MUNICIPAL GRAIN COUPON or PEKING MUNICIPAL INDUSTRIAL GOODS COUPON or PEKING MUNICIPAL SUPPLEMENTARY FOODSTUFFS COUPON. The Chinese know these various tickets and what they entitle the holder to in the way Americans might know traffic regulations. When the housewife goes to her appointed grain shop and presents her ration coupons to the clerk, she knows that the latter will make sure that she gets no more than 55 percent of her monthly ration in wheat flour, no more than 20 percent in uncooked, husked rice, and the rest in less desirable coarse grains. She will know too of the minor exceptions and small exchanges that she has the right to make; for example, that one kilo's worth of wheat-flour coupons may be used for a kilo of fresh bean curd for her household every month. Similarly, she can get uncooked beans or cooked grain products with other types of substitutions.

Do not suppose that these complex transactions take place in some gleaming, well-stocked governmental distribution center where hundreds of clerks sell the grain, the oil, the bean vermicelli, and so on, wisely rationed to ensure that, under China's conditions of scarcity, every person can obtain enough. In Peking — as in Chungking — the markets are seedy, unkempt places of uncertain supplies and certain long lines. One

ITEM	AMOUNT	AVAILABILITY

Grain Coupon	Issued every month according to age and work of recipient:
	  11.5 kg unemployed female adult
	  13.5 kg female office worker
	  17.0 kg male university student
	  17–20 kg male machine operator
		Fixed proportions of grains as follows:
		20% rice
		55% wheat flour
		25% coarse food grains, maize bean products, etc.

Cooking Oil Coupon	0.25 kg per month per head	Cotton and rape seed oils available in shops and, sometimes, soybean oil Peanut oil has not been sold for years Sesame oil available in very small quantities during certain holidays
Cotton Cloth Coupon	5.6 meters per head per year	Standard cotton for clothing, some synthetics (though synthetics not generally rationed) Mosquito netting
Unspun Cotton Coupon	0.5 kg per head per year	Wadding for quilting and padded clothes

Industrial Coupon	1 unit per head each 6 months	10–15 units: bicycle (plus special coupon giving permission to buy)
		  10 units: sewing machine
		  5 units: leather shoes for men
		  2 units: leather shoes for women

ITEM	AMOUNT	AVAILABILITY
Industrial Coupon	1 unit per head each 6 months	1 unit: kg tea, wool blanket, wool thread, silk quilt cover
Furniture Ticket	Available only to newly married couples	For double bed, wardrobe, etc., and as with bicycles and sewing machines, a combination of industrial coupons and special product coupons needed for purchase
Peking Residents' Grocery Ration Book	1 per household each year, containing separate sections for each month	150 grams per head, bean vermicelli, but often not available
		100 grams sweet potato starch
		100 grams soda
		1 kg / month / household, fresh eggs
		1 kg / month / household, sugar
		1 bar / month / household, hand soap
		100 grams / head for 7 months, sesame paste — unavailable the other months
		Fish: coupons issued for certain types but they are not readily available
		In addition, for holiday periods like the Chinese New Year, other products go into temporary ration, such as green onions, Chinese cabbage, potatoes, black mushrooms, aniseed, and peanuts

result of the state's concentration on industry, rather than consumer needs, is that the capital city of the most populous country in the world has markets that resemble those in small Third World backwaters.

Rationing, of course, is intended to ensure that, for the basic necessities, each individual will get his fair share of China's scarce goods, and indeed, there is certainly something to that argument. There is a famous photograph of China from the 1930s, showing a beggar boy, his ribs sticking out of his skin, his alms bowl extended forward toward the camera, while just behind him, sitting with smug, unseeing, uncomprehending satisfaction, is a prosperous, plump female rice merchant. I have seen plenty of dire poverty in China, but never so disgraceful a contrast as the one in the photograph. Nonetheless, there are Chinese citizens who believe that the elaborate system of coupons, with its rules, its regulations, its huge administrative apparatus, and, most important of all, its tendency to breed acceptance of itself as a normal condition of life, becomes self-sustaining. It justifies the slowness, the inefficiency, and the unpredictability of supplies; it creates a situation that, while theoretically temporary, is in fact entirely tolerable and so entrenched as a part of life that, combined with the inherent nonproductivity of socialism, it will endure forever.

Perhaps the single most unvarying aspect of daily life in China's capital consists of the enormous amount of time that the average resident has to allot for the purchase of food. The lines of the long-suffering, the expressionless, the resigned clutching tattered ration tickets in their hands, are ubiquitous. The race, in China, often is not to the swift; it is to the patient, the enduring. I used regularly to visit one market area not far from the Temple of Heaven where it was common to find two enormous lines, often several hundred meters long, that began at narrow twin shop-front counters, stretched along the street and around a corner and down behind the peddlers' stalls. This was the milk supply depot for this district of Peking. Only parents with young children are entitled to buy the half-liter bottles. Once a month the purchaser waits on one line to present proof of his right to buy milk and is awarded milk ration coupons for the thirty days to follow. Then, every day he stands on the other line and, at length, receives a full deposit bottle. In bitterly cold, blustery January, there are the rounded, blue and green padded jackets and trousers; in April with its sandstorms, the long rows are spotted by colored gauze wrapped around the heads of the milk purchasers; in torrid August, there are the white shirts of men and the subdued print blouses of women. But whatever the season, it can take as much as two hours to get the daily bottle of milk.

It is, of course, one of the century's supreme ironies that such things as milk are so difficult to obtain precisely in the countries where, in accordance with the theory of socialism, the entire apparatus of the state is supposed to serve the needs of the people. It is well known that no socialist country, whether Poland, Cuba, the Soviet Union, Yugoslavia, or China, has been able to avoid burdening its ordinary people with scarcities; that beer and nails, soap and milk, and most other items of everyday use by the masses are of shoddy quality and produced in gravely insufficient amounts. The official Chinese reply to foreign reporters impolite enough to ask about scarcities of daily-use commodities goes something like this: We are poor and backward for historical reasons and more recently we suffered great losses because of the sabotage and interference caused by the Gang of Four. But we are now doing something that no other socialist country has ever attempted; we are mixing market forces with the advantages of planning. If you come back in ten years, there will be no more shortages.

Perhaps. It is worth noting, however, that that reply is a common refrain among socialists around the world who archly proclaim that, unfortunately, until their particular school of thought and action arrived on the historical scene, nobody was pursuing the arduous road to utopia correctly. In any case, as the 1970s turned into the 1980s, chronic shortages came to be openly admitted by the Chinese press. I learned in Peking from one news report, for example, that nearly 75 percent of the best beer produced in the country — Tsingdao brand, made in a brewery originally built by German imperialists — is exported. Certainly, I already knew that for the ordinary Chinese, obtaining a bottle of Tsingdao, which foreigners take for granted in their hotels and restaurants, is well-nigh impossible. "We have much steel hoarded in stores," said an article in the *People's Daily*, changing the subject from foodstuffs to hardware, "yet in the village it is impossible to buy a nail." Between 1957 and 1979, according to an article in Peking's *Worker's Daily*, the amount of timber allotted to the building of furniture declined by half, even as the population of the country as a whole went up by at least one-third, so that in 1979, China produced only twenty million pieces of furniture for its nine hundred million people, of which six million pieces were allocated to government offices. The same article said that a shortage of leather shoes was caused by the fact that in the same twenty-two years, the amount of leather allocated for shoes declined by one-third.*

"At present," reported an early 1980 article in *Economic Research* magazine, "the majority of light industrial products are in short supply. . . . Paper production falls short of demand by about one-third. One-

---

* These examples, fully documented from the Chinese press, are taken from the *China News Analysis* of December 21, 1979.

third of the sugar supply has to be imported from abroad. The average per capita consumption of textile fabrics amounts to only 40 percent of the world's average level. There is a general shortage of such other commodities as sewing machines, bicycles, wristwatches, leather shoes, liquor, electric fans, electric bulbs, and household furniture. In many cities and towns, people wishing to buy a pair of leather shoes have to queue for half a day. Young people getting married and wishing to acquire a set of household furniture have to register for it half a year in advance."

These shortages, moreover, combine with a pricing system that makes many commodities exorbitantly expensive. Indeed, browse through the dim, seedy aisles of one of Peking's ramshackle department stores and you will see that, in addition to plain and simple rationing by coupon, there is another system of rationing by price. A simple electric fan, for example, will cost one or two months' salary for the average worker; a small refrigerator, six to eight months'; a locally made black-and-white TV, large and ungainly like Western models of two or three decades ago, as much as a year's worth of pay. There are, in shop windows and on occasional counters, some commodities that are so highly priced that they produce snickers of cynical laughter among Chinese and foreign browsers alike — room air conditioners at about eighteen hundred U.S. dollars, for example, or imported Japanese color TV sets for about the same price. Indeed, the extreme high pricing of many manufactured products in itself has produced a host of ironies. One is the fact that in the so-called Friendship Stores foreigners can buy Chinese-made goods, from beds to sewing machines to refrigerators, at prices far below those in the local department stores. This gives rise to one of the more annoying features of a foreigner's relations with his Chinese friends: namely, that the foreigner must deal with a host of requests from Chinese to acquire for them at the Friendship Store the made-in-China goods that they cannot afford to buy in their own stores. It is a kind of running joke among resident foreigners in Peking that if a taxi driver or a repairman provides you with good service at, say, 3:00 P.M., he will ask you to take him to the Friendship Store by 4:00.

All life in every country is filled with dull routine, but in Peking, with its drabness, its lack of variety, its scarcities, the routine seems duller and more time-consuming than in other places. I once asked two of my friends, a married couple with one child, to describe to me in great detail how they spent their average day. Let's call them Wang and Li, the former being the husband and the latter the wife (a Chinese woman does not take her husband's surname, but children usually take the name of their father). They live, like thousands of other couples, in a single room in a four-story dormitory that belongs to Wang's workplace. The bed takes up half the space of the room; there is an armoire and a folding table, a couch and some small wooden stools, a small black-and-white television, an enormous, old-fashioned radio, with a new-fashioned stereo cassette player attached, and a tiny Japanese refrigerator, a gift from Li's father. Outside the room is a badly lighted, smoky corridor smelling of garlic and soy sauce and lined with single-burner gas stoves, jumbles of pots, pans, small cabinets, tea kettles, and other kitchen debris, since, as in many dormitories, the common-space hallway serves as everybody's kitchen.

Wang and Li have done reasonably well in life. Both hold middle-level clerical positions in government ministries. Their combined income is nearly a hundred dollars a month, of which they pay only a couple of dollars for rent. Their four-year-old son, Wang Ruiqing, goes to a nearby kindergarten every day but Sunday, so they are free of the worrisome problem of what to do with the boy when they are working. They, more-over, are far from malcontents. They work; they enjoy their strong and happy marriage and their single child (they've signed a pledge not to have a second, which entitles them to a small salary bonus every month); they see no danger of grave economic deprivation; they are not particularly in-terested in politics and do not rant and rave, as some Chinese do, about the absence of freedom in the country. Yet, when I asked them how they spent the average day, the question unleashed a torrent of complaints about how wearying and unrewarding their quotidian routine was.

Part of the problem was that we were having this discussion over a very excellent *shuan yang rou* hot pot in the restaurant of my hotel; this dish, which the Pekingese love in winter, consists of thinly sliced pieces of lamb held briefly with the chopsticks in a caldron of boiling water and dipped in an aromatic mixture of sesame paste and other sauces. It hap-pened that Wang and Li were embarrassed because they had invited me to their home for hot pot that evening and then, at the last minute, had had to call to say that despite hours and hours of effort, they had been unable to buy any lamb at all. Since there was always lamb for us privi-leged and pampered foreigners, I insisted that we have our meal anyway at my place. And so, as we dipped our pieces of tender, lean meat into boiling water and larded them with sesame sauce, Wang, fuming over his loss of face, hurled down a challenge. "You foreigners live in this hotel where everything is provided. You go to your appointments in your air-conditioned cars. You never have to cram into a bus in the middle of a hot August day to get someplace or to ride your bicycle against the wind in January. So, you're completely out of touch with the way we old hundred surnames live. But, try this: make believe that you are going to prepare a dinner for four people. Draw up a list of all the things you need, the meat, the vegetables, the oil, the cornstarch, the soy sauce, et cetera. Then go out and try to buy all of it. See if you succeed; see how long it takes you before you finally realize that you are going to fail."

Wang and Li wake up on the average morning at seven o'clock. They get their son ready for kindergarten. In their dormitory, there is fifteen minutes of hot water every morning for those who want to bathe — this is done in dim, grimy, common bathrooms, one for men and one for women. They rush through this activity not only because of the shortness of time but also because breakfast food goes on sale in the dormitory canteen just when the hot water arrives in the bathrooms, so, by this piece of illogical planning, it often happens that they can have a bath but not breakfast or breakfast but not a bath, since the food sells out very quickly.

They both work from about 8:00 to 11:30 in the morning and from 1:30 to 5:00 in the afternoon, Wang going to his job by bicycle (twenty minutes) and Li to hers by bus (forty minutes). They try to divide most of the household chores, with wife Li in charge of the child, the housecleaning, and the cooking, and husband Wang taking responsibility for the laundry and the marketing. It is the latter that infuriates him. He says that he often tries to sneak away from work at 11:00 in the morning to make some purchases, which can take him as much as an hour. Except for a bimonthly purchase of rice and wheat flour, he scarcely bothers with the state market, because that is always too crowded and badly supplied. So, he takes his chances at the free market, paying the somewhat higher prices in exchange for the shorter waits. His rule of thumb is that if there are more than twenty people ahead of him on a line, he does not stand on it, or, as he puts it, "If I can't get vegetables, we all take some vitamin pills; but I just can't stand to spend an hour waiting to buy cabbage." Regularly, Wang has to go out again in the afternoon after work to try to pick up a few things that were unavailable earlier, but he is often not successful. In any case, he estimates that he spends between one and two hours doing the marketing every day.

Once, I spent a hot summer Sunday with Wang and Li, in part just to pass the time in their always pleasant company but in part to see how they spent that particular day, the only one that they had entirely off. I arrived at 9:00 A.M. at their dormitory, just in time to see Wang take off on his bicycle, a string bag in his hand, to go shopping. Li and I were to take four-year-old Ruiqing on an excursion to the children's amusement area in the Temple of Heaven park.

We took the bus, which was very crowded. It has to be understood that in China, where everything is in scarce supply including sometimes a place even to stand on the bus, what would be a routine, dull procedure anyplace else becomes a memorable ordeal. So it was with the bus on that day. When it arrived, there was a sudden surge and then a horrific thudding together of bodies in front of the open door, the race in this particular instance going to the swift and to the strong. A reticent Western reporter, accustomed to waiting on line, along with a small, frail mother and her four-year-old son, does not have much of a chance, and so we actually failed to get on the first two buses that stopped at intervals of about ten minutes. We squeezed gratefully onto a third only after the violent young men in sleeveless T-shirts had jammed their way in ahead of us.

It used to be in Peking that a foreigner on a bus, no matter how crowded, occasioned a competition among seated passengers to give up their places for him. This hideous practice has fallen into abeyance, the Chinese with seats having regained the right to ignore the foreign presence, which should have been inalienable in the first place. On that particular Sunday, it meant that I got to ride just like the local people, with elbows in my ribs and butts squeezed up against my thighs. Twenty minutes later, we arrived at the gate to the Temple of Heaven, paid our admissions of one mao (about seven cents) each, and began to walk to the amusement area.

Along the way, Ruiqing insisted on a bottle of orange soda pop and then an ice stick, both of which his mother bought for him without resistance. Li had long ago explained to me that the one child per family policy had made many Chinese parents overindulgent. Indeed, in its major cities at least, where the necessarily draconian birth-control policy has greatest effect, China promises to become a nation of only children, pampered, spoiled, doted on by their parents, living in a world devoid of brothers and sisters and sibling rivalries. Li often talked about the enormous amount of thinking, planning, and effort that went into little Ruiqing. When he became old enough for kindergarten, for example, it happened that he was accepted into a school adjacent to the Beihai Park, which is thought to be the best and most exclusive in Peking, the one where the grandchildren of many of the highest-ranking cadres go. At first the availability of a place there seemed a great opportunity, much better than sending Ruiqing to the small, neighborhood school where, not without considerable effort, he had also been admitted. But Wang and Li decided in the end that their son was better off not going to the Beihai school, and their reasons show a fascinating kind of class consciousness on their part. The school is so fancy, they thought, that it would be very expensive just buying the things that Ruiqing would need, the several sets of new clothes, the pairs of shoes, the silk quilt for taking naps. More important, they were concerned about destroying his self-image. He would, they figured, be treated less well by the teachers because his parents were not well connected. He would not be taken to school and picked up in a Red

Flag limousine or even a Shanghai sedan like the more aristocratic children. He would be teased by his classmates because of his lowly status. "Right now," said Li, "Ruiqing has a lot of self-confidence in his relations with other children. But he might lose it if he went to the first-class school."

But if Ruiqing was denied the best preschool education, he was denied very little else that it was in the power of his parents to give him, as, for example, on this Sunday outing. The amusement park for children in the Temple of Heaven consists in the main of a few creaky rides: an airplane that goes gently around while rising and falling; a miniature train that makes a circle; a little boat contraption that drifts slowly through a circular concrete canal. Ruiqing wanted to go on all of them and he was not to be denied, despite the fact that it was a broiling hot day and that each ride required standing on line for a good twenty minutes to a half hour. While we waited stoically for a chance at the airplane, Li told me how she had come to the park a couple of weeks before, patiently waited her turn at this same ride, and just when it seemed as though Ruiqing would be in the next group, some foreigners turned up and, to the silent chagrin of the waiting local people, were ushered to the front of the line, their children given precedence for a turn on the ride.

Finally, after the three rides, after more treacly soda pop all around and ice sticks too, we wound our way out of the park; we boarded a bus with even more trouble from the muscular youths than before, and we arrived back home weary and hot, to find Wang taking a nap after his exertions of the morning. While Li started to get some lunch ready, Wang told me that he had been out for nearly two hours and had returned with ten kilos of rice, three green peppers, four hundred grams of fatty pork, a can of sausage, and a bag of shrimp chips. He told me that after lunch he would do the family laundry, washing the seven-day accumulation of clothes by hand in cold water in a tin basin in the bathroom and then using just about every vertical plane in the room and in the stairwell to hang the clothes to dry. Later, he would go out again to see if there was any fresh fish on the free market, because Ruiqing liked it and it would be a treat for dinner. And after that, he expected to be too tired to do much of anything else.

Wang and Li, in fact, very rarely go out in the evening, in part because they have nobody to watch Ruiqing, in part because, like seats on the bus, movie, theater, and ballet tickets are hard to get; they too require long hours of waiting on line days in advance, and Wang says he is just not in a frame of mind, after all of his other chores, to do that. They read a couple of magazines, mostly those that contain short stories or film scripts, but they are not interested in the *People's Daily* or other newspapers, except for *Reference News*, the most widely available of the internal publications, containing translations from foreign news reports. There are very few books in the house because any good new ones that are published sell out so quickly that it would be a full-time job to try to get copies. And so, the family will end up, as it usually does in the evening, watching whatever happens to be on television, possibly listening to some music on the cassette player. It is very likely that some friends from elsewhere in the dormitory will drop by for a while to chat. Thus will pass another day in the not very eventful life of Wang and Li — except for one thing. It happened, Wang told us excitedly when we returned from the park, that he had some wonderful news this particular Sunday. It seems that one of the janitors in the dormitory had brought back two freshly killed chickens from a visit to his old home in the countryside. He kept one for himself. But Wang happened to run into him in the entry hall and, thinking quickly, offered him a thick pile of extra wheat-flour coupons for one of the birds. The janitor accepted. Tonight, there would be a rare good feast.

It is, as the day of Wang and Li suggests, the scarcity of things more than the absence of freedom that most profoundly affects the everyday life of the Chinese. Peking, for example, used to be a place that teemed with restaurants, of all sizes and suited to every pocketbook. Up until the 1950s, the New China News Agency has reported, there were some 5,000 restaurants in the city, and while that was clearly a drop from the days when every street corner had its little stalls selling one or another delicacy, it was not yet a condition of grave scarcity. Today, however, dining out is hard. There are, the official news agency said, only 0.3 restaurants per thousand people, or about 1,500 total — a decline that is less drastic than that for department stores, shops, and groceries, which dropped from 70,000 before 1949 to only 10,000 in 1980. The tourist brochures and guidebooks talk about the wonders of Chinese cuisine, and for those with privilege and money the wonders are still available. But a good meal out for a member of the old hundred surnames is a very rare treat.

Indeed, all Peking residents know that there are two kinds of restaurants in the city: the ones that have special rooms and special dishes for foreigners only and the "masses' restaurants" that cater to the ordinary people. The latter are seedy, grimy establishments where you would go out of necessity, not in search of culinary pleasure. Normally you have to stand on line twice, once to buy tickets corresponding to your choice of a dish (many of these places have only heavy, doughy, but filling, steamed dumplings) and again to pick up your plate. Then, holding your dish in your hand, you wander around looking for an unoccupied wooden stool and a corner of table where you can have your meal.

In addition, there are in this city of five million people perhaps about fifty better, larger masses' restaurants where you are attended to by a server at your table. In one of these places an average worker could easily spend half a month's salary to take his family out to dinner. Good, even excellent, meals are at times available. There is hot pot, Sichuanese camphor-smoked duck, Hunanese Dongting Lake chicken, and Yunnanese shrimp in hot-oil sauce, as well as such metaphorically named specialties as "Ants Climbing the Tree," "Noodles Crossing the Bridge," or "Buddha Jumps over the Wall." There is no question that, as the propaganda proclaims, the restaurant food has gotten better since the fall of the Gang of Four; the notion that good food is somehow a reactionary, bourgeois relic fell with the radicals. Still, Peking old-timers mutter that there are dozens of delicacies that are no longer available, that eating out is too much of an ordeal, and that even if some of the dishes are good, many are oily imitations, unsatisfactory copies of genuine Chinese *haute cuisine*.

The situation is well summed up by an experience my friend Wang once had when he invited me to his house for Peking duck (this was a few months before the incident of the lamb hot pot). A Peking duck dinner is one of the standard items of the tourist trip to China; there are several restaurants that make it, the most common for short-term visitors being what is known as the Big Duck Restaurant (there are also the Old Duck, the Little Duck, and even the Sick Duck, located near a hospital), a six-story, concrete establishment that pushes out literally thousands of Peking roast ducks every day. Virtually every tourist who goes to Peking is taken for a banquet at the Big Duck. There is even a bit of morbid humor among foreign residents about the place since it happens that some elderly tourists, who first exhaust themselves during the day on the Great Wall and in the Ming Tombs, then die at night in Peking after a large, rich Peking duck meal; the syndrome is known locally as "death by duck."

No Chinese, though, has ever been known to die from this particular hazard. Only tourist guides and other local people who do "foreign-affairs work" entertaining visitors in Peking go to the Big Duck, or, for that matter, to any of the other duck restaurants. And so, when my friend Wang invited me to eat a duck at his home, he then had to find one in a restaurant to take out. He went to the Old Duck; they told him they had only enough for the foreign guests. He went to the Big Duck; they told him the same thing, that maybe he should try the Small Duck or the Sick Duck, but that in any case, there were not so many ducks that just anybody could come and buy one. Wang, however, was not to be deterred. He is smart and skilled in dealing with state officials and proud of that skill. He cajoled them; he threw himself on their mercy; he told them that the *foreign* guests had already been invited and how humiliating it would be for China if, in this city of thousands of ducks, he was unable to provide them with one. Finally, the restaurant functionaries gave in; they handed over a duck in a plastic bag and Wang proved once again that in Peking, it is the clever, the resourceful, the persistent that can from time to time savor the pleasures of a minor triumph.

All during the time I lived there, Peking seemed to be in the midst of a housing construction boom. Everywhere cranes raised themselves up over square brick or cement rectangles in varying stages of completion. It is an ugly, stark architectural landscape but, at least, it represents a belated acknowledgment that socialism is not a success if whole families crowd together in single rooms, sharing kitchens, toilets, hallways, with other similarly crowded families. In this, Peking suffers from an important leftover from the Cultural Revolution, when thousands of families were given license to invade and share the premises of other families. The old-style court yards got divided up so that one family rarely occupied more than one room; even the inhabitants of the small, spare apartments in concrete high-rise buildings had to make way for other families, turning over bedrooms to them and sharing the use of the kitchen and bathroom. This condition of one apartment / two families is still widespread and will remain so until a lot more new housing is built.

The unavailability of apartments has numerous sociological consequences. Children often live in small cement cubicles in their parents' homes until they are well into their thirties because they have no place to set up their own quarters. Betrothed couples wait years to get married because of the limited supply of apartments; or, they marry but live separately at their respective parents' homes. In any given family, a couple with an apartment can be subjected to some disconcerting treatment. I know a couple with a young child that live separately, the husband in Nanking and the wife and child in Peking. Because of that, they had to relent in the face of enormous family pressure to give up the Peking apartment for a brother and sister-in-law who were both in the same city but had no housing. The wife thus moved with her baby into a flat with her parents, and she and her husband temporarily retake possession of their apartment on the rare occasions when he is able to come up from Nanking for a visit.

The common practice of assigning husbands and wives in widely separated parts of the country places considerable hardships on these people as it is. They usually have the right to visit with each other, at the state's expense, once a year. Children spend long periods without seeing one or the other parent. While the theoretical explanation for this practice is that there are limited numbers of skilled people and they must be posted where they are needed, some Chinese have suggested to me that much of it is unnecessary. It largely stems, they say, from the inclination of the party to see self-sacrifice for the revolutionary goal as a good in itself; one gains merit by self-abnegation for the sake of public service. In any case, these separated people, often well into middle age, can find themselves in living conditions that would appall Western college freshmen. I knew one minor official whose wife lived in Heilongjiang while he was posted to the Ministry of Agriculture in Peking. He lived in a ministry-run dormitory for men, in a large room that he shared with nine others. The room had ten narrow beds, a few chests of drawers, a mirror, and a grand total of two lamps, each equipped with a twenty-five-watt light bulb. There was a radiator that threw off tepid emanations in the dead of winter but there were no fans for the hot and sultry summer. There were cockroaches and mice aplenty. The dining room was downstairs but it operated only between the hours of 5:45 and 6:30 for dinner, which made it very difficult for my friend to get home in time for his evening meal. Once the ten men in my friend's room petitioned the management of the dormitory for more lamps and larger bulbs. The problem, they explained, was that with so little light there was no possibility for any of them to read or study at night. They were denied. Two lamps with twenty-five-watt light bulbs were specified by the regulations, the dormitory management told them.

There are, of course, avenues in China by which an individual can express preferences. He can try to become a writer or an artist or a performer or, more commonly, he can take the entrance examinations to the university and, for that tiny fraction that pass, even choose the department in which he will study — though even this choice is circumscribed, since a would-be student can apply only to one department at each school, with no possibility of change later, and can be accepted by only one university in the entire country. But for most Chinese there is really very little choice of profession. Graduates of middle school who do not pass the university entrance exams — and that, of course, is the vast majority of them — simply wait to be assigned work by the impersonal employment bureaucracy, which itself receives requests from enterprises for a certain number of new employees and then randomly assigns available unemployed young people to jobs. The resourceful and the industrious can get around this impersonality by trying to organize cooperative enterprises, a teahouse or noodle stand or tailor shop. But many are not interested in these activities because the compensation is low and they have few of the benefits, such as free medical treatment or child day-care services, offered by a large state enterprise. Thus, many people wait for a year or two or more to get work, meanwhile living with and being supported by their parents.

One key way to get a job is via what is called the *ding ti,* or substitution, system. In this, young people take the place of parents who are retiring from jobs, often after being pressured by their place of work to do so early to make way for the younger people. In many factories or other enterprises half or more of the newly hired workers arrive at their posts by precisely this method, which means that to a very considerable extent, China is becoming a place of hereditary status. Given restrictions on migration from the countryside to the city, the children of peasants are very likely to be peasants too; children with factory-worker parents are often destined to work in the same factory. The children of officials or intellectuals, given their better schooling and richer childhood environments, are most likely to go to the universities and, in time-honored fashion, to labor with their minds rather than with their hands.

In any case, it cannot be overestimated just how keen is the desire for many people to get started in a job. I knew one family in Peking with a fourteen-year-old grandson. The young boy was an indifferent student and showed very little promise of ever doing well enough in scholarly pursuits to hope to rise very high in life. His grandmother, aged fifty-five, was a factory worker. She retired and thus had the right to appoint a member of her family to *ding ti,* to replace her. The family deliberated a long time over how to deal with this situation. Should they remove the fourteen-year-old boy from middle school and send him to work in the factory? He was, they believed, too young to work forty-eight hours a week on an assembly line. On the other hand, an employment opportunity in a desirable state enterprise might not come up again for years, so that after the grandson finished middle school, he might have to wait for years to be assigned a less desirable job. And, once in a job, it is virtually impossible to lose it; one is set for life. The arguments in favor of starting work thus were stronger than the ones for staying in school. The fourteen-year-old started at the factory, where he can now expect to remain for the rest of his working life.

The shortage of jobs is, of course, a problem of national concern; there are at any given time in the country probably some twenty million or more people in urban areas alone who are waiting for work and, given that 70 percent of China's population is under the age of thirty, the problem will be solved only with a dramatic expansion of the economy. But shortages in China extend from such major needs as work and fresh vegetables into practically every small and petty detail of life.

What, for example, if you want to get tickets to a live cultural performance? One summer, through a contact in the Ministry of Culture, I was offered four such tickets to a gala showing of award-winning folk dances. I invited a friend to go with me, and with our two extra tickets in hand, we arrived by car at the theater, where there was the usual milling about of people trying to get in to see the show. There would be no problem getting rid of the extra tickets, I knew; but I did not know that doing so would turn out to be an experience in a subtle form of violence. I held up the tickets and began to ask if anyone was interested in them. Immediately, there was a rush toward me that felt and sounded sickeningly similar to the rush that accompanies the opening of the bus door on Sunday morning. My friend was quickly elbowed out of the way and before I knew it, there was a powerful, prehensile grasp of fingers encircling one half of the two tickets that I had been holding up in my hand. I could not tell, with all the people around me, exactly whose hand it was that had laid claim to the precious slips of paper. I held on for only a few seconds, wishing that I could choose the person to whom I would give my treasures rather than be chosen by him. It was a futile and perhaps a silly principle to want to hand them over to some kindly old lady and her granddaughter, rather than have them seized by, once again, the swift and the strong. But I had little choice. I let go; immediately paper money was flashed in my face since, evidently, the strong and the swift expect to pay; but I turned into the theater without accepting the cash.

That was not the end. We went to our seats and watched the first half of the show, which, we soon discovered, consisted of the most trite and sappy of the artistic productions of which Chinese socialism is capable; it was for the most part a series of so-called minority people's dances, performed by stiff, woodenly smiling Han Chinese from various song-and-dance ensembles from the provinces. Thus, at the intermission, we decided to spare ourselves the boredom of still more and went out of the theater by an outside gate. Upon reaching the street, I had the unexpected chance to bestow my intended earlier favor. There, taking an evening stroll, was a frail old man with a cane and shabby, patched clothing; his equally old wife and a young woman, who was, I assumed, his granddaughter, were with him. I struck up a conversation with them and then, rather shyly, not knowing what reserves of wounded pride the offer of a gift from a foreigner might incite, I asked them to take the tickets for the second half of the show.

The three talked for just a second and then accepted with grace, evidently deciding in the same instant that since there were only two tickets, the old man and his granddaughter would go in and the wife would return home. All three of them were clearly pleased with this unexpected turn of events and I too was content as I watched the old man and his granddaughter make their slow way to the gate. Then, my pleasure evaporated as I saw them stand outside the gate for what seemed like too long a time and, finally, turn back to the street and make their slow way toward the rest of us.

"They won't let us in," the old man said with a shrug.

I flashed the tickets to the people at the gate and asked why my "friends" had been turned away. I addressed a stout, unsympathetic woman. "Because they are your tickets, not theirs," she said.

I entreated her: "We have to leave, can't you let this old man and his granddaughter go into the theater? If you don't, the seats are going to be empty anyway."

The answer was a cold, bureaucratic no; there was nothing to do but turn sadly and a bit angrily away. I told the man that I was sorry if I had caused him any embarrassment. He replied: "It's not your fault." He took a few slow steps, his granddaughter on his arm, then continued: "They just don't care about us common people."

Very likely, the old man had two problems preventing him from getting into the theater. One, he looked humble, shabby, unimposing, meek; he was clearly the type of person who would acquiesce to the authority of the woman at the gate and thus he invited the imposition of that authority. The old man also had no connections. Let's assume that weeks before he had heard about the gala dance performance and decided that he wanted to go. First of all he would have known that only a relatively small proportion of the tickets would go on sale to the general public. The vast majority would be held in reserve by various organizations — the Propaganda Department of the party, the Ministry of Culture, the Peking municipal government — and officials in those departments would distribute the tickets both inside the organizations and to their friends and relatives outside. The meek old man was not blessed with friends. He lacked the basic *sine qua non* of access to things in China, *guan-xi,* or connections.

13

The Unit

THE SECOND THING this old man lacked, as a retired, unimportant person, was what the Chinese call a "unit." In the West, a person's "unit" would simply be his place of work or the place where he goes to school. But in China, the unit is, as the name suggests, the basic element of the individual's public life, the nexus of his integration into the intrusive, supervised, molded, centrally planned, totalistic society of China. A Chinese belongs to his unit in the way a monk belongs to his monastery, and he bears a relationship to the unit's leaders — meaning the Communist party secretary or committee — that the monk might to his abbot. Practically every important aspect of his life is decided in the unit. Marriage and divorce; travel abroad; the right to take the university entrance examinations, to try to find another job; or to change residences; all of these things first pass through the scrutiny of the leaders of the units. And, since it is the unit that is likely to get a ration of theater tickets, going to a gala dance performance is likely to happen via that route as well.

Examples of the power of the unit are numberless. There was, to take one instance, the couple from Peking that wanted a divorce. Both the husband and the wife were in agreement regarding a permanent separation; things between the two of them were going from bad to worse and they both recognized it. The unit of the husband (what is called the personnel department is responsible for matters like this) was also ready to grant the divorce, but the wife's unit was reluctant. It felt that the couple should try harder to reach a reconciliation, that they should allow more time to pass. This disagreement required negotiations between the two units. In the meantime, the wife moved out of the flat and began to live with her parents. There were weeks, then months, of talks between the two personnel departments until, at long last, the divorce was granted.

The supervision exercised by the unit at times approaches an assumption of infantilism, as if the adult Chinese requires the superior wisdom of his party secretary in order to make even the smallest decisions. I once met a doctor in Peking who worked in a small, neighborhood hospital. He was a cautious, gentle man who loved to practice his adequate but bookish English and he often did so by telling me about life in his "unit," the hospital. It seemed that the party secretary there was an old revolutionary cadre, a woman, who had never had any training in medicine, yet did not desist from giving the doctors advice about how to treat patients. And not only that, she chastised the female doctors for the way they dressed, since she preferred the standard, conservative blue "Mao" suit to the more colorful blouses and sweaters that were coming on the market; she even pried into the personal lives of the doctors under her to make sure that they were behaving themselves in a fashion consistent with socialist morality.

Since the party secretary is a virtually unimpeachable arbiter of such things as promotions and salary increases, nobody dared express their displeasure with her — even if she was looked upon by most as an ignoramus and a nuisance. "We have to be very obedient," was a constant refrain of the tales my doctor friend told me. He then often illustrated the manner of his own obedience. It seems that he had once suffered a lung disorder and, particularly on days of bad pollution, he felt sick and did not go into work. The rest of the time he felt fine; fine enough, in fact, to ride his bicycle to the hospital every day rather than take the bus, which took twice as long and in good weather was far more tiring. But he did not ride his bicycle; he always took the bus. He was afraid that if the woman party secretary saw that he was fit enough to ride a bicycle, she would suspect that he was shirking his duty when he called in sick. And so, the doctor's bicycle sat at home; he used it on weekends and for purposes where his party secretary was not likely to see him on it. "We must," he told me for the tenth time, "be very obedient."

Imagine in the West a highly trained, professional man who is so frightened by the power of his leader that he declines to take the most convenient way to work, and the complex, multifaceted nature of the individual's attitude toward his unit becomes dramatically clear. It is not to be supposed that the individual necessarily fails to profit from his unit or that all party secretaries are by nature killjoys or obstructionists. Many a person has been sent to school or to a foreign country because of the support and help of the leaders in the place where he works. The good party secretary might well try hard to get "his" people access to housing or to kindergartens for their children or he might try to arrange for a special vegetable supply depot to be set up on the unit's grounds. The leader can be a liberal-minded person who wants to protect the people under him from the often excessive or unreasonable demands of central policies. But whether bequeathing favors or denying them, the leader and the unit have a power that is nearly absolute and not subject to any commonly used form of appeal or recourse to a higher, disinterested authority. What's more, it seems that decisions are often made without any consultation with the person affected. There is a kind of aloofness to the leadership, a secretiveness that adds to its aura of power.

I was once talking to a member of a performing arts troupe who gave me an idea of how this works. He was what might be considered an upper-middle-level member of the troupe, not a star but not a member of the chorus either; he got along well with everybody and never became involved in politics. In 1969, near the end of the most violent phase of the Cultural Revolution, however, he was suddenly and unexpectedly told that he would have to spend a term in a May 7 cadre school — a kind of labor reform camp for cadres and intellectuals very common until the mid-1970s. And so, without warning or explanation, the performer was sent for three years to the countryside to dig ditches, plant rice, hoe wheat, and build barracks, all for the benefit of his ideological outlook. He returned in 1972 to the arts troupe and resumed his normal activities. Then, after about a year, he was called in to his leader once again, only this time he was told that he had been selected to be among a small group of people, all members of the Ministry of Culture, who would go to the United States for a few weeks to prepare for some cultural exchanges planned for later in the year. A wonderful thing, a chance to visit the United States; virtually any Chinese would view such an opportunity with unmitigated joy. Our performer was happy too. But, what most struck him was the absence of control that he had over his own life and the power of the unit to decide everything. "One day I was minding my own business," he said, "and the leader told me that I was going to prison. Another day and he says that I'm going to America. In neither case did I do anything in particular to bring about my fate, either good or bad. In both cases, it was imposed on me entirely apart from my own volition."

Many Chinese are clearly intimidated by their leaders and they sense a strong "we" and "they" atmosphere, in which the members of the party and, in particular, the party secretaries operate as an in-group to the exclusion of all but those that they want to include. The ordinary person has no right to information, even when he himself is affected; he cannot demand an explanation for things that go wrong; his recourse generally is to stand before the portals of the organization or the unit and to ask politely for consideration — or, just as common, to try to get the necessary information by some informal network of friends and contacts.

For example: Among many young people who fail to pass the university entrance exams, there is tough competition to get into other kinds of schools, particularly night schools that, with connections to technical colleges, operate correspondence courses for limited numbers of students. Deng, who is twenty-eight, wanted to go to such a school and took the necessary entrance exam. Afterward, however, the school never posted the results of the exams. It simply announced that a minimum score of 240 was needed for admission to the correspondence course and then it informed those who had passed of the good news. Deng noticed that, while he did not get in, one of his fellow workers (he had an ordinary factory job) did. It happened that Deng had always felt that this particular fellow worker lacked distinctly in brainpower; she had always seemed stupid. Deng just could not believe that she would have scored higher on the exam than he did. It happened also that Deng's father had a contact who knew somebody inside the school and through him, he learned that Deng had indeed scored exactly 240 on the entrance exam, just enough for admission. The contact inside told Deng's father that if he were an immediate relative, he might be able to get Deng in, but that there was little he could do for the son of a friend. Meanwhile, Deng had to accept the injustice of the situation, even while suspecting that the girl from his unit got into the night school because someone pulled the right strings for her and that the exam was only a front, a sham. He could not protest to the school authorities on the grounds that his score was sufficiently high, since he was not, theoretically, entitled to know his score in the first place. There was no appeal to a higher authority.

A second example concerns a young man of thirty named Zhang and shows an even greater capriciousness and impenetrability in the Chinese bureaucracy. Zhang was a translator for a technical institute who had taught English to himself and, for someone who had never been outside China, spoke it remarkably well. In 1980, like thousands of others, he applied to go to a university in the United States, and, like many others also, he managed to find some foreigners visiting China to help him. His technical institute promised to support him in his desire to go abroad, a crucial factor, since, if the unit just takes a passive attitude on such a matter, the would-be student abroad will have insurmountable difficulties getting a passport and permission from the government to leave China.

Some time after Zhang's application, two things happened nearly simultaneously. First, he was accepted at a small college in the American Midwest, which, evidently excited to get a student from the real China, offered him a full scholarship; one of the foreigners Zhang had met also offered to sponsor him, a requirement both for the Chinese authorities and for his American visa. According to the American consulate in Peking, there would have been no problem — but for the second thing that happened. Around the time of his acceptance, Zhang's American friends wrote him to say that a business associate of theirs would be in China soon and that they would be pleased if Zhang could meet with him. When this business associate arrived, Zhang contacted him at his hotel and then went over to pay a call on him. They talked for about twenty minutes in a small public sitting room. Then, the security police in the hotel — which was not in Peking — came to the sitting room and asked Zhang to leave on the grounds that he had no authority to be talking with a foreign businessman. Zhang's technical institute was informed that he had contacted a foreigner without passing through the appropriate official channels. The technical institute then withdrew its support of Zhang's desire to go abroad, so that when he applied to the local branch of the Public Security Bureau for a passport, it was denied him.

There was never any explanation of this denial, despite the many letters that Zhang wrote in an effort to learn the official reason — the real one, he suspected, being that he had exposed his unfitness for going abroad by meeting the foreigner outside of official auspices. Disgusted with the unresponsiveness of provincial officialdom, Zhang went to Peking and applied directly to the Public Security Bureau there for a passport and permission to go abroad. He wrote five letters to the P.S.B. and many others to the State Council and the Ministry of Education, but he never received a single response, and he never got a passport. Clearly, he was the victim of an injustice. Thousands of Chinese had already gone abroad, including the sons and daughters of many of the country's highest officials. Finally, using his "back door" contacts, he managed to find somebody in the P.S.B. who would tell him the official reason for his problem. It was that his sponsor had been to China on business and there was a little-known regulation specifying that such a person could not guarantee a Chinese student. But Zhang, who finally gave up after several months of effort, was certain that the real reason had been that the unit, concerned over his illicit foreign contact, had withdrawn its support; once the unit has denied you, nobody else will come to your aid.

In Chinese history the extended clan, dominated by a dictatorial patriarch, often played a role disconcertingly similar to that of the unit and the party secretary today. *Family* by Ba Jin, the celebrated 1920s novel of social protest, takes as its main theme the crushing weight of tradition and authority represented by a dictatorial, somewhat hypocritical grandfather. In *Family*, Grandfather decides everything, who will do what work, who will marry whom, and so on, and he makes his decisions without considering individual preferences. The key element in Grandfather's decisions is not that he is cruel or heartless — even though the results of his decisions often are. What motivates him is what he conceives of as the interest of the family as a whole, even of the larger social fabric, rather than what each individual dreams for himself.

It would be simplistic to say that the Chinese Communist "unit" has simply replaced Ba Jin's dictatorial family. The main conflict in the novel is a classic one, involving the desire of an idealistic youth named Jue-min to marry a girl he loves, while Grandfather insists that he mate with somebody of the Family's choosing. In theory, at least, and, I suspect, often in practice, such feudal customs have by now been eliminated in large cities like Peking, where young people make their own decisions about marriage, dealing, except in rare cases of veto by the unit, with no more than the parental or peer pressures that are common in almost any country. True, during the decade of the Cultural Revolution, when politics and half-baked notions of class struggle reigned supreme, the party secretary was very much in the Ba Jin Grandfather mold; he was the surrogate paterfamilias who decided if a couple should marry or not, often on the basis of their respective class backgrounds.

In Hong Kong in 1977 I occasionally talked with a young Cantonese woman who had escaped by swimming from China a year or so earlier. She, it seems, had been refused permission to marry the boy she loved in China, since he was from a "bad" class background, so the two decided on a double flight, he leaving first and she whenever she got the chance. The problem was that when the young woman arrived safely in Hong Kong, she was grieved to learn that her boyfriend had in the meantime given his heart to another. Nobody knows the number of sad personal stories caused by the replacement of Grandfather by some ideologically narrow-minded party secretary, though, at least, it seems that in regards to marriage the necessary approval from the leader has become more or less a formality.

Still, like the family, the party and the party committee decide a great deal about the individual, guided, at least in principle, by what, presumably, will be best for the whole state. In *Family* a couple is prevented from marrying; in China today, who knows how many people have married freely enough but do not live together because the state has decided that the general interest requires that they remain separate, assigned to jobs in different parts of the country? One of the most common small features of real life in Peking, as in other Chinese cities, is for couples thus separated by the general welfare to post up little notices on walls and buildings, at bus stops and on the pillars of movie theaters, stating that so-and-so would like to move to such-and-such a place to be with his wife and family, and asking if there is anyone who needs to do the process in reverse, so that an exchange may be arranged.

I do not know how many Chinese today are successful with their little public notices in exchanging jobs and addresses with somebody else so that they can not only be married but live married as well. But certainly for almost any ordinary Chinese the desire to change jobs or addresses entails a long, tough battle with the grandfathers of the Chinese bureaucracy, a battle that, I believe, is far more often lost than won. I have mentioned the couple wherein the husband, who lived in Nanking, was separated from his wife, who had been assigned to work in Peking. For months and months, I got reports from the wife on their efforts to go through official channels to receive permission to be rejoined. The husband was trying to find a unit in Nanking willing to give a job to his wife. With such a job, she would then be entitled to the residency certificate and ration coupons for Nanking essential for her to live openly there. At one point the wife, at the cost of nearly a month's salary, journeyed by overnight hard-seat train to Nanking to take some examinations at a research institute there, and after several months, she was offered a post at this unit. Briefly, very briefly, the couple was happy. They thought that their struggle was at last at an end. But then they discovered that the wife's unit in Peking was unwilling to release her from her post there, on the grounds that it had nobody suitable to take her place. That, the last I knew, was still the situation; the couple remained unhappily separated, the husband in Nanking and the wife living with her baby in the tiny apartment of her parents — remember that she had been pressured to give up her own place to her brother-in-law and his wife. The couple's strategy became for the wife to write numerous letters to her unit and to seek frequent interviews with the personnel department there, hoping that if she made a pest of herself, the unit would release her. "In China," she remarked sadly to me at one point during her ordeal, "you can't quit; you have to be allowed to go."

This bureaucratic rigidity and absence of sympathy is in many ways very surprising. After all, people perform better in their jobs when they are happy and not demoralized, while a freer labor market would introduce a healthy degree of flexibility into the economic system. It is hard to believe that the wife's unit could not find a suitable replacement just as it is hard to believe that Jue-min's marrying his beloved would have brought the extended family crashing to ruin. But in Ba Jin's *Family* it was not a single marriage, a single happiness, that was at stake; it was the supreme authority of Grandfather to make decisions for the benefit of the entire group of family members. Similarly, in the Chinese unit of today, the belief that the collective benefits from the sacrifice of individual aspirations is unshakable, as is the authority of the party leaders to decide what the collective benefit is.

This leads to the most underground aspect of life in China's capital, to its innermost secret: it is that, despite all of the cant and rant about communism and revolution, about the progressive forces and the long march in advance, that appear in official propaganda, China socially remains a profoundly conservative place. It is a society trussed up in impersonal authority, in extreme sexual puritanism, in an ethic of personal discipline and control. In many respects, China today is not postrevolutionary, it is not even nonrevolutionary; it is antirevolutionary.

When the Communist armies marched into Peking in triumph in 1949, they called their feat "the liberation." The term, of course, was by then just another slogan in the Communist arsenal of ready-made phrases and, indeed, the term "liberation" is still universally used to mean quite simply the Communist takeover, or just the date 1949. At the time, however, "liberation" had many connotations. During the years when the Communist party was in its base area at Yanan, it cultivated a breezy, informal, unpretentious style that was, by Chinese standards, as much a liberation in social matters as the liberation they were fighting for was politically. Love and sex were in. Women, at least theoretically, were equal; certainly they were given responsibilities. Distinctions of rank, in a society where such distinctions were historically both elaborate and crucially important, were largely eliminated. While there was little of the rhapsodic talk of free love that took place in the flush of victory among the Russian Bolsheviks in 1917, nonetheless marriage was certainly decided freely among men and women and it was often of the common-law sort — in which the word *ai-ren*, meaning "lover," came to substitute for the traditional terms "husband" and "wife." Everybody was called "comrade." Even the topmost leaders lived in humble cave dwellings; they mixed with the rank and file; they took their rakes and hoes in hand and they cultivated vegetables in their own patches of garden. Of course, behind the scenes, even the Yanan period was undemocratic and dictatorial, as witness the power struggles, the purges, the rectification campaigns, that took place within the ranks of the party even then. Still, by the standards of Chinese conservatism, the Yanan style was liberating. It is even possible that those who participated in the adventure of revolution believed that they would bring the whole country fresh breezes of personal happiness so that Ba Jin's Grandfather would become a bad historical memory.

The delirium of revolution gives way, however, to the realities of ruling, and in China those realities amounted to a veritable conspiracy against genuine social liberation. Perhaps most pervasively felt in the years after 1949 was the traditional Chinese desire for strong institutions, for powerful, decisive government, by the unit as a replacement for the clan. There was at the same time the related concern for orderliness also deeply ingrained in the collective consciousness of the Chinese people; this was the notion, deriving from Confucius, that there is a grand social design in which everyone, the ruler and the follower, the father and the son, the husband and the wife, has a rigidly prescribed, unalterable role and place. For centuries in China a collective ethic took precedence over individual aspirations and, indeed, over individual rights; it was the duty of each person to conform, not to press his demands upon others. Combined with this was the latter-day imperative to control of the Communist party itself, a group that came to power filled with ideas about reengineering the entirety of Chinese society and that thus needed obedience and discipline from its people if the job were to be done. And, there was the inclination toward self-sacrificing puritanism encouraged by the austerity of revolutionary life that we saw in the model bureaucrat Song. Now, these requirements — discipline, order, obedience to the party — are commonly and explicitly demanded in the press as the necessary conditions for achieving the Four Modernizations. They are conditions that fit perfectly the needs both of the totalitarian state and of the Confucian one; thus, it is not surprising that virtually all residues of the earlier ideas of personal liberation have been wiped off the revolutionary slate.

And so, in Peking, the daily life of the average person is dominated by two factors: one, getting enough, and two, getting along. Neither is easy, even if, in some respects perhaps, the latter poses fewer difficulties than the former; for while the one requires activity and initiative, the other is best achieved by a passive acquiescence, an acceptance of things as they are, a willingness to obey.

But is that the case also for the state as a whole? To solve the problem of material needs and to restore national greatness, the state needs not only discipline and order; it needs creativity as well. The Four Modernizations cannot be achieved if the basic social condition is premodern, that is, if it does not allow for the basic amount of independence and freedom that enables people to dare to create new things. Here, we can return to the good doctor whose fear of "the leader" was so great that he could not ride his bicycle to work. We can assume that this man of science is an obedient citizen, but would such a man be likely to blaze new paths in medicine?

Or, to return to another earlier image, how about the young people at the university holding their tame dance party behind the chained and padlocked gate that kept away the "hooligans," the forces of chaos and disorder? It is all right to dance, but only under well-controlled, safe conditions. Like the dance, Peking itself is well controlled; it is safe; it is dull; it has neither sinfulness nor vibrancy. And while that, for the lovers of absolute order, might contain considerable charm, it may in the end be destructive of the larger stated purpose of China's rulers, which is to make, out of what Sun Yat-sen called the "plate of loose sand" that is China, a great nation.

III

PRIVATE LIVES

14

Matters of the Flesh and the Spirit

LATE IN THE 1970s, for the first time in about fifteen years, the Communist rulers of China began allowing their people to express private interests. Personal desire came out of the closet where it had been locked since the beginning of the Cultural Revolution. The pages of the monthly *China Youth* magazine started publishing letters from its readers that asked about love and it printed replies that, while properly prudish and grounded in "socialist morality," at least acknowledged the legitimacy of the aspirations for romantic and sexual satisfaction. This came to a grand climax near the end of 1980 when the magazine devoted itself to nothing less than a debate on the "meaning of life." A young woman named Pan Xiao had written a letter — apparently authentic — to *China Youth* that elicited something like sixty thousand responses over a ten-month period.

Pan Xiao began her epistle by saying that the "attractions of life no longer existed" for her, that she had lost all of the "beautiful illusions" she had cherished before she reached her ripe old age of twenty-three. Her experiences were a chronicle of common woes for the generation that grew up during the Cultural Revolution. She was disillusioned by the personality cult of Mao. She was refused admittance to the Communist Youth League when she went to middle school because she criticized a leader. She read the approved books but found them irrelevant to her aspirations. She lost her idealism and, she wrote, learned to be selfish, "to bargain for wages and bonuses, to flatter and to speak false words." She looked for love but the object of her affections reported what she told him to the leaders; he wanted to curry favor since his family was in political disgrace. Then, when the family was rehabilitated, rather than marry Pan Xiao, he abandoned her for another. One day, Pan Xiao wandered into a Catholic church and witnessed a mass; she thought about becoming a nun (which would have been impossible). Then, in a state of "extreme depression," she contemplated suicide. Instead, she wrote to *China Youth* and dared its editors to publish her tale of woe.

The letter became the basis for an exhortatory campaign — presented in the form of the "meaning of life" debate — to persuade the youth of China to fight against demoralization by throwing themselves into the historic struggle for socialism. The meaning of life, the *People's Daily* declared in a summation of the debate, consisted in "spurning the egotistical outlook and believing in and spreading the revolutionary outlook" (that is, the spirit of self-sacrifice in the pursuit of the "public interest and the Communist cause"). No letters were published saying that the meaning of life consisted in doing something better than anyone else had done it, creating a great book or painting, achieving wealth or fame, or success with handsome men or beautiful women. But, at least, Pan Xiao's letter had broached such once forbidden themes as love and betrayal, the need for private fulfillment, even old-style religion. It was the modest beginning of a public acknowledgment that private matters, joys and sorrows and the quest for personal meaning, were legitimate matters for concern.

Around the same time, a small volume was published in which the editors of *Youth* newspaper (published every other day by the Communist Youth League) gave advice on matters of the heart; for example, on how much importance should be given to beauty in searching for a mate (not much), or, in the case of a jilted young girl, how to get over her sorrows by throwing oneself into the "hot struggle for production." A rather scientific and entirely nongraphic little paperback called *Knowledge of Sex* became a fast-selling item on the black market, as did an expurgated version of *Everything You Always Wanted to Know about Sex and Were Afraid to Ask*, under the new title *Sex and Physical Culture*.

This fell far short of the Western obsessiveness about beauty, style, love, sex, and wealth that has spawned those hosts of dream-fulfillment books and magazines that are found in the United States and Europe. But consider what things had been like a few years before. I remember one long train ride during my first visit to China in 1972, a period when the Chinese masses seemed to be engaged in one big, absurd, and obvious lie about personal needs. I was going *en groupe* from Zhengzhou in Henan Province all the way across the North China Plain to Shenyang in the northeast, a journey of nearly two days, so there was plenty of time for idle chatter with our guides. Some members of our group began to try to elicit from one of these friendly but fearful fellows an admission that he noticed pretty girls. This effort quickly turned into an obsession. Wickedly we teased and coaxed him. We tried to strike compromises — of course politics was the main thing, but if he would only admit that a woman's sex appeal flitted briefly, oh so briefly, through his mind before he focused exclusively on the important things, we would leave him alone.

Our poor guide sweated and squirmed. He laughed humorlessly. He cast longing glances at the stark early spring landscape of northern China that passed by the window. But we were relentless. We pushed on with arguments based on the undeniable scientific fact that there were certain natural biological urges, weren't there? That, the world being a place of great variety, there were bound to be some girls prettier than others. Of course this poor fellow, whom I remember as a gentle, nervous person, knew well his own lusts and desires, his dreams and his passions; it was no secret to him that he noticed pretty girls. Yet, he could not be budged. He insisted that he didn't notice beauty, only such things as a woman's world outlook, her class consciousness, her devotion to the study of the thought of Chairman Mao. And not only that; he maintained, in the face of vociferous incredulity among the foreigners present, that but for a handful of unrepentant bourgeois careerists and capitalist roaders like the then disgraced Deng Xiaoping, all Chinese were of this same view. It was the triumph of political theory over biology.

This was viewed by many Chinese as the triumph of the absurd. And I too found the repudiation of the personal to be one of the most monstrous of the Maoist tumors that had been grafted onto the Chinese body politic. It was the needless subordination of millions of individuals to the will of a few old men, who themselves enjoyed the liberties as well as the higher titillations of power. History needed to be served. Each individual in China was expected to swim in the same stream of inevitable historic progress, to live for the future, to substitute the arid triumph of ideology for the complex richness of the person. And this was accomplished with such success that many credulous Western visitors assumed that the personal needs of the Chinese existed on a smaller scale than those in the individualistic West.

This I find a demeaning and even unconsciously racist notion. It is true that in their outward behavior, the Chinese, including Chinese young people, are less flamboyant, less obviously concerned by such matters as style, appearance, and relations with the opposite sex, than we are in the extravagant West. But this is a superficial difference. In their inner lives, the Chinese experience the same yearnings and drives, the same miseries and joys, and even the same preoccupations and obsessions as other people do. For example, young men in army camps on the Manchurian or

Mongolian borders, I am told, dream and talk as compulsively about sex as soldiers elsewhere do. The Chinese vocabulary is filled with symbolism and euphemism for sexual activity: "crossing the snowy peaks" means to touch a woman's breasts; "sun tool" and "jade gate" are the poetic terms for the sexual organs of men and women. Anybody at all familiar with Chinese history and literature will know, for example, of the heightened eroticism contained in the country's culture. This was not just a matter of the emperor's thousands of concubines. It was also evident in such things as illustrated sex manuals, pornographic art, long treatises on lovemaking, aphrodisiacs, potions, positions, legends in which beautiful maidens floated like butterflies into the mountain retreats of Confucian scholars to provide them with the pleasures of love.

Passion, it is true, was an exclusive phenomenon; in particular, the Chinese woman was expected to remain faithful even to a husband who died when she was still young. But that does not reduce the importance of love to the individual. If anything, the Chinese, who assume they will have only one mate for life, are apt to surrender themselves more rhapsodically to love than Westerners, with their diluting concerns for varieties of experience, are prone to do. In a strange way, the role of passion became clear when China in the late 1970s began for the first time to provide information about crime. Many capital offenses centered on the classic themes of infidelity, jealousy, and rejection. There was, to take one example, the case I read about in Xiamen on a public execution notice. It concerned a man sentenced to death after he murdered his friend and his lover when the latter rejected him in favor of the former.

Similarly, as China began to give legitimacy to personal needs, the opposite of passion, estrangement, also became a common, visible phenomenon. Peking itself experienced an epidemic of divorce, especially as couples pushed into marriage during the Cultural Revolution, when the party authorities often decided on the suitability of mates, began to separate. There was one well-publicized case of a woman who was seeking a near unprecedented second divorce on the grounds that her second marriage, like her first, had been a largely involuntary matter that took place in an atmosphere charged more with politics than with love. Her case aroused enormous controversy as thousands of people wrote letters to the newspapers arguing either that she should be allowed to liberate herself or, in the majority of cases, that in her second marriage she had incurred a responsibility to her husband that could not be annulled without his active consent.

These matters of the heart, of the body, and of the spirit emerged on the surface as China made its modest transition in the late 1970s to a greater degree of permissiveness. By the time I got to Peking, the atmosphere had changed enough to make some research into personal needs and aspirations possible. China was like a huge darkened amphitheater. Wherever you struck a match, a few faces of individualism would appear in the glow while all around were glimmers of thousands of other faces farther back, waiting for the light to reach them. Wherever one went in China, there were personal stories, sometimes of success, usually of tragedy, at the very least of the small matters — the lusts and ambitions, the cravings and the heartaches, the courage and the cowardice — that affect and afflict all human beings, with, I assume, more or less equal intensity. It was perhaps my own strongest personal ambition to recover the buried treasures of individual Chinese lives. How had these intelligent and gifted people survived thirty years of Maoist experimentation? Were they defeated, resigned, disillusioned, or were they hopeful in the face of ongoing changes? Were they, not just as subjects of total control but as Chinese, different from us? All during the time when I lived in China, I cast my light into that gloomy amphitheater, straining to make out the features of the faces that I illuminated. The result is a highly selective, entirely random sampling of lives in the Chinese revolution.

Late one morning in October 1979, I was walking in one of the southwestern provincial capitals. I was on a busy street, lined by rows of drab two- to three-story buildings, crowded with bicycles, carts, pedestrians, all of whom seemed to be staring at me, a lone foreigner with a camera and a notebook. I had managed, on this occasion, to elude the Travel Service guide, who would normally have been along with me to help. I was just walking and looking. I had been to the market and watched as people queued up for fresh bean curd. I had surprised grandmothers and grandchildren by appearing in small lanes, peering into courtyards, craning my neck in front of whitewashed walls. I had tried to make friends with one little girl by offering her a piece of candy, only to watch the poor little thing dissolve into tears of terror when the tall, curly-headed apparition that was I loomed up in front of her (she did grab the candy, however). At about 11:00 A.M., I found myself at the entrance to a small lane wherein some women were doing laundry in tin basins in front of outdoor spigots. I stared at them. They stared at me. Then, from behind, I heard a voice asking in bad English if I was an American.

"Yes, I am," I replied, turning to find a Chinese man in his middle fifties, rather slight, with a creased, sensitive face, staring at me intently.

"Are you a Christian?" he asked.

Of all the things that I might have been asked, that question was about as unexpected as any imaginable. It happened often enough in my lone wanderings around Chinese cities that people walked up to me and put their faces within a few inches of my own, just to have a look at me, or, if I was with somebody else, to listen in to my exotic foreign accent. A common phenomenon was for some curious person to lean over and put his nose into my notebook, amazed apparently that anybody could possibly master the intricacies of foreign script (when, of course, their own ideograms are infinitely more complex and interesting). I have been asked where I am from; what work I do; what my salary is; whether I have a wife or children; and how much my watch, camera, jacket, shoes, or whatever, cost. I have been asked to express my views on China, on the American elections, on Soviet socialism-imperialism. But, particularly in 1979, religion was different. It had for thirty years been officially suspected, persecuted, driven underground, or wiped out. It had never come up before as an open matter of conversation.

"No," I replied, feeling somehow apologetic. "I am not a Christian." Concerned that I might drive my unexpected interlocutor away by revealing my lack of faith, I had momentarily considered lying, abandoning the beliefs of my Jewish ancestors, and declaring myself for Jesus. But I needn't have worried. My friend stood motionlessly. He wore the ordinary shabby, voluminous, blue cotton clothes; he had on round, yellow-framed glasses, and his English was mangled nearly beyond recognition. At length, as the inevitable group of people began to circle around, he started again.

"I used to have American friends, Mr. Hall and Mr. Beck." He looked at me expectantly as though he thought I might be able to give him news of Mr. Hall and Mr. Beck, who I presumed had been missionaries in the city an eternity before. My friend invited me to visit his nearby middle school, where he taught science. I accepted with pleasure.

We walked back up the same street that I had just descended, attracting innumerable curious stares. A foreigner with a camera and a notebook was rare enough. One walking together with an ordinary local Chinese was unheard-of. Michael Wu — to give my Christian host a name — led me into the courtyard of the middle school, where the stares multiplied tenfold. He said something to the throng of teenaged pupils that quickly gathered, and then brought me up a flight of stairs that ascended the side of a classroom building and into the one large room that was his home. There was a dusty, creaking wooden floor, a metal-frame bed and a couch, a couple of wooden chairs, a small desk, a bureau, and a bookcase whose several shelves groaned with old volumes.

Mr. Wu gave me a glass of hot Chinese tea and then, before I could stop him, dumped an enormous spoonful of soggy sugar into it, apparently out of deference to what he thought was Western taste. I wondered whether Mr. Hall and Mr. Beck had loaded up their Chinese tea with sugar. Wu took an ancient leather-bound Bible in Chinese from his bookcase and showed it to me. It had been printed in Shanghai in 1947. He gave me a small paperbound book in English called *Favorite Bible Verses* (Chicago, 1946), so worn that many of the pages had become illegible. He pointed to the inscription on the title page and read aloud: "Don't forget to read your Bible daily."

"I pray here every morning, by myself," said Mr. Wu, and he continued to pull down various books from his shelves, old English volumes printed decades before, like *The World's Best Short Stories* (Shanghai, 1924), edited by one Henry Huizinga, and a 1925 dictionary of English phrases. Around noon, one of his students, smiling with naive benevolence, came in, and sat on the bed to watch us, so that all this heterodox talk of Christianity had to cease. As an alternative, Mr. Wu showed me his English-language textbooks, a series called *English 900*, which for a while had been distributed free by the Voice of America to any listeners in China who wrote to a certain post-office address in Hong Kong. Wu was such a listener. Even as his unwelcome student looked on idiotically, he told how he used to listen to the Voice of America secretly, using an earphone, in the days when to do so risked getting reported to the Public Security police by the local "activists." Now, however, the Voice of America was encouraged by official China as a way of learning English. The conversation flagged. Wu urged his student to go have some lunch, but the student insisted on blessing us with his presence. I began to suspect that the young man was one of those intrusive activists, who had been sent to look in on his teacher during the visit of a foreigner. Finally, Wu's daughter came home, bringing with her a bowl of rice and some vegetables for her father. Seizing an opportunity, the nervous Mr. Wu then pressed his own lunch upon the friendly student, gently overcoming all his polite refusals until he and Wu's steaming bowl of rice mercifully disappeared down the stairs.

I was introduced to the daughter, who was eighteen and stayed in the same room with Wu, sleeping on the couch. I asked about the girl's mother. "My wife," said Wu, waving his hand in a vague backward gesture, "she left. Divorced me." His eyes clouded over for a minute as we sat there in awkward silence, and I began to understand the fullness of the tragedy of this frail, frightened man who lived in a past world of Messieurs Hall and Beck and Henry Huizinga's *World's Best Short Stories*.

The tragedy had to do with more than just freedom of religion, even though Michael Wu certainly suffered because of its absence. Fundamentally, Wu's sad life derived from China's own erratic search for a way to confront the challenge of the modern world; his tragedy stemmed from the violent alternations between the country's desire to mix on an equal footing with the countries on the outside, and its equally strong xenophobic desire to turn inward. Mr. Hall and Mr. Beck had come to southwest China and an intelligent and impressionable young man named Wu had fallen under their influence, not only becoming Christian but, far more important, becoming a kind of internationalist at the same time. For him, the outside world was a stimulant, a provocation, and also a hope for a China that had lost its greatness, fallen into backwardness — a China that needed, for the sake of its identity, a new, dynamic idea that could only come from abroad. There were millions, most of them not Christians, who were of Wu's persuasion, including the great majority of China's leading intellectuals, its scientists, artists, writers, diplomats, who believed, not without some pain, that the best chance for the country lay in trying to become a part of a cosmopolitan, international community.

Under the Nationalists, there were plenty of xenophobes and conservatives, not to mention the corrupt ignoramuses in the military and in the government who thought not of China but of themselves. So, the conflict between those who looked out and those who looked in never really stopped. But by and large, when the Communists took over, China entered a long period of xenophobia, particularly after Peking's break with Moscow became open and irreparable in 1960. Under Communist rule, cosmopolitanism became at best an undercurrent; during the more radical periods like the Cultural Revolution, it was relentlessly suppressed.

Wu, whom I believe to be representative of many others, got caught up in this painful alternation. For the first decade and a half of Communist rule, he survived all right, a little fearfully perhaps, but keeping his job at the middle school and remembering to read his Bible daily, even going to church on Sunday. His identity was essentially cosmopolitan and, though he was cut off from his old friends in the outside world, he didn't suffer too much because of it.

Then came the abrupt swing toward irrational xenophobia during the Cultural Revolution, starting in 1966, and Mr. Wu's life fell total victim to Maoist attempts at social engineering. As he put it in what should have seemed a non sequitur, "Because I believed in God, I had to leave the middle school." At first, he didn't want to say where he'd been forced to go. But gradually he overcame his reticence and began to tell me, perhaps his first foreign contact since Mr. Hall and Mr. Beck had left three decades before, what had happened to him. Starting in 1966, he was interned for eleven years on a state farm, run by the police, about twenty miles outside the provincial capital. "I did hard labor," he said; "it was like Siberia." In 1976, he was finally allowed to return to his former middle school and resume his broken life.

Again I asked about his wife, but Mr. Wu waved his hand in a dismissive gesture. He didn't want to talk about her and I suspect that she had, either voluntarily or under pressure from the local authorities, divorced him without his consent. That sort of broken marriage was not a rare phenomenon in China. I knew of two brothers in Canton who had spent long years on a state farm on Hainan Island, a subtropical area notorious as one of the country's most difficult and primitive places. Their father had been a local performer in Cantonese opera. In the mid-1950s, he had tried to escape to Hong Kong by walking over the land border. Captured by the Chinese police, the father was sent away, probably to a labor camp in the northeast of the country. The boys' mother was advised by the party authorities to divorce the criminal father. The last I was able to learn about these people, in 1978, was that the family had never heard a single word about the father. That day when he left for prison, he disappeared from their lives forever.

I cannot be sure whether there was a similar story with Wu's wife or not, though I assume that his refusal to delve into that one corner of his life meant that, whatever happened to his daughter's mother, it still caused him great pain and humiliation. In any case, Michael Wu's story was meaningful to me, not only because it was my first excursion into the personal heart of China, but also because its elements of political tragedy showed very well the ways in which the insistent demands of the revolution produced fear and uncertainty among those who chose not to heed its particular call. Above all, Wu was a living example of the fatefulness of personal decisions in China, where individual choice affects lives in a way that Westerners might find hard to understand. In the West, personal decisions stand or fall on personal criteria. Whom we marry, what church we attend, whom we vote for, what we will read, write, say — these are largely matters for judgment by the individual himself and only marginally do they affect things like jobs or social status, much less such fundamentals as personal freedom. While, of course, we agonize over them, our personal decisions and choices do not normally test the extent of our courage or heroism. In China, as in other countries dominated by Communist parties, people face personal choices that require a courage and strength of conviction far beyond what we experience in the West.

Sometime in the 1950s, Michael Wu decided that he would retain his Protestant faith, even though he knew that it was already stigmatized, not only as an opiate of the masses, but as an opiate imported by the imperialists from abroad to poison and enslave the mind of China. His decision was no doubt different from that of many others, those who rode with the tide, who saw that their personal interests and advancement required that they divorce themselves from the foreign religion, that, at least, they mouth the slogans of Marxism. *China Youth*'s letter writer, Pan Xiao, after all, learned how to be selfish, how to bargain for wages and bonuses, how to flatter and speak false words. Her boyfriend betrayed her confidences in order to curry favor with the political leaders. In personal and philosophical matters, hypocritical compromises with power and authority become the vehicles for getting along.

But not for Michael Wu, who decided to remain true to the convictions that he had learned from Mr. Hall and Mr. Beck. It was easy to see the staggering price that he had paid for this decision to cast his lot with the God of the foreign imperialists, rather than the gods of the Communists. What remained to him in his modest home above the middle school classrooms were the fragments, the shards, of a life ruined by intolerant politics.

As Wu paced nervously in his room, telling me in a frightened, tremulous voice of his life, it was hard to view him as in any way heroic. Here, after all, was a man who preferred to pray in secret in his home even as elsewhere in China local Christian believers were succeeding in getting their church properties returned to them under new central government guidelines restoring freedom of religion. And, when some sixteen-year-old kid happened to wander into his room, he clammed up entirely on the very subject that pervaded, with tragic consequences, his entire life. Michael Wu tried to cope with his situation by withdrawing into an underground world, filled with memories of days gone by and taken up by such private pursuits as learning English and poring over volumes of another era. And yet, despite this caution, this fearfulness, it is possible to find heroism in his inconspicuous life. The issue of courage does not arise unless there is fear. Wu did not stoop to flattery or to falsehoods. He refused to compromise with communism as a way to preserve his Christianity. And he was bold enough to tell his story to a foreigner encountered fortuitously on the streets. In other words, Wu stuck to the fateful choice he had made many years before, and if, out of fear, he decided to retreat from the world, that did not annul the fundamental courage of his choice.

"Things are better now," he told me as I was getting ready to go back down to the street. "But there are still limits." He went on, in his hesitant way, "Actually, we don't have much hope." Having once been brutalized, Michael Wu is just trying to get by from one day to the next. Things are better, yes, but things in China have changed from better to worse many times before, and Michael Wu, like millions of Chinese, is careful to avoid giving future xenophobic "activists" any reason to brutalize him again.

Religion, of course, is not a major concern of very many Chinese, who for centuries have approached metaphysics in general with a casual eclecticism that is, in itself, unusual in the West. Nonetheless, precisely because religion has been the focus of such concentrated negative energy by China's rulers, it is an area of life wherein one can discover the meaning of personal conviction. The survival of religious belief came for me to be a terrain where the various possible responses to political pressure could be seen in different individuals — capitulation, compromise, hypocrisy, resignation, defiance, opportunism, courage. Each person wears like a name card the nature of his reaction to the awesome pressures of the Communist party.

In the city of Kunming, capital of Yunnan Province, for example, I managed to pay an unannounced and unaccompanied visit to the mosque to see how the region's many Moslems had endured their own political pressures. And, I was not surprised to find that among them there had been a strong spirit of resistance against efforts to suppress the one true faith. The Kunming mosque is a ramshackle structure near the main shopping district of the city that shows immediately its Chinese characteristics. Indeed, it looks a good deal more like a Taoist temple than it does like the typical mosque of central Asia or the Middle East. It has red lacquered pillars, straw mats on the floor covered by red rugs, and a sloping temple-style roof of clay tiles. My visit there took place in 1979 and the mosque had just been restored to the faithful after many years of being used as a factory workshop. There was a pile of broken wooden furniture covering one stretch of red rug. Large gouts of machine oil formed ugly circular stains on the wood floor beneath the mats. I was received graciously, even enthusiastically, by the imam and several male believers who were sitting and talking in a small anteroom.

They told me that in the mid-1970s (some said it was '74; others that it was '75), there was a movement among the region's estimated one hundred thousand Moslems to get the mosque reopened. Groups of militants demonstrated in the streets to complain not only of the still shut mosque but also of the fact that Moslems were being required by the state to raise pigs on neighboring communes. "So," said the imam, "we rose up to oppose them." The Moslems met stiff resistance from "them," the local authorities. Many Moslems were arrested and some of those jailed were released only in the fall of 1979. Worse, one largely Moslem production brigade called the Sha Dien Brigade refused to turn over to the police some of the activists who were wanted. So, the Sixteenth Regiment of the P.L.A. arrived at Sha Dien and shelled it for several days. About three hundred people were killed in the battle. Afterward, the army rounded up five of the Moslem leaders and publicly executed them.

The Moslems who told me that story were clearly proud of their defiance, and, at the same time, they were contemptuous of the Christians in Kunming, who, it seemed, had not managed to persuade the local author-

ities to restore a single church. "The Christians haven't risen up to resist," said one of the believers, a grizzled old fellow with a dirty white
skullcap. "We Moslems believe in God and we don't fear anything, not
even death." Yet, I was disinclined to credit any superior courage on their
part. The mosque, after all, had been closed down for more than a decade
and not reopened until several years after the suppression of the rebellion
of 1974 or 1975, which evidently was not followed by further rebellions. I
suspected that the current bravado could have taken place only after the
fall of the Gang of Four in 1976. Until then individual Moslems, faced
with the terror inspired by the slowly grinding wheels of China's control
apparatus, might well have played it safe.

There was no doubt, however, that by 1979 religion of all sorts, Buddhist, Moslem, and Christian, was flourishing in a new period of tolera-
tion. By mid-1981, more than forty Catholic churches had been retrieved
from the schools, factories, and offices to which they had been turned over
in 1966. There were Buddhist temples in every district. They became
tourist sights. Over eighty Protestant churches had reopened as well as a
Protestant seminary in Nanking complete with forty bright, eager young
students. If you bothered to look, you would find in practically any city
in China, as I did in Chungking, some rubble-strewn old church filled
with workmen busily restoring it. I went to Lanzhou in northwestern
Gansu Province and asked if, by any chance, there was a church. I was
directed to the municipal library, a series of low-slung stone buildings
around a courtyard. There, two hundred thousand books were being put
into boxes and moved out so that the library, which before 1966 was the
Protestant church, could become the Protestant church again. There was
also a feeling of momentum in this, a sense that religious faith, after all
that desiccated Maoist pseudointellectualism, was touching many new
Chinese hearts. Even Pan Xiao had gone to church and thought of becoming a nun. And, in Peking, I met a number of young people who,
while not actually going to church, were attracted to the notion of spiritual beliefs. Once in the Nationalites' Palace discotheque, I was talking
to the pretty Chinese girl I used to dance with from time to time. "Communism puts so much emphasis on struggle," she told me when, for some
reason, the conversation turned to religion. "What I like about Christianity is that it centers on kindness in human relations."

But while, by their lights, China's leaders were making sincere efforts
to respect once again the article on freedom of religion that was present in
every Chinese constitution, it was freedom of religion on terms that still
posed serious choices for individual believers. The churches were organized along the lines that were created in the 1950s, the Protestants into
the so-called Three Self Christian Patriotic Movement, the Catholics into

the Chinese Patriotic Catholic Association, the Buddhists into a Buddhist Association, and so on. For the Catholics, this meant no official contacts with the Holy See. It also meant remaining at best silent on such questions as abortion, divorce, and birth control where the policies of the state and of the church would normally have clashed. In the 1950s, many Catholics and Protestants had gone to jail precisely because they spoke out against the governmental reorganization of the churches. (Many, in fact, did not have to speak out; they were jailed in those various bursts of revolutionary excess that swept people away whether they had committed "crimes" or not.) What that suggests is that in the 1950s, choices had to be made, fateful choices. Those who decided to resist the government's religious policies have, by now, mostly disappeared. When you visit the churches of China, you are talking to the ones who decided to survive by compromising with the legions of Mao. Now, for example, when the church associations hold their national conferences, they routinely pass through the rituals of fealty required by the Communist authorities. They issue a statement praising the government's policies and declaring that the only way to be a good Catholic, Protestant, et cetera, is to support the leadership of the Chinese Communist party.

I do not wish to imply disrespect for those religious figures who decided to accept the "patriotic" associations required by the party. At the very least, a decision to compromise allowed the churches to exist, so that these days, from Canton in the southeast to Urumchi in the northwest, Christian hymns do rise into the officially atheistic air of China. A religious figure could well argue that circumscribed churches are better than no churches at all, that it is better for Christian believers to have a place to worship on Sunday than not to have such a place. Once I talked with the Protestant bishop of China, Ding Guangxun, a former head of the World Christian Federation in Geneva, who is now the president of the Nanking Theological Seminary. He argues forcefully and persuasively that only by putting the churches into the patriotic associations could the church leaders free Christianity from the stigma of being a foreign religion, that only in this way could the church be both fully Christian and fully Chinese.

And yet, what about those who did not compromise, who refused to see in religious belief any need for the Communists' ritual of fealty? Interested in the courage of conviction, I tended to put them on a different level from those who accepted the government's transformation of the churches. Moreover, unlike the impressive and forthright Bishop Ding, many a "patriotic" churchman's pro-government rationalizations were so obsequious as to be devoid of all moral content. I cannot mention names; but I remember well the priest in one large city church who had been ordained in the early 1950s by Bishop Gong Pingmei. The priest had become an active member of the "patriotic church." The bishop went to prison in 1955 because of his opposition to the "patriotic church." When I asked the former about the latter, I was treated to a rationalization full of the cant and rant of Communist jargon at its worst. It seems, the priest said, that Gong Pingmei did not go to jail because his ideas were different. He went to jail because he was a "counterrevolutionary" who had put himself into opposition with the "new China." Bishop Gong Pingmei remains, as of this writing, the last of the old Vatican-appointed bishops still in prison.

There are other views among the Catholics of China. In Shanghai, many Catholic families refuse to attend mass at the city's restored red-brick church precisely because they do not regard it as the real church. There is also in Shanghai and elsewhere a slender, fragile network of Catholic priests and believers who maintain a kind of underground church separate from the patriotic church. I had one direct experience with this underground church and it was a deep lesson in both the courage of convictions and the horrors of totalitarian intolerance.

It was in a city in the north, the identity of which I have promised not to disclose. I had gone to this place to collect information for a story having nothing to do with religion. Before I embarked on my journey, however, I asked the authorities in Peking if there were any reopened churches in the city in the north. If there had been a church, I would probably have tried to make time to visit it out of general curiosity regarding the state of Christianity in China. But the answer was no, there was no church, and I forgot the matter. When I arrived in the city, I discovered quite by accident that the authorities in Peking were incorrect. Strolling around the free market of the town, I stopped at a small food stall to chat with some of the local people. The proprietor, a stout woman in standard blue cotton, asked me what my religion was.

"I don't believe in religion," I answered, giving her the easiest reply. "What about you?"

"I am a Catholic."

"Really? I thought there were no Catholics in this city."

"Oh, there are many of us. And we have a church, too."

I asked for the address of the church and promptly informed my foreign-affairs-office guide that I wanted to visit it. And so I did, by myself, and only after ignoring the guide's insistence that I could not visit the church because we had not made the necessary arrangements with the "department concerned" — meaning the government's Bureau of Religious Affairs. I found the church where the food-stall proprietor had said it would be, down a small, drab lane of poor, mud-walled houses. It con-

sisted of a very modest, squat, stone-floored chapel that was fairly bursting with restoration activity. A foreigner striding into almost any courtyard in China is a rather conspicuous sight, so it was only a matter of
seconds before I had been discovered and taken to the priest. This man
turned out to be most gracious and informative. He gave me an enthusiastic tour, told me that there were more than a thousand parishioners there,
that they had donated their own money for the repair of the church, and
that they were performing the labor themselves. I asked why I had been
told in Peking that there was no church in the city.

My question produced a sudden silence among the people who had
gathered around to hear my conversation with the priest.

"That's because they don't know about us," he said at last.

"Why not?" I plunged ahead with innocent curiosity. "Haven't you
informed the Patriotic Association that you are reopening the church?"

Another silence. Some shuffling of feet, clearing of throats. The priest
replied, "What good would it do *us* to notify *them?*"

Then I realized. This Catholic community was rebuilding its church
under the usual official auspices, but quietly, inconspicuously, it had simply opted against participation in the Catholic association. Of course it
had no ties with Rome either, no chance of contacts with the Holy See.
But it wanted to remain in spirit, if not in form, a part of what it regarded
as the true Catholic church. The previous year, the priest had traveled to
another province where he knew a bishop who had been nominated before the Communist revolution by the Vatican. In that way he had been
ordained a real priest.

There was a wide gulf apparent between this quiet, strong man in the
city in the north and that priest who had talked of the "counterrevolutionary" Gong Pingmei. But the difference was still to grow. This priest
took me to a kind of shed that was being used as a chapel on Sundays
while the repairs were under way on the main church building. There
was a makeshift, raised pulpit, a wooden cross, two paintings of Jesus,
some strips of red paper. At the side of the chapel was a door that led into
another room. The priest beckoned me inside and I noticed the dirt floor,
the two beds pressed along the stone wall, the dresser and the mirror, the
thermos full of hot water, and two men dressed in proletarian blue with
wispy beards and faces lined with age. They too, I learned, were priests.
One of them had spent thirty years on a reform-through-labor camp in
Qinghai Province; the other had done a few years less than that in Gansu.
They had both returned within the preceding two years.

Stunned, I stood in the middle of that poor, bare room, that pitiful
monastery, where these two aged ghosts were living out their last days.
One of them, evidently assuming I was somebody else, spoke to me in

Latin; the other, in Chinese so heavily accented that I could understand only fragments. But, in fact, I understood without words. You can read articles and books that make reference to forced-labor camps, that throw off bloodless statistics and theories about the revolutionizing of society. These two men, who smiled at me kindly and pressed on me cup after cup of tea, were among the statistics. They were people whose lives had been destroyed by one of those Marxist-Maoist slogans that project some people into the vanguard and drop others into the dustbin of history. But, in an important way, they had risen above their persecutors because their stubborn, foolish, and, perhaps, prideful faith had endured. They had not compromised. No questions could be asked about their courage. I understood only two things that the old priests said to me. One in Chinese: "It was the Chinese church that broke relations with Rome." The other in Latin: "Ecclesia catholica una est" ("The Catholic church is one"). The issue for them, the point of difference with the "patriotic" authorities, had remained the same for all their decades of captivity. But most fundamentally, the issue was something different. It was the right to be free of somebody else's determinism. It took centuries for the Catholic church in medieval Europe — so similar in many respects to the Communist parties of the world — to learn to respect that right. I wondered if the Communists ever would.

A brief epilogue on the underground church: At the time of my visit there, I did not think very much of my small quarrel with my guide over his insistence that we must go through official channels before seeing the church (I had refused since there was no time for bureaucratic procedures). A few days after my own visit to the priests, however, a foreign friend of mine went to the same city, and I recommended that he see them as well. But when he showed up at the same humble courtyard, the atmosphere had changed dramatically. The priest who had been so warm and hospitable to me firmly told him that the work of restoration was not yet complete, that visits were thus not possible, that no, it was not permitted to take photographs. This is unprovable, but evidently, after my appearance there, the church had received a call from the authorities, who laid down certain regulations about talking without official approval to foreign visitors. That is the circumscribed nature of freedom of religion in China; that, indeed, is the nature of freedom of speech.

15

The Dispossessed

THE FOREIGN-AFFAIRS OFFICE of the Public Security Bureau is located in a charming, imperial-style courtyard pressed against the ancient moat of the Forbidden City. All foreigners resident in Peking go there from time to time to get travel permits, exit permits, reentry permits, and so on. When the long-term visitor first arrives in Peking, moreover, he has to go to this picturesque and soon to be familiar courtyard, to obtain a residency permit for Peking. This is a routine procedure and not very troublesome. It happened when I tried to do it the first time, however, that I misunderstood the directions and ended up at the wrong P.S.B. reception office, where I got a glimpse of the "real China."

The reception center for Chinese visitors to Peking is located on Zhengyi (Righteousness) Road, the border of the gracious pre-1949 foreign diplomatic quarter. Just down the street is the state tailor shop where Western-style suits are made for officials going abroad and where the Mercedes Benz or Red Flag limousines that have brought these officials for fittings (the suits made there are in fact studiously unstylish) can often be seen. There are no Red Flags parked in front of the P.S.B. office on the other side of a whitewashed wall in a courtyard far less charming than that of the foreigners' reception center. Outside on Zhengyi Road, on the day I arrived there, were a group of people with the stark, poor, unabashedly dumbfounded look that identified them as country folk. They were dressed in faded, padded black. The men were grizzled and smoked fat cigarettes rolled unprofessionally from newsprint. The women were haggard, grimy, tough, sexless.

Inside, there were more of the same kind of people, standing and staring, sitting on a wooden bench and staring, proffering papers to a Public Security official who sat at a battered wooden desk, spoke in harsh, blunt tones, and stared back. The office was dark and dreary. The floor was of dirty cement, the walls chipped and unkempt. I was astonished that foreigners would be sent to this particular place to register with the authorities, since it made such an obviously bad impression; but it was indeed a P.S.B. reception center and that was where I had been told to go by the officials of the Foreign Ministry. And so, while the peasants looked on, I pressed my case on the Public Security officer. He puffed on his cigarette and scrutinized my passport. He stared at me in silence for a long minute, lifted the receiver of his telephone, and began asking the crackling voice on the other end what should be done with a foreigner who insisted that this was the place for him to obtain his residency permit. At length, the Public Security officer notified me of my mistake. This was the reception center for Chinese; I would have to go elsewhere to conduct my business.

Eventually I found my way to the charming courtyard where the problems of foreigners are handled. In the meantime, I had accidentally discovered a little-known slice of life in the capital, one that was to take on considerable importance to me as a part of the camouflaged reality of China. The peasants waiting in the street and in the shabby police reception center were among the thousands of folk from the provinces who, beginning in 1979, descended on the capital city seeking redress from the central government for various grievances, many of them dating back to the Cultural Revolution. What they were doing was called *shang-fang*, meaning "visiting a higher level," and for some time in 1979 and early 1980, they could be seen everywhere, staring listlessly at the foreigners near the gates of the Peking Hotel, sleeping on the sidewalk in front of the railway station, loitering around restaurants in hopes of picking up some scraps from the table when the day was done. Most were poor peasants. Their complexions were three shades darker than those of people from the city. They wore tattered, dusty, black, padded clothes. They had the slack-jawed, stony-eyed amazement on their faces of rural people in the city for the first time. They were like ghosts from a past that many people believed — mistakenly — had long ago disappeared from China, the ghosts of primitive, backward, benighted villages untouched by the progress promised by the revolution. They had various grievances, usually involving the loss of jobs or mistreatment of themselves or close relatives by local officials, and they stayed around the capital for weeks and even months, sitting in front of the guarded entrance to the State Council or trying to sell little handicrafts near Tiananmen Square. At one point, there were probably more than a hundred thousand of them in Peking. While, in my early contacts with them, I had assumed that they simply arrived helter-skelter in the city and threw themselves on the mercy of local authorities, now I knew from my discovery at their police station that such was not the case. They duly registered. They were identified, numbered, controlled, and sent to one of the areas on Peking's outskirts where they were authorized to stay.

For several months, the Chinese government did little to conceal their presence, and that is surprising given that, to some extent, they constituted living, breathing pieces of evidence of the deep problems that existed in the provinces. Gradually, however, the authorities rounded up most of the petitioners and got them off of Peking's main streets; they persuaded them to stay in designated camps in the city euphemistically called "reception centers." With considerable fanfare, the government also announced that it was assigning some ten thousand bureaucrats to deal with their complaints, a gesture that created an impression of responsiveness on the part of the government; however, I never met a petitioner who had managed to see one of these ten thousand bureaucrats, and it was a common feeling among foreigners in Peking that the new program existed for propaganda purposes only.

In the fall of 1979 I went for my first visit to a *shang-fang* "reception center" and with that act, inadvertently set in motion a long and frustrating effort to collect some of their tales. The center was located along a narrow alley that ran between two walled-in factory compounds. Lining the walls were hundreds of plastic lean-tos that snapped briskly in the breeze like gas-station pennants. Many people were huddled under them. Others sat listlessly and played cards, or talked, or stared into space. Someone with a mordant sense of humor had painted a slogan on a huge, discarded drainage pipe — REFUGEES OF CHINA. When I showed up, a crowd of dark, angry faces surrounded me, everybody shouting at once, people thrusting pieces of paper into my hands that gave accounts of their grievances. Hands tugged at my sleeves. Voices hummed in my ears. It was impossible to hear anything except a general, overwhelming babble with occasional comprehensible phrases about injustice, beatings, unemployment. I had never before heard anti-Communist sentiment openly expressed inside China, but that afternoon I got an earful.

The next spring, I went back again and very nearly the same thing happened. There were fewer people. The place had been tidied up some. There was a man, looking very pale next to the weathered peasants and, in his crisp, black cadre's tunic, very militarily trim. A crowd like the one in the fall gathered tightly around. There was the same thrusting of papers into my hands, as though I, as a foreigner, could do something with them. There was the same babble of voices. And then, suddenly, there was the pale-faced cadre approaching to ask what I was doing there. Visiting, I said. He instructed me to leave. I refused. He left. But then, as each person in the crowd started talking to me, pale-face came up from behind, tapped him softly on the shoulder, and led him quietly away. One man said: "I don't care what they do to me. My brother is a high official." No sooner did he complete that bit of bravado than he too was led, unprotesting and without a word of his brother, away. When it happened a third time, it became obvious that my presence there was doing neither me nor them any good. So I walked back out the alley to the street and got into my waiting taxi. As I drove off, I looked back. The cadre in black, another ghost, was standing in the middle of the dusty brown street, writing the license-plate number of the taxi in his notebook.

That was only the beginning of what became a minor obsession on my part to get to know some of the petitioners. A couple of times I went back to the reception area but there was always the problem either of the official presence or of such a pushing, shoving crowd that it was impossible to talk to any one or two people at length. So, one gelid winter evening, I decided to go to the area by car, find one or two petitioners, and invite them to a "masses' restaurant" to talk over a few plates of dumplings.

I found two hoary and weather-beaten men from Sichuan, who were standing and talking outside a tiny shelter of wood, tin, and stone that leaned against a retaining wall down a small lane. They said they were willing to talk and so, while my startled driver glanced at them unbelievingly in his rearview mirror, I took them to the Hung Xing Lou Restaurant, a three-story establishment intended very much for the masses (though with private rooms and special dishes for foreigners on the third floor) about a half-hour walk from my hotel. The place was crowded, mostly with men in faded blue padded jackets, and we had to wait for a table. I thought my two Sichuanese to be more or less indistinguishable from the other patrons of the restaurant, many of whom, like us, drifted around the large noisy room waiting for places to be vacated. But there must have been a subtle giveaway that my guests were people up from the provinces — who had a bad reputation for their habit of hanging around restaurants at mealtimes to beg for leftovers or quickly scoff down what remained from other people's plates. That there was some sort of giveaway became apparent when suddenly one ferocious waitress came over and began loudly shouting at the two Sichuanese to get the hell out of there. She began pushing them. They, thoroughly cowed, were trying to make their way to the exit through the gathering crowd. I tried to interpose myself between my guests and this virago of a waitress and to persuade her that they *were* my guests and that I would pay for their meal — a notion she found so incongruous that she glared at me with mute astonishment. A curious crowd had gathered. Finally, though we were all allowed to stay, we had become such objects of attention that the whole exercise was pointless.

So we left. Unfortunately, however, I had sent the car away so the driver could have his dinner, and therefore we had no choice but to walk back to the hotel. I mumbled apologies for the fact that my idea had turned out so disastrously. They replied that it didn't matter. Anyway, they were used to suffering, I felt. It was bitterly cold that night. When we reached the hotel, they waited outside across the street while I went into the dining room to buy some steamed dumplings to bring out to them. There was no more chance of their being let into the hotel than of their getting an audience with Premier Zhao Ziyang for the presentation of their grievances (which had to do with jobs lost during the Cultural Revolution and not recovered since). I got an enormous quantity of dumplings and put them into a plastic shopping bag left over from one of my trips to Hong Kong. When I emerged from the hotel, I found my friends across the street in front of the offices of the *Guangming Daily*, one of Peking's major newspapers.

There, they created a tableau of extraordinary incongruity. In front of the newspaper office there is a permanent photo display depicting Chinese socialism in its brilliant strides forward — with pictures of laboratory technicians in white suits, of bounteous orchards bedecked with apples, of sinewy workers guiding the levers of industry. And then there were these two grizzled peasants, thrown out of a restaurant for the masses, denied entry to a hotel belonging, as a state enterprise, to the whole people, gratefully accepting a shopping bag of dumplings from a foreigner and being sent on their way (in the backseat of my small but chauffeured car) at the end of a disastrous venture.

Still, I persisted. I was aware of the irony that if I had looked in the countryside itself for people seeking redress of grievances, my guides from the China Travel Service would surely have prevented me from finding them. But they had come to me in Peking and I was loath to pass up the opportunity that they presented. I kept from time to time going back to their areas of stone, mud, tin, and plastic-sheet huts. Equally important, I began to collect written materials from them. The petitioners, as a common procedure, prepared long, detailed accounts of their troubles. They spent hours laboriously copying them on thin, flimsy paper so that they could hand them out to any government official who would let them in the door. Whenever I came to visit, one or two of these multipage documents would be stuffed into my hand or pocket, evidently in the vain hope that I, as a foreigner, might have some influence with the authorities.

The petitions brought them to life. Ungrammatical, scrawled in the tremulous hands of those who do not often hold pens, the petitions were redolent of the flavor of life under communism, full of the vocabulary and the concepts imposed by three decades of incessant propaganda in the countryside. In that sense, they reflected the deep imprint already made by the style of Chinese communism itself. Most important to me, however, the petitions showed these peasant sufferers in all their human complexity as they wrestled with the bizarre movements and demands imposed on them from remote Peking — with antirightist campaigns, Great Leaps Forward, Cultural Revolutions, struggles for power among local leaders. They were full of the touching and homey details that reveal individuals, not embracing ideological abstractions, but grappling with the woes of real life.

Take, for example, Xu Zhuxiang, thirty, from a rural county in Hunan Province. Like almost all of the petitioners, when Xu gives basic data about himself, he includes his name, age, and sex, his county of origin, the name of his commune and his production brigade, and his "class origin." That pernicious concept, which, given Xu's age of thirty, really refers to his ancestors' status, not his own, follows him about not only in the dossier maintained on him by his unit but, evidently, engraved in his own self-conception as well. In Xu's case, the category is "landlord," the worst possible in the rural areas. His complaint focuses on the themes of vengeance and the abuse of power. For reasons that he does not specify, he says, in 1968 — "when the Gang of Four was running rampant" — his mother was "brutally beaten to death." Xu knew the identity of the murderer, one Li, and after accusing him of the crime, had the satisfaction of seeing him sentenced to a jail term of six years. But the murderer Li had powerful friends, including a cousin, named Zhen, who was Communist party secretary of the production brigade.

"Li's cousin concocted the charge that in 1969 I destroyed a portrait of Chairman Mao," Xu says in his petition. "And so I was branded a counterrevolutionary and was sentenced to three years of forced labor without pay. Actually, the charge was untrue. I never did such a thing. I have been pleading my case from 1969 until the present but the matter remains unresolved. Though I am very poor, I have to bring my whole family to Peking to request the leaders of the party Central Committee to rectify my case.

"I have a four-person family," Xu goes on. "When I was falsely accused, I had to borrow money to support them. Now I haven't even a single tile over my head and have to wander about the streets because the pig shed we borrowed from the brigade, for the family to settle down in for a while, has been taken back by the brigade. I hope the leaders of the Central Committee will pity the bitter and sad experiences of my family and me and help me to solve my present difficulties and my sons and grandsons will never forget the big benevolence of the Communist party."

Violence and injustice — these are the principal themes that emerged in the brief, tumultuous conversations that I had with the petitioners whenever I sought them out in their living quarters. Like Xu Zhuxiang of Hunan, many other people complain of their weakness before the local bureaucratic juggernaut of party secretaries, vice-secretaries, brigade accountants, and their friends and relatives. The accountants in particular enjoy a notoriety for corruption similar to the bawdy friar's reputation for licentiousness in medieval Europe. Not a petitioner, but a Chinese friend, once told me of a friend of his who, while working in the city, tried to send via the post office a cash remittance to his wife, who was in the countryside in Shaanxi Province. The money arrived all right at the wife's production brigade — something like thirty dollars — and came to the attention of the accountant. This fellow then seduced the wife. Each time she consented to his sexual demands, he left a little of the money behind for her, making it appear as though it were a gift and never informing her of the money that had come from her husband. When the latter after some time came for a visit, he learned from his wife that she had never, as far as she knew, received his remittance. Gradually he was able to piece the situation together. But what could he do? The accountant was too well connected in the village for the husband to bring him to justice. Faced with the impassive might of the party committee, with its monopoly on power and its instincts for self-preservation, the man felt a profound sense of impotence. And so, like many men everywhere, frustrated by their own powerlessness, he turned his rage against the one person who was within his control and beat his wife mercilessly.

There is, of course, no way to verify these sorrowful tales and, indeed, on my first two or three visits to the principal source of them, the petitioners, I maintained an attitude of considerable skepticism; I made allowances for exaggeration on the part of people who were, after all, trying to elicit sympathy and recompense from the central government. But the sheer numbers of them who told me that their fathers had died under persecution or that their wives were beaten to death or that they themselves had lost their jobs and their property to an avaricious party secretary made me believe more and more in the existence in the countryside of feudal-bureaucratic satrapies with the power to crush the individual. The petitioners, moreover, appeared as simple and inarticulate; they were people of few words. When they talked, they began their stories in the middle, without providing background, as though you, the listener, were already familiar with all the major elements and they only needed to fill in a few details. The petitions, laboriously handwritten on red-lined tissue paper, put these stories into perspective.

Here are a few more:

Complainant Zhang Xi, male, age forty-four, class origin middle peasant, from Hunan. On August 21, 1979, while working on his family plot he got into an argument with a nineteen-year-old youth who was not only the son of the vice–party secretary, but "spent a lot of time practicing kung fu so that he could always be ready for scuffles." The issue was Zhang Xi's belief that his plot was being encroached upon. "I reasoned with him," Zhang Xi writes, "but who could have known that he would not only be deaf to all of my arguments but would suddenly attack me with his spade and cut my hand." When Zhang Xi took his bleeding hand to the brigade office to make a complaint, he found the leadership not only arrayed against him but prepared to punish him for his insolent attempt to bring the relative of one of them to justice. On that day, the son of the vice–party secretary and his allies beat up Zhang Xi's son; then they assaulted his wife and his third daughter, Fuyun.

Zhang Xi sought redress for this incident several times at the county level but, as he puts it, he "met with rebuffs." Then, in October, he traveled to Peking and presented his petition to the Party Central Discipline Inspection Commission, and, he reports: "With deep concern for the suffering of the people, the leading comrades of the center gave me a letter of recommendation to carry back to the county and have the question settled there." However, "because of the bureaucratic shield" that the leaders of the county and brigade could give to each other, the question was not resolved. Instead, things got worse. The leaders suborned some local peasants to claim falsely that they had witnessed the conflict between Zheng and the vice–party secretary's son and that the latter had only defended himself.

Then, having told that much, Zhang Xi adds, almost as an afterthought, a detail of stunning significance. It seems that five years earlier, in 1974, he had already had an altercation with the vice–party secretary during which his daughter was beaten to death. "I had made a number of complaints about this," Zhang concludes, "but because the vice–party secretary corrupted cadres with food and drink and the public security officials falsified the record, no solution was ever found." Now, on his second visit to Peking, he says: "I request the leadership to make profound investigation and to treat the matter accordingly."

Complainant Zhen Huifeng, female, aged forty, class background landlord. Her complaint: she was dismissed from her post as a doctor in a rural county seat in Shandong Province because of certain "mistakes" she had made, and served a long term of labor as a common peasant on a production brigade. Zhen Huifeng admits in her petition that "because I was young and naive," she "made some mistakes regarding the problems of life" — meaning that she had had sexual relations outside of marriage. That was before the Cultural Revolution started in 1966. She is ambiguous in ascribing the reasons for her plight — very possibly they derived simply from her landlord-class background — but she goes on to list a whole series of charges that were trumped up against her after her initial foolish "mistake." They included having a "bourgeois medical style," being "indifferent to the poor and lower middle peasants," listening to the "enemy's radio broadcasts" (probably the Voice of America), and continuing "illicit sexual relations."

Her tale of woe suggests the existence in her life of a kind of brooding, menacing political force. She does not identify it clearly but shows that it had her under constant supervision. Once, for example, she bought a new radio and as she was testing it out, came across an "enemy" broadcast, which she hastily switched off as soon as she realized what it was. Nonetheless, she was forced to stand in the snow for whole nights until she confessed to listening stealthily to enemy broadcasts. Then the radio was confiscated. Finally, in 1971, she was expelled from her post as a doctor in the county and sent to the countryside. "I have reported my case several times to the county party committee, but each time they tried to pass the responsibility on to someone else. The county committee told me to look for the Policy Implementation Office; the Policy Implementation Office asked me to look for county leaders. A cadre, Peng Taisheng, told me that since I had had sexual affairs with others, it was difficult to redress my case, so, with this moral convention in their minds, they have refused to do anything. Now, I hereby ask the [central] leaders: Am I not qualified to contribute to the Four Modernizations simply because I committed some mistakes in the past?"

Complainant Rui Chonggeng, male, aged thirty-two, class origin middle peasant, from a production brigade in Hunan Province. Rui, like many of the petitioners, is seeking redress for a wrong perpetrated against a close relative, in this case his brother, who was driven to commit suicide, a tragedy, Rui Chonggeng writes dramatically, that brought about "the ruin of a family and the loss of its fortune." Rui says that his brother, Junting, joined the revolution in 1949 and rapidly rose in the local hierarchy, serving first as the head accountant of a trading company and then, after receiving some schooling, rising to a county judgeship. In the middle 1950s, under the strain of work, he suffered a "mental disorder" and had to take a leave from his assignment. Then, just as he was on the way to recovery, he was forced to resign by the government leaders of the

county — for exactly what reasons Rui does not specify. The brother refused to accept the discharge, sending back the subsidies and allowances
that came with it and declaring that "he did not want money that could be
used in the construction of the motherland." Depressed, he tried to hang
himself but was rescued by his father. Still, his mental condition got
worse; "his heart was filled with anger, sorrow, anxiety." Debts accumu-
lated. Neither "the county government nor the party ever enhanced their
revolutionary proletarian outlook; they never took care of us in any way."
During the Cultural Revolution, brother Junting was summoned to take
part in "study," meaning that he had serious ideological problems. "He
felt so wronged; he could find no place to complain to; finally he drowned
himself in a well." Since that incident, the family has made over forty appeals to the county and provincial governments to (1) restore the reputation of the dead brother and (2) compensate them with all the salary due
him during his illness, the money spent for medicine, the hospital and
burial fees, and a death pension. Rui Chonggeng concludes: "The great,
glorious, correct party and the people's government of a higher level will
certainly look into this case in a discriminating way."

The effusive gestures toward the glorious party and the great revolution that many of the petitions make are very much like the elaborately
formal, written addresses to the emperor. The petitions are latter-day
mandatory oaths of fealty to the ruling mandarins. Yet they suggest
something of the attitude that the peasants have toward the supreme
rulers. The old operative phrase was: "Heaven is high and the emperor is
far away." But while remote, the imperial court was supposed to be concerned with the welfare of China's lowly inhabitants; there was certainly
no hope of seeing the emperor himself, but he nonetheless represented a
supreme, unquestioned, and heavenly authority. Similarly, today, if their
petitions are any indication, the Chinese peasants see in the exalted leaders of the central government a kind of final recourse, a last hope, a repository of supreme and, perhaps, saving power. But if they can be manipu-
lated by a bit of flattery, by turning some of their own rhetoric against
them, so much the better.

What the petitions show too is that the peasants welcome the authority
of the regime. "They don't want democracy down on the communes," an
editor at the *People's Daily* once told me, "they want strong, honest
rulers." The humble rural folk who live beneath plastic lean-tos and wait
for days and weeks to hand up their crudely lettered statements to some
governmental reception center are not looking for equality. There runs
through all of these letters a sense that, yes, it is all right for life to be unfair; it is just that it cannot be too unfair. There is an acceptance that goes

beyond calculated flattery of the right of rulers to rule and of the duty of subjects to be obedient to them. No doubt that explains how so many of these petitions confer a kind of unreflective legitimacy on much that would, to the Western liberal mind, seem outrageous: the labyrinthine party structure, the importance of class origin, the extraordinary array of terms and slogans, the various bits and pieces of revolutionary jargon and hortatory sloganeering that, together, constitute a whole new vocabulary imposed from above and accepted, absorbed, parroted back from below.

One of the most extraordinary petitions I collected is entitled "Abstracts from a Wrong, False, Mistaken Case," by a Hubei peasant named Wang Fushan. Wang's story contains an amazing collection of what might be called the conceptual artifacts of Chinese communism, as well as many of the Byzantine, petty, personal circumstances that can endanger and even ruin a person.

Wang's problem, stated in a kind of prologue in his petition, is that he was wrongly branded a "rightist" in the massive purification campaigns of 1957 and 1958. He was, he says, wrongly disciplined with the "double expulsion," an abbreviated term consisting of two Chinese characters that stands for the eight-character expression "To be expelled simultaneously from the party and discharged from public employment." In 1960, suffering from his unjust discharge, Wang forged a document, for which he received an unmitigated punishment. Then during the Cultural Revolution "when the Gang of Four was running amok," he was found to be an "active counter," another two-character abbreviation, for "an active counterrevolutionary element and a counterpart of historical counterrevolutionary elements" (whatever that means). All of this, he says, was unfair, and he begs for his good name and position to be restored.

Wang begins his petition by listing the nine various branches of the government and party that he has already appealed to. Then he reminds the central leaders of their own policies of "seeking truth from facts" and "making corrections wherever there are mistakes" — two principles that were "always promoted by Comrade Mao Tse-tung." Only in this way, Wang reminds his lofty readers, can "solidarity between the party and the people be strengthened and the lofty prestige of the party and Comrade Mao Tse-tung be protected."

Having shown his grasp of the spiritual fundamentals, Wang goes on to tell his story in graphic detail. He is forty-nine; his class status is lower-middle peasant (the best); he is a demobilized soldier who joined the army in 1949. So far, an impeccable record. In 1958, as Mao's Great Leap Forward picked up momentum, Wang was transferred from his regular post to a rural district-seat accounting department in order to do "central work," meaning work that is looked on by the party as of urgent importance. With that seemingly innocuous move, he slowly became entangled in a net of conflicting loyalties and angry acts of vengeance that eventually brought about his total ruin.

The initial incident seems remarkably petty. Wang's boss at the accounting department, one Hou, needed another hand and thus arranged the transfer of still another functionary to the county seat. But afraid that this new functionary might be borrowed by still a higher-level unit, Hou wanted to make it appear as though his presence in the accounting department would be only temporary, that his rice coupons were still coming from his former workplace. (As an indication of the high drama that such minor malfeasance could entail, Wang matter-of-factly reported that Hou's predecessor vacated his job by hanging himself.) Hou asked Wang to participate in this petty cover-up. Wang did; then he noticed that officials at the higher level, who indeed were interested in the functionary's transfer, were becoming suspicious about his status. Wang was uncomfortable. He was in the final stages of being admitted into the Communist party and knew that even a small lie, once discovered, could ruin his chances for membership. Writing in that special jargon of the party, Wang says, "I realized that I was taking an action [withholding the truth] that was harmful to the unified leadership of the party committee; I was afraid that I might commit an error of decentralism." And so Wang got ground up in the gears of the very bureaucracy he hoped to rise in. He came clean about the functionary to the party superiors. Hou was criticized. Then Hou avenged himself, says Wang, by organizing his allies inside the accounting department to charge Wang with dereliction of duty. Wang was formally given the label "bad element" and he suffered the "double expulsion" — from the party and from his job.

Wang was naturally aggrieved. "Conflicts took place in my mind. I originated from an exploited family [lower-middle peasant] and had never joined any reactionary organization. In the long period of revolutionary work after the liberation, I never committed even one small error concerning the party's line and policies. It was profoundly wrong and unjustified to be avenged by [Hou's] functionaries just because it was I who had adhered to the principles of the party." Wang also, in a rather pathetic attempt to establish his credentials, writes that Hou was a former member of the exploiting class who had once been dismissed during an early 1950s ideological purge. He seems entirely unaware that the cruelty dealt to Hou years before might be similar to the one being dealt to him now. The party's abstractions mean something to Wang, a man blessed by all the revolutionary definitions who yet finds himself now having to appeal again and again to the higher levels of the party, at the district and the province, for the unfair verdict against him to be reversed. But even when these levels recommended restoring Wang to work, the Hou clique

THE DISPOSSESSED · 199

got away with only lessening the gravity of Wang's label from "bad element" to "ideologically reactionary person," which still sounds grave enough to me but which, apparently, represented a diminution of Wang's burden. Wang was disconsolate. "I cried to the heavens; the heavens did not answer; I cried to the earth; the earth did not answer." Finally, during the "three disastrous years" — the period from 1959 to 1961 following the calamities of the Great Leap Forward — Wang's situation collapsed entirely. "Famine ran high," he writes. "My father starved to death." While authorities have never publicly disclosed the number of people who died by starvation during this terrible period, that Wang evidently believes his statement about his father to be rather ordinary indicates in itself that death through malnutrition was common.

Pressed by debt and still persecuted politically by his enemies, Wang decided to flee to the Yangtse River city of Wuhan. But how to get there? In China a citizen can get the ration coupons he needs to survive only in the place where he is duly registered as a resident. So, Wang forged transfer papers for Wuhan and found a job teaching there in a local elementary school. That situation did not last very long, however. Wang was rounded up in a routine check for "black registrations," the term used for people living outside the area where they are entitled to receive ration coupons; so he was forced to abandon his teaching job and return to the county seat. (I imagined the consternation it must have caused at the school when, one day, teacher Wang simply did not show up.)

Back in the county, Wang was now wanted for forgery. So, he hid. "No unit would shelter me; no relative dared let me stay with him. I starved for one period of three days and three nights." But, he goes on, "I knew the truth about myself" — that is, that he had been framed — "so I couldn't just throw myself into the Yangtse River." Wang made another attempt to go someplace else, using the Public Security Bureau to forge still another residency transfer certificate, but the occasion never arose for him to use it. Finally, devoid of alternatives, he turned himself in to the local police, hoping that they would treat his offenses leniently. "Besides the forged certificate, I had committed no other breach of the social order. Yet, during the trial, the prosecutors in the county court insisted on a strict sentence. The court looked on my case as one with a history [meaning that his record of the past was used to determine his overall bad character], and in 1960, I was sentenced to five years' imprisonment."

In his long petition, Wang Fushan never once questions the values or the legitimacy of the Communist party. No matter how badly he himself has been mistreated, slandered, traduced, and imprisoned, he takes great pains to display himself as a model of correct attitudes and behavior. He glories in the praise of the same party organization that treated him so unfairly. He boasts, for example, that during his five years of "reform through labor" (a euphemism for serving time), Wang always "upheld truth, did four [undescribed] deeds of merit, and was given a number of [again unspecified] awards." Still, his luck was bad. Just as he was to be released at the end of his term into the custody of the local county authorities for his final "rehabilitation," the Cultural Revolution began. "During the time when the Gang of Four rode high, I had a personal disagreement with a landlord" — again, he is grounded in the expectation that his revolutionary class status makes a difference — "who attacked me. In defense I struck back. But for that I was declared an 'active reactionary' and confined for nine months." That conviction was later overruled during the post-Cultural Revolution reexaminations of criminal and political cases, but Wang says that he has still not received his pay for the nine months he was in prison.

He concludes, as many petitioners do, with a summary of his attempts at various local-level organizations to get justice. But, he says, "Until now my case remains to be corrected." He also adds, in the final few lines of his petition, the information that the local district court and the county authorities have written a letter to Wang's commune warning that "legal discipline would be meted out against me if I continued to go up to the capital to be a petitioner and make outrageous demands." Yet evidently Wang refused to heed this warning, as his presence in the capital indicates. A loyal Communist he certainly is. But it is his very loyalty, apparently, that drives him to seek redress.

Wang, in the penultimate paragraph of his plea, also observes the ritual of fealty to the Communist mandarinate. He mentions his current good behavior (apparently unaware that in so doing he suggests what he wants to deny — that his behavior was at any time not exemplary); he declares that he has the support of public opinion; and he pledges his whole life to work for the Four Modernizations. But if that last act of fealty was, as I suspect, pro forma, it nonetheless accurately symbolizes the loyalty to the Communist system that Wang Fushan has felt throughout his life. "The peasant does not want democracy. He wants good, strong rulers," said the man from the *People's Daily*. So it is with Wang. For twenty-three years (he got his first "double dismissal" in 1958; I met him in Peking early in 1981) he has been buffeted by the changeable winds of intraparty struggle. Yet, he can think of no alternative but to continue his quixotic effort to "reverse the verdict," meanwhile declaring his undying loyalty to the party and its policy of the moment, expressing himself in the peculiar mock legalese of Chinese communism. Wang does not have the concepts to do otherwise. He remains basically a very simple man. His is a case study of alienation, in the sense that he has had nearly nothing to do with forming himself; he is entirely a creature of the Communist system that raised him, educated him, provided him with an avenue to worldly success and modest political power, and then, with the caprice of the gods, crushed him. Finally, he is alienated by the ultimate lack of recourse in China's system, by the absence of objective guarantors of fair play. Wang Fushan can only appeal to the party that created him to undo the wrong that it itself did to him. And so, in the same breath, he bemoans his terrible fate and praises the system that visited it upon him. Wang's story, and the way he tells it, demonstrates — to alter Hannah Arendt's famous phrase — the banality of the absurd. Wang Fushan watched as the party swung wildly and inconsistently from one direction to another and, at each sharp turning, he tried his best to follow. When I met him, patched, faded, and poor, in Peking and he handed me his petition, he was clearly a man angry and defeated. Yet, at the same time, he is unaware of what exactly went wrong. He is stricken with the sense of the tragedy of his life. But does he know whom to blame? And now, is there anybody he can really trust?

16

Revolutionary Victims

IF THERE ARE MANY in China whose experience has alienated them from their own potential for awareness, there are others who are only too cognizant of what the revolutionary experience has done to them. China in this sense is the land of the wounded intellectual. Almost without fail when I met a person with a degree from a university, I met somebody who had suffered because of Maoism. The country is filled with learned ex-convicts, with gentlemen former inmates of forced labor camps, with men of arts and science who learned how to till fields and shovel manure and cut trenches out of the frozen winter soil of northern Manchuria. Some of these people are now again heads of departments in the Academy of Social Sciences or at the *People's Daily* newspaper. But many others have done no better than to have had their "labels" removed, to have been brought back to their native places, given some sinecure, and allowed to live out their senior years in relative peace. And, while they have been rescued from the worst of their suffering, still they represented a sad, a tragic phenomenon of the Chinese revolution, the Maoist inclination to wreak havoc with the best of its resources as it strives to attain some misconceived and entirely abstract ideological goal.

The most common Chinese metaphor for suffering is "to eat bitterness," an expression whose derivation suggests the central concern of life during millennia past, to get enough to fill the stomach. It is considered bad form to suffer too loudly; you are supposed to know how to eat a share of bitterness without dissolving into self-pity. In this, many Chinese are different from their Western counterparts, who, with their belief that justice must be done, are likely to shout about the wrongs done to them, to sue, to write letters to the editor. It also makes it difficult for the foreigner in China to delve into the personal hearts of those who have lived through the Maoist chamber of horrors, the antibourgeoisie campaigns, the mass roundups for the labor camps, the paranoid suspicion of foreign contacts, the Cultural Revolution. Gradually, however, the scars begin to show even among the sedate and cultivated Chinese scholars who would rather not talk so much about themselves, but would rather hear something about you.

One of my friends in Peking — I'll call him Professor Chen — was the very epitome of the classic Chinese scholar. A non-Communist patriot, he had spent the 1940s and 1950s editing and writing multivolume tomes on China's history and culture. He was the kind of man that Confucius deemed the Gentleman: self-possessed, generous, concerned with what was right rather than with what was profitable, filled with a sense of propriety, and prone to a near ceremonial, but entirely sincere, ritual of politeness in interpersonal relations. Professor Chen lived in a dilapidated traditional-style house on a courtyard, with an old dusty couch and easy chair, a few pieces of wooden furniture, a leak-stained ceiling, peeling walls, and magnificently delicate patterned wood latticework windows.

I occasionally paid afternoon calls on him and as the worn, unattended sitting room gradually fell into darkness, he would talk about all sorts of things, except himself. We talked about the grand old prerevolutionary tradition by which young people who could not afford to go to the university would audit whatever classes they wanted at the best schools in China, often being the best scholars in each class. It was a way, he said, of enabling the talented poor to get an education. He talked about the former liveliness of the streets of Peking, of all the culinary delicacies that used to be sold every day on the lane that ran by his house but that were unavailable now. A fanatical, and even pedantic, lover of Peking opera, he described great performances that he had seen in the past, told me his favorite parts of the immense repertoire of librettos and scores. He showed me his personal collection of reproductions of traditional opera masks that had somehow survived the depredations of the Cultural Revolution. Moreover, Professor Chen seemed a happy man, always talking about what he and others were doing now that "the old man" (Mao) was no longer making life miserable for them.

It was only after several visits that I began to hear the other experiences of this gentle scholar. Professor Chen had spent three years doing labor reform on a farm in Hubei Province; he had been branded a member of the "stinking ninth category," the classically Maoist terminology for an intellectual. All of his several children in one way or another had had their dreams crushed by the experience of having a member of the "stinking ninth category" for a father. The years when they might have been students, they spent doing physical labor on a rural commune. They were not workers, peasants, or soldiers, the three preferred categories from which a new class of intellectuals would be drawn, so even when the universities reopened they were politically unqualified for admission. These bright and eager and dutiful children all failed to receive a higher education; one of them was still in a rural area having not yet succeeded in coming back to Peking, and the fourth, the youngest child, was the only one who, because she was only sixteen when the Cultural Revolution started, had been allowed to remain in the old family home. Clearly the apple of the old professor's eye, this one — he finally told me — it had all become too difficult for her, and one day she wrote a last letter to her parents in the labor-reform camp and killed herself by swallowing a large amount of DDT (still the most common method of suicide in China).

One late afternoon, Professor Chen called me over to one end of his sitting room, opened a drawer, and took out of it a strange, unrecognizable object. It was a crude wooden handle into which had been embedded a piece of bent metal. It had not been his, the professor said; it belonged to a good friend, another scholar, who was, when he was still alive, the greatest authority in the country on the great seventeenth-century novel, *Dream of the Red Chamber*. The object was a tool, used to twist raw hemp into fiber for rope. The old Chinese scholar had spent his three years in reform-through-labor manipulating that tool in his hand. Because it had enabled him to work, he believed that it had enabled him to stay alive. And yet, an inscription that he had roughly carved into the wooden handle seemed to me to symbolize something much deeper than just an effort to stay alive. It was a bitter piece of self-mockery, a supercilious sneer at the blackness and the void. It said simply: "My life."

What amazed me more than anything else about Professor Chen was his enthusiasm, the absence in him of any mournfulness or bitterness even in his words or in his demeanor. Was he wise like the Taoist philosopher Chuang-tse, I wondered; Chuang-tse, who did not mourn the death of his son because, as he put it, there was once a time when I didn't yet have a son and I was happy; now again I have no son, so why should I not still be happy? Or, did Professor Chen simply display the dignity of being able to "eat bitterness"? Or, was it the belief that the past had been an aberration, that things were going to improve so much as to be good? Finally, I asked what explained his cheerfulness. He replied: "You should not think that I am optimistic or cheerful, or even that I lack bitterness. I am simply resigned. I know that what did this to me was the system and I know that without changing the system there can be no real hope for China."

In fact, in several respects Professor Chen was lucky. First of all, unlike many other victimized scholars, he is alive. He has back the home where his father before him lived, and unlike many people who owned the traditional low-slung houses built around courtyards, he is not sharing his with the strange families who moved in during the Cultural Revolution. Most important of all, perhaps, Professor Chen managed to get through most of the ideological campaigns more or less unscathed, falling finally only during the Cultural Revolution, when, in any case, almost everyone like him fell too. But there are many people in China —whether it is only hundreds of thousands or millions I do not know — who were made to suffer intermittently for practically the entire period of Communist rule. These, moreover, are not men, like the priests in the northern city, who consciously set themselves in opposition to the Communist party. Many of these people became the "targets of revolutionary struggle" simply because of ill-begotten definitions, because in the abstract, ideological sense, they were enemies of Progress.

The names of the numerous campaigns against innocent victims read like parodies of themselves. They go back at least as far as the "Rectification Campaign" of 1942 when the Communists under Mao, grouped in their revolutionary base area at Yanan, were absorbing the thousands of urban intellectuals who flocked to the revolutionary cause. In the early 1950s after the seizure of power came the Three Anti and Five Anti campaigns against such "bourgeois" phenomena as corruption, waste, theft of state economic secrets, and embezzlement. In 1954 there was a vicious, controlled assault on a group of writers, most importantly China's most talented literary critic, Hu Feng. The following year saw the movement "to weed out counterrevolutionaries." In 1957 was the "antirightist campaign," up to then the most massive onslaught against the intellectuals in Chinese Communist history. Then in 1962 came the so-called Socialist Education Movement, followed, of course, in 1966 by the Cultural Revolution, with its various subsidiary movements — campaigns against Confucius, against Beethoven, against the Chinese novel *Water Margin*, against the Italian filmmaker Antonioni, and, simultaneously, another one, revived from earlier in the 1960s, *for* a conveniently dead young soldier-hero named Lei Feng, whose personal history changes even today as the values and ideas for emulation continue to be transformed by the leaders.

Many a patriotic Chinese found himself, by definition, "a target of the historic revolutionary struggle," and thus was ritually and routinely investigated, publicly criticized, and punished every time Chairman Mao turned up the ideological heat. It was at these times that the totalitarian monster showed itself at its most bestial. It was terrifyingly unreflective; it assumed its own infallibility; it allowed no counterarguments and there was no recourse to some independent and objective arbiter for the victims. What was — and what continues to be — most terrifying about these periods of ideological excess was the ability of the leaders to mobilize every aspect of the entire society, the schools, the newspapers, the neighborhood committees, the radio, the mass organizations, the Communist Youth League, the labor unions, the Women's Federation, the factories and communes, and to pose against the tiny, powerless, targeted individuals their monolithic strength.

Even the vocabulary became an exclusive tool of the leaders, who drummed up a few pseudoscientific phrases and used them as surrogates for all genuine analysis, all independent thinking about the complexities of the real world. "Complicated social relations," a phrase suggesting but not specifying some sort of historical impurities in one's lineage or past associations, was one way to convict an individual with neither facts nor evidence, much less any sort of due process. There were the "four olds," the "members of the exploiting class," the "bourgeois careerists," and the people with "historical problems," this last a piece of political flypaper designed to catch virtually anybody who ever spoke a word to or associated with another person before the "liberation." One condemning charge was to have "connections beyond the seas," a sign of likely treasonous intent; or one could be a "black hand that instigates fighting among the masses."

Through the entire awful period of being the target of a campaign, moreover, the individual not only had the whole society attacking him with this Orwellian cant, he had the further agony of watching his colleagues and friends, forced to participate in the ritual or become targets themselves, betray him en masse. In the most zealous periods, even wives and children were forced to "draw a clear line" between themselves and their husbands and fathers, to "stand on the side of the proletariat" rather than with their loved ones. For the victim, the isolation in the midst of a hostile society can be total, awesome, intolerable, inhuman.

It is no excuse that the seeds of this kind of social pressure have lain for centuries in the soil of Chinese tradition. Criminals, for example, were often put into the cangue, a flat rectangular board with a hole that fitted around the neck and exposed the face to the censorious regard of the public. The pressure of social convention, the negative sanction of being shamed in front of the group — these aspects of personal discipline were more pronounced and highly developed in the group-oriented culture of China than in the individualistic West. And so, not surprisingly, some of the "criticism and struggle" of Communist China became routinized for its participants. I have mentioned the young violinist who played at underground dance parties in Canton, until he was rounded up during a search for "black registrations" and sent back to the state farm on Hainan Island where he was supposed to work. He told me that each time there was one of these dragnets in Canton, eighty or so youths would be discovered and sent by monthly ferry to Hainan. For each month's arrival of these people, a mass meeting would be held with the entire three-thousand-member population of the farm in attendance. The wrongdoers would stand onstage with placards, latter-day cangues draped over their necks, describing their offenses, and the leaders would make speeches criticizing them and urging better behavior on the others. The victims, however, tended to shrug it all off; the time spent in Canton was worth this particular routine.

Before I got to China, when much of my information came from Cantonese refugees, I heard many descriptions of how campaigns, announced with much fanfare at the center, would be routinized at the local level. In one production brigade, for example, there were ten individuals with "bad class backgrounds," so every time the word came down from Peking to struggle against "rightists" or "newborn capitalist roaders" or simply to "take class struggle as the key link," a few of the ten would be hauled in front of the masses, shouted at, cuffed a few times about the head, and then let go, the production brigade having fulfilled its revolutionary tasks. But of course, this routinization of struggle leaves its mark; it has an effect on the mentality of the person who absorbs the half-baked concepts that underlie it, and, of course, it imposes terrible suffering and constant fearfulness on the victims for the crime of, say, having worked harder and been smarter than others and having thereby risen to the dangerous status of rich peasant.

Since the partial political relaxation that followed the death of Mao, the routine class struggles against the usual targets have diminished, as China's national policy calls now for unity and the united front. But social life is still very much regulated by the Communists' elaboration of the methods of the traditional society. Take, for example, sexual impropriety. I know of one apparently common sort of case in Guangdong Province wherein an urban girl of twenty (below the marriage age that was then twenty-five for women) was courted, seduced, and made pregnant by a member of the party from the production brigade. At first the desperate couple tried to keep the matter a secret, which was obviously not going to be possible over the long run. Eventually the girl was found out by the doctor, who immediately reported her condition to the brigade leaders, and, before long, the machinery for dealing with offenses against "socialist morality" (which in this case is rather similar to Confucian morality) was set into motion. The girl pointed her finger at the responsible person; terrified of the consequences, he denied having had relations with her, a futile gesture given the condition of the chief witness. Meetings were held and under the pressure of the girl's accusation and the official investigation, he at last admitted his responsibiiity. That led to more meetings. The man was criticized within the party; then, he was presented before a mass meeting of the brigade and turned into a negative example. Speeches full of commonsense wisdom were made by the leaders, who explained that his actions were a violation of the marriage law and that his interest in the girl sapped his energies for the work of the revolution. He wore a dunce cap in the form of a cockscomb for this intentional and exemplary act of humiliation — another rather droll latter-day cangue calling attention as it does to the face of the wrongdoer. He was dismissed from his position as a squad leader in the production brigade. The girl was taken to the hospital, where she had an abortion at the expense of her now former lover.

While this sort of social pressure brought to bear on a sinning individual derives directly from the authoritarian puritanism of traditional China, its use in political matters is a refinement and an elaboration that the country owes to its Communist leaders. True, China was always politically authoritarian; Confucian precepts were inculcated in the masses in a way that foreshadowed the propaganda campaigns that today instill the notions of communism in hundreds of millions of Chinese. But there are major differences, most important perhaps in the extent to which the latter intrude into everyday life. Moreover, the system of investigations and punishments, particularly against those singled out, not for what they did, but for their unprogressive backgrounds, for the abstract definitions given to them by the revolution, has been so capricious and arbitrary in its application as to have a far more shocking result on the victim. In traditional China, there were dismissals and severe punishments. But there were no wholesale purges and no labor reform camps and none of the heavy-handed psychology used today to break the wills of the offending individuals.

The supreme irony of Chinese communism is that these refined techniques, while massively used against sinning non-Communists like Professor Chen, were honed and sharpened in attacks against many of the Communist revolutionaries themselves. No revolution has devoured its creators as has the Maoist revolution. From its very founding, the party's history is the history of the eventual fall and disgrace at one time or another of every single official — with the exception of the clever Chou Enlai — who rose into the very highest ranks of the party to stand next to Mao himself. The political corpses — and the volumes and volumes of overblown rhetoric used to discredit them — litter communism's wake like the sewage of an ocean liner. There was Manchurian party chief Gao

Gang in 1955; minister of defense Peng Dehuai in 1959; Liu Shaoqi and Deng Xiaoping and many others in 1966; defense minister, and constitutionally designated successor to Mao, Lin Biao in 1971. Then there was the rise and the second fall of Deng Xiaoping in 1974 and 1976, respectively; and in the latter year came the "smashing" of the Gang of Four followed by the cashiering during the next three years of secret-police chief Wang Dongxing, of Peking military region commander Chen Xilian, of former Peking mayor and Politburo member Wu De. Finally, in late 1980 and early 1981, the man who in 1976–1977 was called "our wise leader," Hua Guofeng, was eased out of his positions, first as premier, then as party chairman.

The conspiratorial, secretive nature of the Communist party and the absence of any peaceful way to compete for power are certainly the major causes of this disturbing phenomenon, which has converted the history of the party into one of internecine warfare. Ever since the party's founding, moreover, the paranoia of the leadership has seeped downward like poison into the lower echelons of the organization, creating lives of constant anxiety and insecurity for many party members. Those who made revolution earliest were among the ones who suffered the most. Indeed, this fact made me wonder what now, after all these decades of struggle, was the mental state of those now aging party members who joined the revolution as fervent youths and then watched over the years as the party trampled on their ideals. There must, I thought, be a kind of disillusioned old revolutionary who felt, not just mistreated, but betrayed. Or, I wondered, were they all capable of playing mental tricks on themselves, believing sincerely that at each twist and turn of the policy, at each instance where some former hero was transformed into a villain, the party somehow remained correct? It is, of course, not easy to find a ranking official to discuss these matters with frankly. But I did interview by proxy one old woman cadre without her knowing it. She is the friend of the mother of one of my Chinese friends. I supplied the questions; my friend went to her and asked them and provided me with the answers. Thus, this story comes secondhand, but I have every reason to believe that it is, as an experience in the agonies of commitment to the Chinese Communist party, true in every respect.

Like so many young people who became idealistic revolutionaries, Tang Meisung (again, the name is a false one) came from a good, educated bourgeois family, in this case from Zhejiang Province, which, along with Jiangsu, was traditionally China's most fertile breeding ground for scholars, poets, and painters. She received some elementary education while young, which, as she put it to my friend, was not bad for a girl in those days. More important, she fell under the spell of the questing restlessness rampant among youths in China in the 1930s who were reading the new, socially realistic literature of Ba Jin and Lu Xun, with their emphasis on the corruption and injustices of the old society. Tang wanted to join the revolution; she wanted to remake the world; she wanted to devote herself to a cause. And so she left the tedium of the provincial middle school where, even with her own rudimentary education, she had a job as a teacher, and, at the age of twenty, went to work in a factory. Her purpose was to make contact with the underground Communist organization and in this she succeeded, becoming a clandestine member of the Youth League in the mid-1930s.

But two years later, she was arrested by the Kuomintang in what was the first of many experiences of betrayal, the person who informed on her to the KMT police being the very person who had introduced her into the party in the first place. This episode echoes an unpleasant recurrent theme in Communist party history. In the early days of the revolutionary struggle, those who were arrested by the Kuomintang were more likely to fall under the suspicion of the Communists' secret police than those who were not. Just as Joseph Stalin so distrusted the Russian soldiers who had been taken prisoner by the Germans in World War II that he sent many of them to labor camps, so too did the Communist party feel that those who had fallen into the grasp of the KMT had either been tainted by the enemy's propaganda or, under pressure, become double agents.

So it was with Tang. Released after three years in prison, she headed for the Communist base area at Yanan, eventually settling down as a schoolteacher in 1941 in a village controlled and governed by the party. Then, after about a year, the party's security apparatus, led by Kang Sheng, embarked on an ideological campaign called, with the Communists' unerring instinct for the catchy euphemism, the Liberate and Save (*Jie-jiou* in Chinese) Movement. Its purpose was to give those who had come from the Kuomintang areas an opportunity to save themselves through confession. That, in any case, was the theory, though many years later, Tang understood that the real motive had been to bind absolutely the loyalty and obedience of each member of the party by making them feel at first hand the intrusive might of the organization and by making them confess to something that they had never done.

Tang was accused of having informed on other members of the Youth League during the time she spent in a KMT jail. She was innocent; she knew that many others — she was put into a kind of detention center with twenty other young women — were innocent also. Yet, one by one they confessed. And the manner in which they did so shows that even at this early date (1942), well before the seizure of power, China's Communists were already masters of the psychology of obedience and control.

One technique, for example, was to make a model of one of the suspects, to put her before the others on a stage and to have her make a speech in which she declared her guilt and her shame. To encourage the others, the party then magnanimously forgave and released her.

Within a few days, one by one, all of the twenty confessed — except for Tang. And as each of them dutifully reported on activities that, at least in some cases, they had never undertaken, they joined the chorus urging Tang to admit her mistakes and to accept the blessed exoneration of the party. She alone refused and in so doing was subjected to a series of pressures and tortures that gradually increased in severity.

First she was deprived of sleep and interrogated in the classic good guy–bad guy technique — a method known to the Chinese in Yanan as the "wheel war" (*che lun zhan*) method. A second tactic combined physical discomfort with intense group pressure. This was called the "throw the skin ball" (*reng pi qiu*) method. Tang would be taken into a bare room where, all along its four walls, the women who had already made their confessions were standing. For hours at a time, they would shout at her and push her violently back and forth across the room. In this way, not only was the recalcitrant victim loudly criticized and physically disoriented, but the others, those who had already confessed, further bound themselves, via their participation, to the totalistic system of the party. For this, indeed, there was also a euphemism: *bi gong*, meaning "to gain merit."

Still, Tang did not admit any wrongdoing; she insisted on her innocence. Nonetheless, she was weak, disheartened, isolated, as the pressure continued with still a third technique. This consisted of a strong man shouting at her to confess as he repeatedly lifted her, then dropped her on the ground. That was alternated with "soft" methods. Her best friend, the wife of the head of the organization department of the party branch, who had been one of the first women to confess, came to give her affectionate advice: confess and everything will be all right. Other leaders of her party cell visited her and talked to her kindly: Why are you so stubborn? Why are you being so silly? they would say. By now, of course, the issue was her obedience to the party's commands, rather than whether or not she had ever informed on Youth League members to the enemy KMT. The party organization had committed its own prestige and authority to the charge, and it was prepared to wait as long as necessary until she satisfied the requirement to obey. It took several months, but eventually she saw that nothing terrible seemed to happen to those who had confessed their guilt and so she finally decided that she had no choice but to confess hers as well. This humiliation, this capitulation to an unjust demand pressed on her with violence, resulted in a subtle psychological effect: she was both angered at the party and more than ever before subject to its discipline. In fact, the day after her confession, she felt flooded by relief that the ordeal was over. That night there was a dance party at which she was asked to play the piano.

Tang in fact remained so committed to the ideals of the Communist revolution that even a second campaign did not shake her faith. This was the "investigate and lift up" (*jian ju*) campaign of 1943, another in that long series of paranoid witch-hunts launched by Mao's secret police chief Kang Sheng. In this campaign, each party member was asked to make a full report on all suspicions that he or she had regarding the past behavior of any other party member. Dutifully, Tang wrote that she believed it entirely possible that one of her comrades, who had been imprisoned together with her in Shanghai in the late 1930s, was a double agent. By that gesture, of course, Tang herself was able to "gain merit," and she gradually began to rise in the hierarchy of the party, becoming with time a member of that special breed known as the "revolutionary cadres." She was sent to the party training academy in Yanan; then, she was dispatched to Manchuria to work in the "liberated areas." Along the way she married, remaining with her husband in the northeast after the takeover and enjoying all of the privileges of the elite class, her own two-story house, the use of a Shanghai sedan, a maid, a wet nurse for her newborn babies, all of the services granted by the party to the Communist aristocracy that would enable them to devote their full time to the tasks of the revolution. After a few years, Tang was transferred to Peking, where she became one of the top leaders of an important bureau directly under the control of the State Council.

All during these years, Tang watched as the party waged its power struggles, disposing of one old revolutionary turned traitor after another, always doing her duty by paying lip service to the campaigns of slander against the offending individuals, and emerging unscathed herself. She avoided direct involvement in any of the factions; she simply did her work, and, in any case, she was not seen as a threat by any of the top leaders. But then, in 1966, came the Cultural Revolution, and Tang found herself in deep trouble. Having been both jailed by the KMT and struggled against for so many months in Yanan, she was a natural target of China's ineradicable political paranoia. As the Cultural Revolution picked up momentum and grew more and more radical, Tang came to realize that her own arrest was inevitable. She got ready a small bag of necessities and waited at home. One night came the knock on the door and she was taken away by a group of "revolutionary rebels" from her bureau, escorted by officers of the Public Security Bureau. She went to the number-two Peking prison, under suspicion of being a spy. For three months, she lived in a very tiny three-sided cell — known as a "triangle" — just big enough to lie down in, with no windows, a small peephole in the steel door that led to the outside, and a dim light bulb hanging from the ceiling that remained on both day and night. For that entire period, she was never let out for air or exercise and had only two brief sessions of mild interrogation. Otherwise, she passed the time eating the three meals that were pushed through the door at her each day and reading Mao's Little Red Book. The guard who looked in at her from time to time through the peephole did not allow her to do anything else.

Tang had a difficult time. She had frequent hallucinations, in which vivid pictures appeared to her on the walls of her cell; she experienced near constant dizziness. She says that conditions in the Peking number-two prison were far worse than they were when she was jailed in Shanghai by the Kuomintang. Finally, she was moved to another prison, where she was confined, no longer in the triangular torture chamber, but in a "normal" cell for solitary confinement, complete with such luxuries as a bed, a window, and a light bulb that went out at night. During the day, she continued to pore over the works of Mao; she exercised twice a week in a narrow, high-walled alley from which only the ends of the prison roofs and the sky were visible. Altogether, Tang spent six years in four different prisons, never formally charged, tried, or sentenced. For the last four years or so, she was in a prison in the provinces where at least she could mingle with the other Cultural Revolution prisoners as well as with the pickpockets, murderers, and thieves who made up a major portion of the prison population.

At the end of the second year, Tang stopped receiving the modest packages of food and clothing that had, until then, arrived from her husband. It was in this way that she was led to suspect he had died (he had), though she was never informed of that by the authorities. Beyond that, boredom was the main problem to be overcome. One thing she did was unravel a towel and, using straightened hairpins, knit the separate strands into a set of underwear — which she still keeps as a momento of that period. She remembers one time when the prisoners were given some pieces of fresh bean curd to eat. She was so overjoyed that she didn't want to eat all of it at once but kept some of it apart and managed to ferment it. She says that it was the most delicious thing that she ever ate in her life. Near the end of her imprisonment, she was allowed a visit from her son. She says that her main determination was to see him without weeping, and in this she was successful. In 1972, she was released and allowed to return to her apartment in Peking. She was forbidden, however, to talk of her experiences to anyone, and in this the obedience with which she had been inculcated back in the Yanan days remained in force. She didn't even tell her son what had happened to her during the six years she had been away from home. Indeed, it was only after the death of Mao and the gradual discrediting of the entire epoch of the Cultural Revolution that she felt free to begin recounting her experiences to friends.

Today Tang remains a loyal, hardworking revolutionary cadre, having been restored to the post she occupied in the bureau under the State Council before the Cultural Revolution. Religiously she reads the "internal" documents that circulate among high and trusted cadres. She attends meetings; she supports the party's policies as correct and wise; she gossips with her few close friends about who is up and who is down in the ceaseless jockeying for power and position that takes place at the stratospheric levels of the party.

But how does she feel about her life? She knows that ever since she was twenty, and idealistically joined the underground Communist movement, she has been swept up into currents and eddies far too strong for her to swim in; that History, with its cruel jokes and mean accidents, dominated her life far more than she dominated it herself. She takes a position midway between blind loyalty and disillusionment. She is too realistic to believe that, with the Gang of Four out of the way, China's search for wealth and power will soon be at an end. She is glad to be well off at the moment. Most of all, she sees no alternative. She is asked if, given her own story and the disasters that the party has inflicted on China, she regrets the path that she embarked upon all those many years ago. She says that, of course, she regrets the sufferings that the cause imposed on her. But she fatalistically accepts the proposition that she had no choice and, certainly today, she believes that the country can survive stably only under the leadership of the Communist party. She says, "In my youth, I was against the injustice and corruption of the old society, which I felt was being perpetuated by the Kuomintang leadership. In those days there was another path; there was a Communist party to join. Now, again, I am discouraged. I see the corruption, the mistakes, and the injustice of our society today. But the party is too strong. Today there is nothing to join to fight against it."

17

The Silent Rebellion

IN EARLY NOVEMBER, 1979, I found myself in a small, dim room, filled with the smoke of cigarettes and a charcoal brazier and crowded with a group of young people who, by Chinese standards, would have to be called rebels. They were all editors or writers for a group of unofficial, nonapproved magazines, dealing mostly with politics and literature, that enjoyed a fragile burgeoning during the Democracy Wall Movement. The editors sat shoulder to shoulder on a narrow iron-frame bed along one wall, while I faced them balanced atop a rickety wooden stool. The room had a crude stone floor, walls of stained whitewash, an iron potbellied stove, and a single, dim light bulb dangling from the ceiling. To get to it, I had been led down a labyrinthine network of small *hutung* (lanes) inside a common Peking residential neighborhood of one-story, tightly packed houses, and then into a rabbit warren of small homes and the remains of old courtyards. Though I went twice to this home, I do not think that even now I could find it again myself, and that fact alone contributed to my sense of having penetrated finally, both physically and spiritually, to a deeper and more moving Chinese reality than I had ever encountered before.

For years, I had wondered why China, unlike the Soviet Union and Eastern Europe, seemed to produce virtually no dissent, or at least none that leaked out to the West. The single exception to this was the brilliant, acidic, anti-Maoist masterpiece by the small group of Cantonese known by the collective pen name Li Yizhe, which originated as a wall poster in Canton in 1973. While in Hong Kong, I also heard about a number of works of underground literature telling of sufferings and deprivations during the Cultural Revolution. But there were, as far as I could tell looking at China from the British Crown Colony, no sustained efforts at creating a body of dissident ideas.

In this darkening room on this afternoon in November 1979, I reached people with the kind of yearnings and aspirations for self-realization that, while not identical to our own, belied the claims made by many foreign "friends of China" that the citizens of the People's Republic are not concerned with the issue of freedom.

It is not even that my encounter with the editors that autumn afternoon was entirely rewarding. It was, in fact, stiff, wooden, uninspired, particularly when compared to the conversations I would later have with young Chinese whom I met after moving to Peking. But this group of editors had already been interviewed by Western reporters during the heady days of the Democracy Wall and some of them were a bit jaded. They had already been asked all the questions I posed and there was a certain passionlessness, a rote quality to the way they responded to them. More important, perhaps, the movement for free expression was at that time under pressure from the authorities that would soon bring it to an end altogether. Its spiritual leader, a brilliant young electrician named Wei Jingsheng, had been tried and convicted on charges of passing secrets to foreigners and his fifteen-year sentence only a few days before had been upheld by the Supreme People's Court, China's docile, judicial rubber stamp. Thus, the dangers of unauthorized contact with foreigners were becoming all too conspicuous.

My meeting also had an unhappy outcome. One of the most prominent of the young editors present was one Liu Qing, a moving force in the most thoughtful and moderate of the unofficial publications being sold at Democracy Wall, a mimeographed monthly called *April Fifth Forum*, named after the date of the vast anti-Maoist demonstrations that had taken place in Peking on that day in 1976. Three days after I saw him, Liu was arrested when police rounded up a group of Democracy Wall activists who were distributing copies of Wei Jingsheng's defense at his trial. Liu had not been picked up by the police during the initial raid and seizure of the Wei manuscripts, but later went to the police and took responsibility for the distribution activities. The police took him at his word and detained him, gradually setting free the others they had arrested in the course of the day. When I learned of this, I wrote an article for *Time* on the stepped-up suppression of the Democracy Movement and I quoted the most memorable, and in retrospect the most prescient, thing that Liu had said to me a few days before: "We recognize that to achieve democracy, we will have to make sacrifices — of blood, even of our lives. But we are ready to sacrifice for the sake of changing China."

Liu's sacrifice was three years of what is called "administrative detention," a convenient device by which the Public Security can skirt the nice-sounding due-process guarantees of China's new legal code and put somebody out of circulation without the awkward necessity of a trial or even a public notification. Almost exactly a year after Liu's arrest, I was led again through the residential maze of lanes and courtyards to the house where I had first talked to him. Members of his family told me that he was spending his detention doing hard labor in Shaanxi Province. The family had not yet heard from him directly; they didn't know whether their letters to him were getting through or not. It had taken the better part of that year for the authorities, after receiving numerous visits and pleas, to inform the family of Liu's punishment and his whereabouts or, in fact, to legitimize his imprisonment by the formality of "administrative detention." The whole episode was an object lesson in the ease with which the wayward individual can be shut up, without provoking a protest in the rest of the world, without allowing even the Chinese people themselves to be informed of the situation.

And so it was with the brief fling at free expression that Liu Qing and Wei Jingsheng represented. The Democracy Movement had been snuffed out. The wall itself, a couple of hundred meters of gray rampart in front of a bus depot on Peking's Changan Boulevard, had been scraped clean of the colorful montage of wall posters that had decorated it for over a year. One morning in March 1980, a team of workers arrived on the scene at the wall and with scrapers, brushes, and water hoses restored it to its pristine condition. The unofficial publications that had been sold there were no longer in existence, except for a few miserable mimeographed and stapled remnants that circulated through the mail to a few dozen subscribers and testified to the fact that in some dim, small rooms a few people were still putting their pens to paper outside of official supervision. Many foreigners opined that the movement itself had always been rather tiny and insignificant, an infinitesimal drop of liberal agony in the great sea of Chinese indifference.

And yet, there was the unmistakable evidence that for many months, the movement did flourish, suggesting rather strongly that there were powerful desires among many Chinese to try to irrigate, to plant some shrubs and flowers in the arid political desert of communism. The movement may not have swept the country into a new historic stage, but it was important for both contemporary and historic reasons. It showed the political and personal aspirations, the dreams, and the hopes of China's brightest young people. It also partook of that *idée fixe* of the last century and a half of China's history, the patriotic search for a way to renewed greatness.

For a year, the wall had bristled with posters of every conceivable size containing a host of new ideas. There were large, portentous multisheet philosophical disquisitions on the nature of "true socialism." There were bitter complaints against the Communist regime and ardent calls for genuine free speech and assembly, for an open political system. There were also torn shreds of envelopes on which were scrawled pleas of a personal nature, open letters to the party's Central Committee for the redress of grievances, complaints of wounds suffered in past political campaigns, offers to exchange jobs or residences with others. The wall represented a great, bewildering profusion of Chinese characters that, for the first time, disclosed an active mind still simmering and stewing beneath the placid, uniform surface of Chinese socialism.

It does not pay to be excessively romantic about this phase of Chinese history. One rather skeptical Chinese friend, who loved to make acid comments on the rhapsodic observations of foreigners filled with hopes for human rights in China, observed that the foreigners underestimated the differences between the Chinese and themselves as well as the extent to which the mind of China's youth had already been overpowered by thirty years of propaganda and thought control. True, he said, Democracy Wall had generated some wonderful new ideas, but only a few. The vast majority of the long, serious tracts on politics that appeared on the wall were written from within the Communist framework; their authors used the stilted vocabulary of the propaganda machinery, and thought along the patterns already laid down for them by the system they lived in. Even though they wanted to change that system, they failed to realize that, in essence, they had already accepted its terms and its values. In that sense, my friend said, the wall showed not, as the foreigners suspected, that communism had failed to capture the minds of the Chinese people; it showed, in fact, how very successful the regime had been in determining the way that people would think by replacing deep and complex concepts with a few simple, prefabricated, mediocre political notions.

And yet, as my friend would readily admit, the Democracy Movement at times did soar above the mediocre. If most of the wall posters were banal and obvious, some were fresh and vigorous. "Even though the people remain the theoretical masters of history, in actual fact their role is merely to provide legions of respectful and silent servants, and to serve as clay in the hands of the real masters," went one celebrated phrase by Wei Jingsheng, who seemed to speak for many of the city's well-educated youth. An extraordinary thing about the wall was that for the first time, the dominant feelings expressed by the Chinese revealed interests and worries that many Western writers had assumed they did not have — about their lack of freedom, the privileges of the party members, their own poverty, about the "odious political system" (in Wei Jingsheng's blunt phrase) that had been forced upon them. There was even a statement about that most hidden of all Chinese hidden zones — sex. A ten-page wall poster by one Yang Ye demanded an end to government-enforced puritanism, advocated legalizing premarital sex ("let the people have free sexual affairs with those they love") and an end to China's absolute prohibition on eroticism in the movies. But, overwhelmingly, the voices of the wall were political, and the underlying theme of much of the best writing concerned a remedy for the continuing decline of China's historical greatness. "Why is it," asked one essay in the *April Fifth Forum*, "that the Chinese people show so few accomplishments inside China itself, yet earn Nobel Prizes once they have gone abroad?" The magazine's answer: "Because the production and development of science requires a definite kind of soil and that soil is democracy."

What is most striking about that idea is its similarity to the notions generated by idealistic, dissatisfied young people more than a half century before. During that great florescence of self-searching and experimentalism of the May Fourth Movement of 1917–1921, the most common slogans were precisely those of "democracy" and "science" that the restless Chinese of 1979 were again demanding. In the earlier period the two ideas were called respectfully "Mr. Democracy" and "Mr. Science," but they were linked inextricably together, the one viewed as a condition for the other. The Chinese of the Democracy Wall period were entirely aware of the similarity, moreover. When the *April Fifth Forum* posed the same questions once asked by the revolutionary generation sixty years before and concluded with the same prescription of Science and Democracy, it suggested that after thirty years of socialism, the twice-chosen prescription for national renewal had not yet been put into practice.

Not surprisingly, the party's tolerance for this sort of criticism was limited. True, early in the movement, the writing of critical wall posters had even been encouraged by Deng Xiaoping — probably because most of their criticisms were directed against Deng's enemies in the Politburo. But within a year, Deng had eased most of his enemies out of power and from his late 1978 affirmation that "if the masses feel some anger, we must let them express it," he turned by early 1980 against uncontrolled expression. After all, in the long run, it was the party, and not some ragtag assembly of ideological vigilantes, who embodied by definition the solution to China's ills; the party's answer was the one true answer among all the answers first proposed in the days when Mao and company were still young. And so, by a formal decision of the Communist party Politburo in March 1980, the writing of wall posters was banned and within days the movement and the heady atmosphere it had engendered were gone —victims of still another imposed transition.

Yet, the movement exerted a lasting influence, at least on many of China's private lives. Its causes did not disappear because of its suppression. The party responded to a perceived lack of enthusiasm for revolutionary politics among the country's youth by embarking on a new campaign for a kind of moral rearmament, urging its people to devote themselves heart and soul to the Four Modernizations. Among those I knew, however, cynicism about the purposes of the party ran so deep that I doubt that any amount of propaganda could have eliminated it. As one friend told me: "They cannot achieve the Four Modernizations; certainly they cannot live up to the promise of democracy; so they dream up all this hocus-pocus in the press asking everybody to be a good person. It's only because they don't have anything else to say and they have to fill up the editorials with something."

This friend was typical of many of the members of the generation of the Cultural Revolution whom I met in Peking. His name was Fang. He was a slender, good-looking man of thirty-three who was just finishing middle school when the Cultural Revolution broke out in 1966, ending his chances of going on to the university. He, like most, was swept away by the madness of this last long gasp of Maoism, ending up, again like most, working as a peasant in Hebei Province not too far from Peking. When he returned, his parents, who are both well-connected party officials, helped him get a job pushing papers in one of the economic ministries.

Fang was one of the people whom I used to wait for a call from. He never gave his name over the phone but just specified a day and a time when I should go to his little room, where he often invited others. His crowd was, by Chinese standards, hip. Its members cultivated a casual, yet studied world-weariness that would have been recognizable on American college campuses in the 1960s. They wore their jaded knowledgeability like badges; they were quick and savvy, and, like so many people in China, they focused mostly on politics, on the world according to the Communist party. They traded gossip about the private lives and mistresses of party members; they talked in great detail about the ways of the Public Security Bureau, about how to recognize plainclothesmen (they called them *lei-zi*, or land mines) and the license numbers of the cars assigned to track foreign diplomats, of the special secret telephone that connected the higher-ups in the State Council and the Politburo, of bits and pieces of information that appeared in the "internal" Chinese press. I used to listen to their conversation with the fascination of an outsider exposed to the practitioners of some mysterious and arcane science, even while recognizing the good deal of self-importance that was contained in the way they posed as members of the Communist cognoscenti, their pretensions of knowing all and disbelieving all.

In this sense, I was an ornament in the cap of Fang, who, by having me as a friend and confidant, displayed to his friends his willingness to live dangerously. But not too dangerously. Fang one day made the mistake of calling me, not from the public phone that he normally used, but from a phone in his work unit. As usual, no names were mentioned, only a time and a date for our next meeting. But the next day, Fang was called in by his section chief and asked why he was having contact with a foreign journalist and if he was being careful about what he said. After that, Fang saw me only once or twice more. He was, one of his friends later told me, being chastised by his parents for his contacts with me. Finally, I left Peking for about ten days, and Fang never called again after I returned. He was, said his friends, frightened. He was lying low.

Until that unwelcome disappearance, we had played a little game in our relations with one another — I on one side and Fang and his friends on the other. I posed as the acolyte, eager to learn the truth about China as seen from Chinese eyes; they played the somewhat supercilious instructors in the mysterious ways of Chinese communism. In fact, most of the group around Fang were jealous of my freedom, of my opportunity to make choices about my job and my career, indeed, of the temporariness of my stay in China. For many of Fang's friends the world outside China had a magical appeal; they invested it with all sorts of fantasies; and, naturally, many of them — though not Fang himself — wanted to go there. Thus, long after Fang dropped out of sight, several of those whom I had met through him continued to call, mostly in the unrealistic expectation that I could somehow get American visas for them.

This phenomenon was not reserved only for the friends of Fang. Millions of young people dream of going to the United States. Once, driving home late at night after visiting a foreign friend in the western part of Peking, I noticed a Chinese man flagging me down from the side of the road. He told me that he desperately needed to go to the area near the Qianmen and since I was heading in that direction I gladly offered him a ride. He learned during our conversation in the car that I was an American journalist, and that piece of information, once given to him, made for a small nuisance that lasted not weeks but months. The Chinese hitchhiker, who spoke not one word of English and had no particular qualifications, dreamed of America the way a true believer dreams of the Kingdom of Heaven. He wanted to go, and, to that end, he began to telephone me, always about seven in the morning, roughly once or twice a week. I, frankly, did not want to become involved, and so each time he called I insisted that there was very little point in trying to extend our midnight ride together into a lasting friendship. The hitchhiker never gave up, however. Until a departure from Peking for several months, I used at unpredictable intervals to start my day with his early-morning effort to make an appointment.

Boredom, Leo Tolstoy wrote, is the desire for desires, and that, I believe, is a large part of the explanation both for the hitchhiker's persistence and for the fascination with me and with America shown by the circle of Fang. These people, bright and capable, are among what has been called the Chinese "lost generation," the hundreds of thousands of people, now mostly in their thirties, who were caught at formative stages by the Cultural Revolution's experiments in extreme egalitarianism and who never, once those experiments were put aside, managed to start up again. They know today that the attentions of the state will now go, not to them, but to the younger generation just entering the years of university education. The lost generation, by contrast, will hover around the lowest levels of the bureaucratic ladder for years, perhaps for life, without much chance of becoming very important. They have little to do in their jobs — which, in any case, are in large part make-work — and cannot live very fully for their leisure time either. They can go to the propagandistic movies and be politically uplifted; they can watch TV; they read the newspapers and the magazines, including the internal publications to which many of them have access via their parents. They scoff at the new campaigns for moral rearmament and mutter darkly about the intrigues and betrayals that take place at the top. But there is nothing much to strive for, no hope of making money or improving personal standards of living, no chance of going to the university or of traveling abroad, or even of changing jobs or occupations. In China, where so much is controlled by the officially organized professional societies, it is even difficult to develop hobbies or personal passions. The music heard on the radio, the books available in the bookstores, the plays being performed on the stage — these are determined by the relevant department of the state. And so, Fang and his circle lead rather soulless lives; they are stuck in their early thirties, mired in the drabness and mediocrity of Chinese society, and they know it.

In Peking, I sought out artists and writers, of whom there are two sorts: officially recognized members of the professional societies, who are paid a fixed salary no matter how much or how little they produce, and the nonofficial creators who paint or write for reasons that have nothing to do with making a living. It was the latter group that interested me more, not because I thought they were necessarily better (in many cases they were not) but because of the courage and the commitment necessary to produce art in a society that does its very best to impose tight boundaries around what is acceptable.

A bit of background on this is in order. There is no area of life in China that better exemplifies the sorry drift of a great civilization into mediocrity than the desiccation of Chinese culture. And this is especially true given that for much of the youthful period of Chinese communism, when the party, in its struggle for power, was trying to attract idealistic artists to its side, the most talented of China's writers saw in the Communist revolution the best hope for the future. Lu Xun, Ba Jin, Cao Yu, Lao She, Mao Dun — these are the writers who rejected the solutions of the Kuomintang even as they rejected the crushing weight of China's Confucian tradition with its inequalities, its slothfulness, its resistance to change. Their novels and essays, written in the 1920s and 1930s, represented a minor flowering of a new kind of literature for China, a literature of social realism that awoke in millions the yearnings for dramatic change. These writers, before the Japanese invasion of 1937, did not as a whole join the party; but they sympathized with it. And then, after Mao Tse-tung set up a base of anti-Japanese resistance in remote northwestern Yanan, most of them — except for the great Lu Xun, who died in 1936 — slowly gravitated into the rebel camp.

In 1942, Mao initiated what has ever since been regarded as the watershed between the early, hopeful period of creativity and what was to become the dull, mediocre official culture after the founding of the People's Republic. He convened the so-called Yanan Forum on Literature and Art, the essential and purposely vague idea of which was that stories, films, paintings, and so on, must serve the revolution, meaning "the masses of workers, soldiers, and peasants," and that to do so, the "petty bourgeois intelligentsia" that produced art needed "to transform and remold their thoughts and feelings." This talk of Mao's was followed by campaigns to rein in those writers and artists who still believed that the revolution was going to mean a genuine liberation in the realm of the arts, a real breakaway from the conservative constraints imposed by the Confucian orthodoxy. This is not the place to recount in detail the party's relentless efforts to grind down the independence of the Chinese artist and to place him within the narrow confines of what the semilettered Communist potentates deemed "revolutionary." But the campaigns of slander and innuendo, of invective, and of overblown rhetoric that were mounted at one time or another against just about every major artistic figure in China had an obvious effect. Most of the major writers were either silenced or, like the ever faithful and ever flexible Guo Morou, were reduced to pathetic sycophancy. Some famous literary figures dutifully served in various high positions in the Ministry of Culture, but with very few exceptions, none produced a major work after 1949. Indeed, I believe that it can be said that since the 1942 Yanan Forum, not a single work of literature, art, music, or drama has been produced under the auspices of the Chinese Communist party that can be recognized as great — this in a society that ranked culturally as one of the greatest of the human race.

After the death of Mao and the fall of the so-called Gang of Four, there were many hopes both inside China and abroad that the new, moderate leadership would usher in a more liberal, permissive phase. Officially, the slogan again became "Let a hundred flowers blossom." And, indeed, in reaction against the absolute cultural tyranny exercised, with the evident approval of Mao, by Jiang Qing, some relatively daring and promising works were produced. To be sure, they were overwhelmingly political, designed to portray the horrors of the recent past and what was called the "dark side" of Communist society, in particular the pettiness and greed of minor functionaries. There was in this very little exploration of the themes that have often made for greatness in art — jealousy, vengeance, love, indecisiveness, revenge, renunciation, courage, the search for identity or for meaningfulness. These were largely ignored as writers devoted themselves almost exclusively to venal party secretaries and unjustly accused factory section chiefs. One of the best of these works was a play produced in Shanghai in 1979 called *The Artillery Commander's Son*. It lampooned a petty functionary who fawns obsequiously on his daughter's suitor, thinking that he is the son of a high officer in the army. The joke is that the young man whom the good daughter wants to marry is really a janitor's son. The audience looked at the play through a large, mock magnifying glass constructed at the front of the stage, as if to say: now we are going to have a genuinely close look at the nature of our society.

Like some of the wall posters of the Democracy Wall period, this new, more unfettered and critical literature had its moments of brilliance. But, in general, it reflected the extent to which the Communist party has imposed its concerns, its values, even its vocabulary on all of Chinese society. What was called "Wound" literature — the stories and plays that described the suffering of the Cultural Revolution — accepted the overall political framework of Chinese communism, its right to absolute control, the beneficence of most of its leaders, its organization of society along socialist lines. The Wound literature merely declared that there were problems, that there was a need for some reform, and that, in fact, reforms were being carried out. Even so, the willingness of most writers to play by the rules did not enable even this modest unleashing of cultural energy to last very long. By the beginning of 1981, there was a definite crackdown. Articles appeared in the press claiming that there was too much stress on the "negative" and not enough on the "positive" features of Chinese society. All along some of the more critical productions had been banned, one of them, an exposé of officials called *The Swindler*, on the grounds that it had not a single nice thing to say about any Communist official.

Still, as many writers carefully watched the mood in its narrow alternations between a hard and a modestly permissive line, they consoled themselves with the notion that at least the authors of plays like *The Swindler* were not attacked, thrown out of the Writers' Association, or arrested in the middle of the night. Then, in 1981, after several months of get-tough signals from Deng Xiaoping, the party decided to make an example of one writer. This was the well-known Bai Hua, the author of the screenplay for a banned movie called *Bitter Love*. The film itself told the story of a painter horribly mistreated during the 1957 antirightist campaign (when Deng Xiaoping was very much in charge) and subsequent political movements. It contained the offending line: "It's not that I don't love the motherland; it's that the motherland doesn't love me." The party's reaction to this work was a model of the patient process of gaining total control over arts and culture. The film, to begin, was never released. Then, the various professional associations held meetings to discuss it; these were forums during which other cultural figures could criticize the play, side with the party in banning it, and help to create a mood of intolerance for it within the Ministry of Culture. Finally, after several months of silence in the press, the newspaper *Liberation Army Daily* launched a rhetorically full-blown, *ad hominem* attack on Bai Hua for having "openly disobeyed the four basic principles [Marxism-Leninism–Mao Tse-tung Thought, the leadership of the Communist party, the dictatorship of the proletariat, and socialism], painted a dark picture of our party and nation, distorted and smeared patriotism, expressed grievances against the socialist system and the people's democratic dictatorship, and venomously mocked and totally negated Comrade Mao Tse-tung." The warning was clear and heavy-handed. Fundamentally, very little had changed since Mao's 1942 Yanan Forum. The principle that art must serve the revolution — which means that the party must control all art — was reconfirmed. Graver still, a "mistake" was no longer just a matter of a personal opinion gone wrong. Once again, all of the terrifying, monolithic weight of the Communist party had been brought to bear against a lone individual. After that, how many more lone individuals would dare to shout into the wilderness?

It is against this background that we come to a small concrete room filled with the artifacts of an entirely private imagination. It is on an upper floor of a building belonging to a dull rank of brick quarters. There, in one narrow, cramped room is an entire universe of creativity. Arrayed on the walls, ordered on shelves, on the floor, on the desk, under the bed, is an extraordinary production of wooden sculptures created by one Wang Keping, a nonofficial artist of, I believe, major promise. Wang's earlier works express the obsession with politics that characterizes Chinese society itself. They are expressions of the Wound literature in sculptured form, but with far greater creative breadth than most of the rather obvious and literal-minded productions of that genre. There is a large, hideously twisted face; another face with gaping mouth and a scream stifled by a wooden block; still another with its nose and mouth hideously attached, the one sucking in the exhalations of the other. There is a misshapen head, with eyes that cannot see, a mouth that cannot speak, and a crushed cranium that leaves no room for a brain to think. But as we progress chronologically through the works of Wang Keping, these political images of suffocation and insentience, powerful as they are, give way to something else, to an experiment in pure form. Wang Keping has transformed himself from an angry, embittered cartoonist in wood into an artist, in isolation, by trial and error and without the help of any other person, making things that nobody else has ever made before him.

Wang has abstract lovers bound together in mysterious embraces. He has sculptured wildly distorted bodies, forms for the sake of form itself, lines and planes in space. This is radical creativity in China, where the terribly conservative artistic conventions have demanded for centuries that the only way to excellence is through copying the works of the old masters. This is still obvious in China today in most of the visual arts. After the Gang of Four fell, such nonrevolutionary themes as misty mountains, flowers, bamboo, monkeys, and birds perched on gnarled cherry branches came back into favor and the artists began again to produce them in quantity — in large part for the tourist-stand trade directed at foreign visitors and the overseas market. So, in just a couple of years, most art in China went from being monothematic and supposedly revolutionary to being entirely traditional and admittedly nonrevolutionary. In fact, both partook of the same extremely conservative habit of mind. The "revolutionary" works of the Cultural Revolution were entirely conformist; they had to emblematize the demand of Mao and his wife Jiang Qing for purity of thought. They were, in this sense, anticreative. Similarly, the current vast output of inky bamboo, bowed branches laden with pink petals, and, most cloying of all, adorable panda bears, represents an equally slavish devotion to the not very high standards of the contemporary salon.

True, there are some exceptions, but even these tend to bring the extreme conservatism of China into high relief. One very bold and promising artist named Yuan Yunsheng was commissioned in 1978 to paint a large mural for the new Peking International Airport. Located in the dining room for foreigners, the painting was allowed to be a bit more daring than most, so Yuan, who is an exceptionally talented and vigorous young artist, did a Rousseauesque tableau of a group of minority nationality tribesmen from Yunnan Province celebrating an annual water festival. One portion of the painting contains two slender women with sleek, curling black hair who happen also to be depicted with their breasts exposed. In virtually any other country, this modest degree of nudity would have occasioned no comment at all. In China, it caused a raging controversy that ended, after more than a year, in the triumph of conservatism.

At first, the painting was shown in its entirety, the two nudes standing exposed to the general inattention of foreigners lunching before their flight. Then, in a sudden swing toward prudery, the authorities determined that the portion showing the nudes would be covered by a white curtain. For months after that the restaurant's foreign guests, their curiosity now aroused, could be seen pulling this curtain aside for a look at the controversial topless beauties. In the fall of 1980, the curtain abruptly came down, and it appeared as though artistic good sense had prevailed. Premier Hua Guofeng had been forced to resign from his top government post at just about the same time as this sudden permissiveness, leading to speculation that the decline of China's chief Maoist and the exposure of the minority maidens' breasts were linked together.

Nonetheless, there was another change early in 1981 when the line on art and culture suddenly tightened. I remember going to the restaurant in March of that year to wait for a flight. As I walked in I was shocked to see that the section of Yuan's mural containing the nudes had been covered over with what looked like permanent pieces of wooden paneling. I asked the waiter when this sacrilege had been perpetrated and he replied with an evidently well-rehearsed answer: "About three weeks ago. You see, the minority nationality people do not in fact appear in the nude. So, in the spirit of seeking truth from facts, we couldn't allow that part of the painting to be shown."

What distinguishes the work of Wang Keping is its freedom from these constraints. He and a couple of dozen others in 1978 formed a nonofficial organization called Xing-Xing (Stars) and up to the end of 1980 had, by dint of considerable, courageous militancy, twice managed to put their works on public exhibition in Peking, the second time in the city's major art museum. Not all of the Stars are good; indeed, a majority seem to have more enthusiasm for bucking the conventions of the official Chinese salon by painting nudes and abstractions than they have creative talent. But along with Wang Keping, there are several others whose work shows not only independence of mind but the spark of creativity as well. It is not, moreover, that the best of them would fail if they tried to become official artists, with the conveniences of a regular salary and access to state-supplied materials. Some of them choose not to embark on the process of gaining official recognition out of a rejection of lowbrow official standards.

I remember talking to one of the Stars, a painter of beautiful, brooding, melancholy, semiabstract landscapes that lack entirely the dutiful optimism and sentimental prettiness of official art. "Do you want to see official art?" he said, responding to my query about his lack of interest in the Artists' Association. He took from a shelf several Chinese art publications and let me leaf through them. I saw the precious, emotionally tinny paintings, the propagandistic posters of socialist plenty, the panda bears and monkeys, the images of happy peasants and gleaming factories, the rocks and mountains intended to pass for traditional Chinese painting; I looked at the thoughtfulness, the aware intelligence, the search for truth in the nonofficial painter's somber landscapes, and I understood immediately his feeling. For a young artist like him, without prestige or reputation, to succumb to the pressures of the conformist salon would be to confine himself to a noninvestigative, hollow mediocrity, to an entirely predictable kind of socialist commercial art, to tourist schlock, to the system's advertisements for itself. But to accept the inconvenience of nonofficial status, to have to work someplace else and to paint in his spare time — that kept open the private sphere wherein artistic satisfaction and integrity were still possible.

Once, Wang Keping waved his hand at the crowded universe of wooden sculptures in his small bedroom-workshop and told me: "Years ago, I myself would have smashed every one of these things; I would have found them bourgeois, individualistic, and counterrevolutionary. But I have changed a lot since those years." Wang, in fact, is too intelligent and driven to be typical of anything; yet, his own transformation symbolizes the awesome experience of China's lost generation, and of what one Western sinologist has called "the children of Mao." Appropriately enough, he was born in 1949 and is thus the same age as the People's Republic of China itself. His parents were both cadres in the People's Liberation Army. As a teenager, in the city of Tianjin, he was thoughtlessly radical. During the Cultural Revolution, he participated enthusiastically in an attack against the local Communist party secretary and greeted with equanimity the news that this official ended up taking sleeping pills and drowning himself in his bathtub. Wang was among a small group that climbed the main spire of the Tianjin Catholic church to tear down the cross, then looted and burned the interior of the building. But he cooled down some when, after the Cultural Revolution, he ended up working for a number of years as a janitor in a factory where, while wanting to be a writer, he cleaned toilets and drains and fixed the plumbing. When, in 1976, one of the Peking television production companies held auditions for new actors, Wang tried out. He was natural and at ease in front of the camera and eventually found himself invited to join the team both as an occasional actor and, more important, as a scriptwriter for TV plays.

Wang says that he wrote dozens of scripts and none was ever accepted or performed. But during this time he experienced what might be considered one of the great advantages of socialism — you don't have to produce anything to receive your salary. Some of the scriptwriters at the television studio have not handed in a script in ten or even twenty years; yet nobody has ever been fired. Wang himself spent a lot of time at home; that was, in any case, where he was expected to work. One day, a piece of wood fell off an old chair and Wang sculptured it into an abstract figure; it consists of an outstretched arm holding Mao's Little Red Book of quotations and a mouth opened in a vicious, intolerant shout. "I didn't understand anything about sculpturing," Wang told me one day, "but I had read and been influenced by the French theater of the absurd, by Beckett and Ionesco, especially *Waiting for Godot* and *The Bald Soprano*. So I decided that even though I didn't know how to sculpture, I could try to carve a theater of the absurd in wood."

And so, the TV scriptwriter, who never produced acceptable scripts, began to populate the stage of his imagination with wooden heads, bodies, and abstract shapes, carving them with simple hand tools and painstakingly sanding them to a smooth finish. He refuses to sell a single one of his works, wanting them to stay with him as concrete artifacts of the activity he has engaged himself in — the search for his own true nature, his own potentialities as a human being. He is a bit obsessed with his work, laboring nearly every day, churning out piece after piece as he tries to discover where his investigations will take him. He shows his work to his occasional visitors with a kind of hesitant pride. "I lack self-confidence," he told me once, even as I was thinking how extraordinary was the example that he represented: a man in near complete isolation from the international activity that is art, working alone in his small room to produce something great in a society that is not likely to accord him legitimacy as an artist, or even very much respect. Wang Keping lacks self-confidence; his past — the day he helped to destroy the Tianjin Catholic church — marks him as a flawed human being. Moreover, he has a long way to develop as a sculptor; he has not yet attained the sophisticated heights of modern art in other parts of the world. And yet, amid the conformist gloom of China, with all of its fantastic pressures to submit, I find him a beacon of light. He is great.

Wang Keping is one of the lucky ones of the lost generation, precisely because he has discovered a passion. He suffers from no lack of meaning, no desire for desires. But for many members of the lost generation, life does not contain a mission as consuming as his. China's population is sprinkled with keenly intelligent young men and women who lead lives of quiet despair. One of my best friends in Peking is a classic example of this sort of person. She is a young woman, rather plain, remarkably intelligent and analytical, but also depressive, devoid of any hope that her yearnings — which are directed primarily toward freedom and love — can ever be fulfilled. Like the letter writer Pan Xiao, she has personally and intensely experienced all of the various political phases of China, each one of which has had a profound effect on her. Born just before the Communists' seizure of power, two years old when the People's Republic was proclaimed in 1949, she, like Wang Keping, is a symbol of the Maoist progeny. Her story entirely removes the socialist experiments of China from the province of abstraction and puts them into the concrete human realm from which they are best considered.

Let's call my friend Xiuping, "Cultivated peace." Though unhappy, passive, filled with despair now, she actually spent the first two-thirds of her life in a state of near delirious revolutionary optimism. She was a proletarian activist, a rising star, a youth blessed by all of the intellectual categories of the Communist revolution, someone raised to believe in a bright future. Her parents were both ranking revolutionary cadres who had joined the party in the late 1930s, and that made Xiuping automatically a member of the Communist aristocracy. Her father, who was one of the top officials in a provincial government, had a two-story house with a garden surrounded by a high wall. But she spent most of the time in a Monday-through-Saturday boarding kindergarten for the children of cadres, located in the hills near the provincial capital. She loved the school, with its extensive grounds, its nice dormitories, its sports arena, and the scrupulous attention that was paid to each of the precious children of the revolutionary cadres. Every week, a detailed report was submitted by the teachers to the parents telling of each child's progress and problems.

Every Sunday morning, a black, chauffeured car belonging to the provincial government arrived at the school to take Xiuping home for her weekly visit with her family, and often she struggled against getting into it. Indeed, the coldness of her family, its almost complete absence of mutual concern, loving, or even playfulness, was one of the important, constant features of Xiuping's entire life. Like the classic French or Russian aristocratic families of the seventeenth and eighteenth centuries, the leaders' children in China were kept apart so as not to disturb the activities of the parents. In infancy, Xiuping suckled at the breast of a succession of some ten different wet nurses — found and provided by the state. On her weekly visits home, she had very little to do with either of her parents and was cared for by the maid or the driver. She says that she can remember every time in her childhood that her busy revolutionary father played with her. One of them was during a two-week period when he, exhausted from overwork, went to a rest sanatorium maintained for ranking officials. But even then, this relentlessly serious, self-improving man spent the majority of his time studying Russian from a textbook, while Xiuping was sent off to play with the nurses. When she was eight, Xiuping's mother died. She remembers clearly that she felt no sadness, even as her father in a rare show of emotion wept unconsolably. Not a single one of her several brothers and sisters shed a single tear. Today, looking back on her childhood with analytical detachment, Xiuping declares that her family's circumstances were on "the extreme side of typical" for the households of 1950s revolutionary cadres.

Without the nurture of a family, Xiuping accepted the nurture of the state. In school, she was taught the glories of the revolution, of the Communist party, and of Chairman Mao. She was instructed always to stand on the side of the masses against the exploiting classes. At the same time, she was told that the highest duty of the citizen was to be obedient to the dictates of China's political leaders and of the party. This pattern continued throughout Xiuping's childhood in the province and then, after the family moved to Peking in the late 1950s, in the middle school, also primarily for cadres' children, that she attended. During this long period she enthusiastically participated in the rituals of self-abnegation and self-purification of Chinese communism. For two years she wrote self-criticisms admitting that she was guilty of having a prideful nature and that she was prone to selfishness. She was a true believer in the official propaganda. She used avidly to read, and to believe, the official newspapers. For one month, she volunteered to work without pay as a waitress in a restaurant in order to serve the people. Her goal was to be ideologically pure and to think only of the party and the people, never of herself. She applied to become a member of the Communist Youth League and, as part of the application, wrote one "ideological report" after another in which she admitted her weaknesses of pridefulness and selfishness but declared her ardor for the cause of the Party and the People.

Still, her ardor led her to a restless desire for independence and excitement. When she was fourteen years old and fired with populist enthusiasm, Xiuping decided that she wanted to be sent to a rural area and work side by side with the peasants. So, she wrote a letter to *Youth* newspaper asking for help in this endeavor. The letter, predictably, meandered through the various channels of the bureaucracy until it arrived at Xiuping's school and, finally, into the hands of her father. He sensibly vetoed the idea. "Make revolution at home by studying," he told his daughter.

Xiuping's restlessness was soon to be satisfied by an event that nobody could have predicted: the Cultural Revolution. It was to provide a profoundly disconcerting and, eventually, disillusioning experience for her — but, in a way not at all intended by its protagonists, a liberating one as well. Xiuping was in her final year of middle school when the first rumblings of the movement were heard in 1966 at nearby Peking University. There, posters had been put up criticizing unnamed party members for wanting to take China down a nonrevolutionary path. "I was at the time soaked in Marxism," Xiuping remembers. "And, while I wasn't yet ready to say 'Down with Everything,' I was impatient at the party leaders' unwillingness to accept criticism." She was also swept away by the exhilarating madness of suddenly finding that power lay in her hands. As the movement, backed by Mao, picked up steam, Xiuping became a fearsome militant among the graduating students at her school, almost all of whom, like her, were children of revolutionary cadres. These young people, sixteen to eighteen years old, were the most prone to activism of all Chinese young people. Imbued since early childhood with a sense of their own impeccable, revolutionary class backgrounds, they were confident, self-righteous, convinced of their own historical-revolutionary importance. Early in the movement, they were held in check by the school leadership, but as the Cultural Revolution rapidly turned more radical and the local leadership was withdrawn, they became, during what Xiuping calls "a happy period," an unsupervised corps of leftist vigilantes who took it upon themselves to impose revolutionary purity on the generation of their parents and grandparents.

For weeks, Xiuping remembers, she hardly slept. Until late every night, she and her fellow activists rode their bicycles through the streets of Peking as they went to the houses of famous and high-ranking people to search them and inventory their contents. They broke in on renowned writers, generals, political figures, almost all of whom received the teenaged bandits with strained courtesy and who allowed many of their "reactionary" possessions — old scrolls, books, paintings — to be registered and confiscated without protest. Then, when that phase of the Cultural Revolution was over, Xiuping and some of the others searched the homes of all the people living in her neighborhood who had been abroad. "I was always polite," Xiuping says of this period. "But not all of the people I brought with me were. Some of them had a natural antagonism to things like pianos, nightgowns, photos showing couples in amorous moods. There were six families in my apartment building who had returned from abroad in the 1950s. I feel very apologetic toward them now and I know that many of them continue to hate me to this day."

There is no question that Xiuping was very happy during much of this period. But things quickly changed. The privileged cadres' children, for one thing, were soon outdone in radicalism by others who did not come from such distinguished revolutionary backgrounds. Indeed, Xiuping became disgusted with the intemperance and violence of many of the movement's militants. Her mood of exhilaration and happiness soon gave way to sobriety and then depression. Liberated from her tyrannical father by the Cultural Revolution itself, she began to satisfy her restless urge to travel and have experiences, but these often proved unsatisfying, revealing, sobering. She was dispatched to Inner Mongolia by a local Cultural Revolution leader with whom she was secretly in love. The theoretical purpose of her trip was to investigate the class struggle there but, in fact, Xiuping spent a frustrating month during which she learned virtually nothing. Then, when she returned to Peking, most of her colleagues were gone. This was the period when millions of Chinese young people began to travel for free on the trains, presumably to spread Chairman Mao's revolutionary message all over the country. The object of Xiuping's affections, the young man who had sent her to Inner Mongolia, was off on such an excursion. So, a bit let down after the excitement of the house searches, and with little else to do, Xiuping and a couple of her friends took a trip by train to the eastern provinces, during which she had a "reactionary" and "bourgeois" experience that brought a rapid disillusionment with politics. Xiuping went to the sea at Beidaihe at night, a place and a time that were far away from the din of the revolution. She lay on a rock and looked at the stars; the cool night air caressed her cheeks; she heard the waves washing against the shore and experienced what Freud called the oceanic feeling: the loss of the sense of her small individual identity and a melding with the vastness, the beauty, and the peace of nature.

That was in June 1967. When, that month, Xiuping returned again to Peking, she discovered that not a single one of her friends was in the city; they were still traveling in various provinces in the countryside. It was the most turbulent period of the entire Cultural Revolution, when much of the top leadership was falling before the Maoist onslaught, when the heads of schools, departments, bureaus, were being dragged before "the masses" for condemnation, when fierce, acrimonious debates were waged on the wall posters that splattered the walls of the city. Xiuping, however, found that her enthusiasm for the revolution had been sapped. She did very little, except to read each day the latest wall posters. Then, unexpectedly, she experienced a kind of intellectual epiphany, the result of which was to change her from an enthusiastic, Maoist activist into a chastened, unhappy malcontent.

One day late in the summer, she was returning to her father's apartment after her daily excursion to read wall posters. Riding in the bus, she suddenly felt her face become hot. She fell into a kind of trance; the immediate world around her disappeared and she fell back upon an entirely unprecedented sense of her inner self. She managed to get home, but for three days could do little but lie in bed and stare at the ceiling. Her father thought that she must have fallen in love. But that was not the case. She did think about love, that at nineteen, she had not experienced it yet; she thought about the young man who had sent her to Inner Mongolia and then, before she returned, disappeared into the ample folds of the revolution. But she thought about other things too, about the revolution, about herself, her identity, about the cool breeze and the vast ocean at Beidaihe and about the life that she wanted to lead.

"Then," she said, "there came a moment that I remember with great vividness, when I came out of my trance and I realized that every single thing that I knew, my entire mental condition, had been formed without my having made a single choice. I realized that everything that I was, my thoughts, my beliefs, my opinions, my knowledge of the world, everything had been imposed on me; my entire being was inevitable."

Xiuping talked about this while she and I were sitting in a park one fall day in 1980, and as she talked I managed to write down just about every word that she said. "All this happened to me while I was lying on my bed in my room staring at the ceiling. I realized that until that moment, I had blindly believed in communism. Before then, I had never found any fault with the system, not even with people marching into my home to record the possessions of my family, or with the so-called education I had received, or with the fact that everything was politics, or even that I myself, a nineteen-year-old girl, could march into people's homes and scare them out of their wits and take away some of their most prized possessions.

"You can be happy or unhappy in life," Xiuping went on. "Or, you can be neither happy nor unhappy. Until that moment, I had been neither happy nor unhappy, and so I don't know why this happened to me. Still, my clearest sensation was of being suddenly very happy. I realized clearly that the world is much bigger than Marxism or communism. I realized for the first time that the world has a much bigger meaning than the party's politics. One of the best things was that I knew that I no longer needed to reform myself. I had always accused myself of being too proud and selfish. Now I knew that I didn't have to change myself or criticize myself. Until then I had never tried to draw independent conclusions. I trusted the party, which, I believed, had a broad experience and could provide me not only with all the answers that I needed but with the right questions as well. But after this experience I realized that I had no other way but to try to find things out for myself. Even if my own conclusions were wrong, they were the only conclusions for me."

Xiuping's discovery of herself endured but the happiness she had at first experienced did not, particularly as she began to run into insurmountable obstacles in the path of her own self-realization. "That moment was very important," she said, "but I know now that from that moment on, I have not been able to develop at all. My happiness turned into unhappiness because once I decided to draw conclusions for myself, I found that there was no place to do that in this country. I was very frustrated because I had no way to find anything out. I knew that no real, honest study has ever been given to my society. The conclusions were drawn in advance by the party and the purpose of study was to verify those conclusions." Yet, for several years after her revelation, Xiuping embarked on an energetic, self-motivated study of China. Her quest led her on a random voyage through China's zones of politics and geography that touched almost every aspect of the often crazily tilted, kaleidoscopic modern Chinese experience.

She had to work with what the authorities had made available, so she began by reading the first volume of *Das Kapital* by Marx. "I found it very easy," she said, "and even though I tried to read it with a critical mind, I couldn't really draw conclusions against it because I had no information, no statistics, no contrary views to rely upon. Having liberated myself intellectually, I discovered all the limitations of this society." Still, she went on, she was at least satisfied to discover that Marxism and Maoism diverged in many ways, in content as well as in mood and spirit. "There was, of course, nothing about Chairman Mao doing this or that in *Das Kapital*; nothing about the 'Great Leader'; there were no instructions given or tasks assigned."

Xiuping also managed to get hold of a copy of Milovan Djilas's *New Class* and, most sinful of all, she read Trotsky — gaining access to both through friends whose parents could buy limited-circulation books at the leaders' bookshop. Then, she began to embark on a series of travels and residences outside of Peking that were to last for nearly fourteen years. First, in 1968, she went again to Inner Mongolia, this time, like millions of others, as a so-called sent-down youth to labor indefinitely on a production brigade. But Xiuping says that, unlike most, she harbored no illusions about "making revolution" in the countryside. "I had concluded already that there was no future for China," she said, "at least not while Mao was still alive. In fact, I used to get discouraged reading all those articles about his longevity. It was a big disappointment that he was so old and yet in such good shape. Still, under the circumstances, my decision was to try to do things for myself. I had a burning curiosity about the rest of the world. I wanted very much to go abroad, but, of course, I couldn't. At the same time, I realized that I didn't really know this country and I wanted to explore it. Other people who were disillusioned didn't want to go to the countryside. I was disillusioned but I wanted to go. Most of those that did want to go had all kinds of high expectations, but I went down to the countryside with my eyes open. I wanted to know for sure that China is China in Peking and everyplace else."

Xiuping spent nearly a year on a commune in Inner Mongolia, where she experienced at first hand the deprivations of rural life. Somewhat to her surprise, she found the greatest hardship was not the scarcity of food, even though while in Inner Mongolia she existed entirely on coarse grains, millet, and sorghum, and vegetables, often pickled; there was very little wheat, no rice, and meat about three times a year. The greatest problem was obtaining the fuel to cook the grain. Most of her pittance of a salary was spent on stamped coal-dust bricks, and much of her time as a commune laborer was devoted to gathering straw and other burnable materials to use for cooking. She and the eleven young women who had left Peking with her went every two weeks or so by horse cart to some hills about three miles from their village to harvest the brush. This was enjoyable work, riding out under the vast sky of the rolling Mongolian plain, lying for a while in the dry grass and enjoying the serenity of nature, riding back on the cart atop the straw to the muffled accompaniment of the horses' hooves on the hard earth. But about the peasants themselves, Xiuping found very little to admire. This particular village consisted entirely of Han Chinese who had migrated from interior regions three generations earlier to escape a famine. She found them lazy, dirty, deceitful. They shirked their assigned work; they borrowed money and did not return it; they all had lice and, as a result, so did Xiuping, three times having to disinfect herself with DDT and boil all her clothing; they seemed content to spend all their time idling, men and women together, on their raised brick sleeping platforms (the *kang*, common to all north Chinese homes), drinking or drowsing or engaging in desultory conversation.

Gradually, faced with the torpid realities of life in the village, virtually all of the eleven women who went to Inner Mongolia with Xiuping lost their political enthusiasm and joined her in disillusionment. They learned that the abstract notions that had appeared on Peking wall posters bore no resemblance to the nature of life in the countryside. The youths, for example, wanted to instigate "class struggle" in the village. But this particular village had no former landlords or even rich peasants to be struggled against, and so they had to content themselves with accusing a couple of unsatisfactory upper middle peasants, who, in fact, seemed in character to be no better or worse than any of the other peasants. The youths also discovered that the cadres did almost no work, their most important duty apparently being to read party documents to the commune members at occasional meetings. Contrary also to the neat intellectual categories formulated in Peking, the young people discovered that the poor peasants did not embody virtue, that they were just as selfish, as calculating, and as lazy as anyone else. Moreover, none of the urban youths were prepared for the material hardships of life, for the fact that every time it rained, for example, their dormitory rooms got drenched. "As time went on," Xiuping recounted, "all but the stupidest of the sent-down youths changed their minds one way or the other about the revolution. Today all of them are back in Peking and not a single one of them believes in Marxism."

Xiuping left Inner Mongolia and, for many years thereafter, was part of a kind of flotsam and jetsam of the Cultural Revolution, drifting, like millions of others of her age, from one place to another, managing to get back to her home in Peking only for brief, semiclandestine stays, provided with neither ration coupons for the capital nor with the necessary residence permit. She put in two stretches on rural communes in the central provinces; she worked as a cotton spindle operator in a factory in Zhengzhou, a bleak, unattractive city not far from the Yellow River. She collected experiences and made random observations; she noted that peasants in central China were far cleaner and more highly motivated than those she had lived among in Inner Mongolia. Nonetheless, she noticed that there was a high rate of suicide among commune members, particularly just before the annual busy planting season. In one brigade where she lived for a while, two young, unmarried women for some unknown reason killed themselves by swallowing DDT after they had witnessed a couple making love in the fields. Once, Xiuping had the bizarre experience of being mistaken for a former schoolmate who had committed suicide. She even heard the authorities' explanation for her supposed act of desperation: it showed, the brigade leaders solemnly explained to Xiuping's roommate, the results of her failure to advance her political thinking.

In all, what struck Xiuping most about her years of drifting was how far Chinese reality was divorced from the beatific images spewed forth by the propaganda. In the cotton-spinning factory, for example, there was a horrendously high accident rate as young, untrained, and easily replaceable girls were set to work on ancient machines with dangerously exposed parts. During her stint in the factory, there were at least ten serious accidents, including several involving lost hands. Xiuping herself once lost the skin from the palm of her hand. The problem, she concluded, was that then, as now, there were no independent labor unions to protect the workers, who, in most cases, did not know and were afraid to ask what sort of compensation they were entitled to from the state, beyond free medical care.

Denied the chance to go abroad or even to the university in China, Xiuping devoted herself throughout much of this period of odyssey to her principal unfulfilled desire, for love. She had several brushes with romance, none of them consummated, most of them not even acknowledged; but it was not until after her periods on the several communes and in the cotton-spinning factory that she fell in love with somebody for real. In the mid-1970s, Xiuping became a member of a drafting workshop in a construction company in Zhengzhou, and there she met a man, already married, who was on loan to the factory from a teaching post in Peking. Their relationship was a classic in subtle gestures and unspoken words. The man worked at a desk near Xiuping's, so, from time to time, it was natural that they should speak to each other. Once Xiuping touched the rice bowl that he brought each day to the canteen, remarking on how clean he kept it, a gesture of intimacy as significant as a squeeze of the hand. At night, she rode on the back of his bicycle. Another time, late in the afternoon, they went together to the company recreation room, where they organized a little Ping-Pong tournament. During the course of play, the electricity went off, and as it got dark, everybody left — except for Xiuping and her friend, who stayed behind and, sharing an act of silliness, tried to hit the ball back and forth by sound rather than sight.

The man was rather conservative; he was married; he also hoped to join the Communist party. He worried that his flirtation with Xiuping would be discovered and bring discredit to him. And so, he arranged with the unit's leaders to be transferred back to his post in Peking — he taught engineering at one of the universities — and, one day, without a word to Xiuping, he left.

Xiuping was nearing thirty. She was still a virgin and she despaired of ever finding a man with whom she could experience the pleasures of love. Perhaps for those reasons, the sudden departure of the man, with whom she had had only this subtle and implicit flirtation, shocked her deeply. She became obsessed with finding him again, not to reproach him, not to persuade him to abandon his wife, the party, and his good sense for her; but to see him. But how? She knew only his name and the university where he taught, but she couldn't simply go there herself and ask for him without having to disclose her own name in return. She wanted to be discreet, both for her own sake and for his. She was afraid to write to him for fear that her letter might end up in the hands of the authorities. She even worried that to curry favor with the authorities the man might turn over the letter to them himself. Still, she was able to get a few days away from the Zhengzhou construction company on "sick leave," and she went to Peking. There, the high-ranking father of one of her friends agreed to help her. Without asking any questions, this sympathetic official, who worked in university circles, got her the man's address. She went to it. She was not concerned with the man's wife because that woman worked in another province and the two saw each other only once or twice a year. When, finally, Xiuping found the man, he was cold, aloof, and annoyed. However, she couldn't stay away, and she visited him several times more, not so much in the hope that he would change his mind about her, but rather in the expectation that his coldness would eventually cure her of her obsession. It did.

Xiuping brooded about her life, over the speed with which it was slipping by, over how, after so passionate an early career as a revolutionary youth, she had ended up in the tepid routine of a factory draftsman, afraid even to write a letter to a man because he himself might turn it over to the authorities. She was not very pretty; she was sullen and embittered. She mourned, more than any other single thing, her unsatisfied womanhood. She regretted, she once told me, that men enjoyed her company because of her mind but never because she was female; in total violation of the party's principles in this matter, she longed to be appreciated for her sexual allure rather than for her powers of analysis. This desire, of course, is not unique to women in Communist countries; nonetheless, puritanical China, with its intrusive, strictly enforced prudishness, its oppressive denial of the erotic and the sensual, has deprived both men and women of achieving satisfactions that in other societies they would have been able at least to seek without interference. It is one of the saddest aspects of the lost generation of the Cultural Revolution that politics interfered in their private lives at the age when people, under normal circumstances, fall in love and get married. I have met many women in their thirties whose love affairs of a decade before were wrecked by politics, by the fact that somebody came from a "bad" class background, or ended up being sent down to the countryside in some remote province, or simply got so carried away by politics that he denied himself the private, individualistic pleasures of love and marriage.

Xiuping sees no way out. Her dream is to go abroad and, like many Chinese, she studies English with a near desperate ardor. But she knows that without money and without powerful sponsorship, her chances are negligible. For a while, she went to a technical training institute in Zhengzhou, transferring from the construction company. But she disliked the daily routine, which, from wake-up time to morning exercise to lights-out at night, was rigorously dictated by the school authorities.

Worse, she found the curriculum crushingly dull; courses were incompetently taught; there was no leeway for independent thought or activity. Finally, she left the school, returning to Peking, where, without a residence certificate or ration coupons, she depends on the reluctant support of her father. And so, at thirty-three, she is waiting for something unexpected, unforeseen, to happen. She does the marketing and some of the cooking; she studies English; she reads the newspapers and gossips with her old acquaintances, still drawn ineluctably to the topic that dominated and ruined her life — politics. She believes that communism is a kind of Frankenstein's monster, a brilliant creation and even a necessary one to give China a fresh start; but one that, in the end, has become an inescapable menace, an oppressive force to which there is no alternative but retreat into a passive, private world where, at least, it is now possible to avoid the most intrusive demands of other more ideologically motivated people.

Of all of this, Xiuping remains intensely self-aware, capable of standing aloof, and even at times of being amused by the spectacle of her own decline from revolutionary enthusiasm to quiet, dignified despair. It is often not in the large elements of life but in its tiny details that her self-awareness becomes most acute. Once, for example, I was about to leave for a brief trip to Hong Kong and Xiuping asked me if I could pick up an English dictionary for her. Of course I said I would be happy to do so, and that launched us on a long discussion of which dictionary would best serve her needs. Only one English dictionary was available in China, she said, but she suspected that it was not very good. She needed one that, while not as thorough and difficult as the unabridged Oxford, would contain all the words she might ever encounter in her reading and explain them without ambiguity. To be more specific, she said she wanted the dictionary to contain *fuck* and *cocksucker*, and so on; otherwise, how could she know what such words meant? I understood, I said, and was sure that I could find something satisfactory. Nonetheless, Xiuping went on and on about this dictionary, describing a bit obsessively and repetitively what she hoped to get, until finally I suggested that we should discuss something else. As I clumsily showed my minor annoyance, I noticed that Xiuping was fighting back a tear. "China is so primitive," she finally said. "I am not humiliated for myself," she went on, in what might have been a commentary on her entire experience in the Chinese revolution, "I am humiliated for the nation."

"Hope may exist or it may not exist. It is like a road across the earth. For actually, there were no roads on the earth, but when many men pass one way, a road is made."

So, in his short story "My Old Home," did China's greatest twentieth-century writer, Lu Xun, reflect on the central concern of his life as a thinker: how and whether to keep alive the flicker of hope that China — which he once likened to a sealed iron house containing sleeping and doomed people — might one day emerge spiritually reinvigorated from its long struggle in the dark. It must be said that Lu Xun's hope at best only flickered. In his stories he offered it in small, subtle doses — in a wreath of flowers, for example, that suddenly appears at the graveside of a dead boy — while maintaining on the whole an attitude of tempered, combative pessimism. "I believe," he wrote in 1922, "that those who sink from prosperity to poverty will probably come in the process to understand what the world is really like."

He might, in that last statement, have been talking about China itself. Or perhaps he intended a reference to individual Chinese, like himself, who, growing up at the time of the fall of the Manchu dynasty and the great intellectual awakening of the May Fourth Movement, faced up later to what the world was really like as China itself sank anew into feudal superstition, weakness, self-deception, and bitter political struggles.

In one of his stories, called "In the Wine Shop," Lu Xun portrays himself unexpectedly meeting a sad and pathetic former schoolmate called Lu Weifu. This Lu had once been "nimble and active"; he used to be idealistic, burning with hope; he remembers how in their youth he and Lu Xun once went to the Tutelary God's Temple and, like Red Guards of half a century later, pulled off the beards of the images, the symbols of backwardness and superstition. Lu Weifu reminds Lu Xun (it is no coincidence that in this autobiographical tale both characters are surnamed Lu) of "how all day long we used to discuss methods of revolutionizing China until we even came to blows." But the central event of the story reveals that Lu Weifu has now sunk into despondency. His life consists of futile gestures; he makes a meager living by tutoring the children of the wealthy in the Confucian classics, the very books he had scorned in his revolutionary days. He admits, "I am willing to let things slide and to compromise." Even his brightest gestures come to naught, as when he buys some artificial flowers to decorate the dull life of a childhood acquaintance, wishing, as he puts it, "that the world would change for the better for her sake," only to find that she, like China, has died an untimely death.

Lu Xun asks his old friend what he plans to do in the future. "The future?" replies his namesake Lu Weifu. "I don't know. Just think: of all the things we planned in the past, has any single one turned out as we hoped? I'm not sure of anything now, not even of what I will do tomorrow, nor even of the next minute."

Nothing illustrates the inclination toward the self-serving half-truth and hollow sloganeering of Chinese communism better than the party's posthumous treatment of Lu Xun, whose death in 1936 enabled the propagandists to create out of him a loyal servant of Mao. Writing in the stilted militarized style that the great writer himself would have despised, Mao called Lu Xun the "chief commander of China's modern cultural revolution," a man who was not only a "revolutionary democrat" (this was true) but who also had the good sense to "mature into a Communist." In fact, at the time of his death, Lu Xun was locked in a dreary, enervating debate within leftist cultural circles in which he argued uncompromisingly against political controls or guidelines on literature. He would not have fared well under Mao or Mao's successors, and, indeed, all of the writers who agreed with him in the 1930s were without exception ruthlessly attacked and purged in the cultural *autos-da-fé* of later years. Only Lu Xun's convenient death enabled him to be held up as a Communist model; the model is a cynical caricature, bearing only the coarsest of resemblances to the complex, ruthlessly honest figure who was the man.

China, of course, is different now; it contains in many ways far more reason for hope than in those days of historical nadir in the early 1920s that Lu Xun described in his stories. And yet, the dashed idealism and the private hopelessness of many of the people I met in Peking seem resonant to me of the May Fourth generation that, symbolically, served as the subject of this tale in the wine shop. In 1949, as during the May Fourth Movement of 1919, China seemed to be on the verge of a rebirth. Many Chinese invested their own hopes for the future in the revitalized greatness of the country itself. Now, as then, the dreams have perished; where once it seemed that just to catch the reflected glory of the revolution would be enough, life now for many aware Chinese consists of an effort to gain small, entirely private satisfactions, to garner a few personal and evanescent joys, even as they ask themselves with Lu Weifu whether, of all the things that they planned in the past, any of them have turned out as they had hoped.

Conclusion

The Lovable People

I HAD ONE GOOD FRIEND in China whose irony-rich life exemplified just about every crass, ill-conceived, and cruel political misadventure ever initiated by the Maoist regime. A highly educated patriot who returned from abroad immediately after the Communists came to power, this man spent nearly thirty years in serious political trouble and was locked up for the better part of two decades in one sort of prison camp, reeducation center, labor-reform farm, or another. That he survived with his sanity intact is a measure of his strength and spirit. That he was subjected to terrible punishments is a mark of how the Maoist regime spoiled its most important asset — skilled, motivated people. My friend is typical of thousands of others; he reflects the full, unpardonable thoughtlessness that lay at the heart of the Communist government for most of its history of rule.

I'll call him Old Li. Now he is all right, enjoying, like many previously mistreated intellectuals, an obscure sinecure in an academic institute in Peking, and claiming that he is neither bitter nor angry nor even demoralized at the spectacle of his wrecked life. "It was a rather extraordinary experience," he once told me. "When you go through something like what I've been through, at least you learn exactly who and what you are. And besides, we must be strong enough to be worthy of our sufferings." Thus, he refuses to descend to self-pity or even to spitefulness. Like my scholar friend Professor Chen, he will eat his bitterness in stoic silence. Still, I would like to make a small amount of noise for Old Li and for the way his life was wasted.

Born in the 1920s in central China, Old Li came from a family that had, in earlier generations, owned and rented farmland, and that had high standards and educational values. These the young Li pursued in a normal fashion through his mid-teens. But when, in 1937, Japan launched its full-scale invasion of China, Li, almost literally, was swept away by history. He began to undertake activities that, while innocent at the time, later came to haunt him. Like slowly maturing seeds, years later they unexpectedly burst into poisonous fruit.

After the Japanese invasion, Li, like thousands, millions, of others, went westward, following the retreating central government of the Kuomintang. He ended up at the Southwestern Associated University in Kunming, an amalgam of schools from other places that set up temporary, exile quarters in Yunnan Province during the war. But, because he was bright and energetic, Li soon found himself working as a translator for the Chinese military in their cooperation with the Americans in Kunming. One thing led to another and he was, still in his early twenties, sent to the United States with a Chinese military-training mission. That was in 1942. He was to remain in the United States for more than eight years, eventually earning university degrees in biochemistry, always planning to return to China. He followed events back home with keen interest, talking them over with his Chinese friends and debating with them whether and when to return to China.

It is ironic in retrospect, but at the time, Li was one of the more enthusiastic pro-revolutionary students in the United States, even giving speeches in favor of the ascending Communists as they fought what Li saw as the "rotten" Kuomintang. "It was easy," he recalled later, "to be a progressive at a distance." (This ease, he might have added, was also experienced by many of the "friends" of China who could see no fault in the Maoist regime even when Old Li was digging ice from frozen streams on a concentration camp in Manchuria.) "It seemed to me then that the Chinese Communist party was doing the right thing and that, in any case, there could be no third way for China." Li's commitment to the motherland led to a classic breakup with a Chinese-American girl friend whom he probably would otherwise have married. "She knew that I would go back to China eventually and she made it clear that she didn't want to go back where, as she said, she would have to draw water from a well and live without a toilet." But Li was determined. "Being an intellectual is a sort of privilege in China. I thought that I owed the Chinese people something."

One key irony of Li's life that would emerge only later was that those who did not return home were much better off, not only in the United States but also in their later relations with China. Li remembers in particular one very good friend also named Li, then a physics student. This

other Li did not return home and became a scientist of international re-
nown. The two Li's used to have lively quarrels until late in the night,
with the physicist telling his friend that he was crazy to go back to China
and live under the Communists. Li was not convinced. "I was getting
pressure from my family back home not to be a 'white Chinese,' which
was the greatest insult. At that time, I didn't use the word *patriotism*. I
learned that word later. But I never meant to stay in the States. I didn't
feel like an American. I felt very much a Chinese." When, finally, in early
1951, an invitation came from a school in Peking to return as a teacher, Li
quickly accepted. His friends, the physicist and others, made eleventh-
hour appeals to him to change his mind. He even remembers meeting
some old schoolmates in Tokyo on his way back to China who also kept
him up all one night endeavoring to convince him that he was making a
fatal mistake. But Li sailed anyway to Hong Kong, steamed up the Pearl
River in a small boat to Canton to pick up the train to Peking, and then,
within months, began to suspect that being "patriotic" was not so easy.

From the very start, his "complicated social relations," his American
education, and his "overseas connections" branded him as a possible spy.
"We were met by officials," he remembers of his arrival in Canton. "We
were wined and dined. But we were watched." After he started teaching
in Peking, he was routinely questioned by the authorities. Where had he
gotten the money for his trip home? What had he done for the KMT?
What were his connections with the Americans? "Over and over again,
they take down your personal history, trying to catch you in inconsistencies, to see if you have hidden anything or lied." After only one year,
though nothing criminal or "counterrevolutionary" was ever discovered
in his past, Li was sent out of Peking to another city to teach. It was found
undesirable for him to be in the Communist capital. Years later, in 1979,
when China had entered its current moderate, more sensible phase, it
came as only a mild surprise to Li when a colleague admitted that he had
been assigned to spy on him and report his activities to the authorities. He
had never uncovered any reason to suspect fault in Li's behavior.

This paranoia, this obsession with enemies in their midst, is a common
form of self-destructiveness among newly empowered revolutionary regimes. Having risen themselves in large part by tightly organized, highly
conspiratorial activity, they suspect that everywhere there are others who
are doing as they did. At the same time, they lack confidence in the extent
of their popular support; they feel the pressure of unfriendly forces from
outside the country; they are aware of the splits, the factions, the poten-
tials for debilitating power struggles within their own party. And so, the
search for ideological enemies serves a double purpose. It provides the illusion that the leaders are doing something about real enemies and it de-

flects attention from the difficult, practical problems of running a government and an economy.

The ideological campaigns that followed one after the other hit Old Li with ever more severe blows. In 1955 came the campaign for "weeding out counterrevolutionaries." His house was searched; he was interrogated; but he kept his job and was not denounced. In 1956 came that strange and disturbing Maoist aberration called the Hundred Flowers campaign, when the party, trying to give vent to frustrations, encouraged the Chinese people to express their views and criticisms freely. Li, like many others, took the bait. He offered his views against the party's curbs on free speech. "I said that trying to stop the people's mouth was like trying to stop the river — things like that." When, after only a few months, the party cracked down against those who had heeded its calls for criticism, Li was singled out for particular, horrible attention. This came during the so-called antirightist campaign, a violent and wholesale purge of intellectuals that, for hundreds of thousands, launched a period of darkness that was to last, with only a few glimmers of hope, for two decades.

Reflecting its typical pseudo–political science, the party — then led by Mao, assisted by such later "moderates" as Chou En-lai and Deng Xiao-ping — determined that there would be six categories of rightists — not five, not seven, but six. In addition, since Mao had declared that 95 percent of the Chinese people were "good," that meant, by a process of elimination, that about 5 percent were "bad." Thus, units were instructed in this scientific fashion to discover and condemn a quota of rightists roughly equivalent to that percentage of its workers and staff. Li was branded a rightist of the most serious kind, a rank-six rightist. After all, he was from landlord background; he had been educated in the United States and had worked during the war for the KMT (never mind that at the time the Communist party itself was part of a "United Front" with the KMT); during the Hundred Flowers movement, he had been guilty of what were called "reactionary utterances," an unintentional admission by the people who think up these sloganistic accusations that the free-speech guarantee in the constitution meant virtually nothing except the right to say what the authorities wanted to hear. Again in mock scientific fashion, rightist category six was further divided into two subgroups, A and B, the difference lying in the right of the latter to get their jobs back after they were reformed. Li was category six, subdivision A, the worst possible.

Still, Li's fall took a few months; it was a process. "They have a way of doing things gradually, to get you used to your new status and prepare you for the next stage." First the leaders of the school simply asked Li to confess, promising that he would be treated leniently if he did. He lost his right to teach but for three months stayed at the school, working as an assistant to the librarian, all the while subjected to interrogation and pressure to confess his crimes. That was at the end of 1957. In March 1958, Li was officially denounced as an "ultrarightist" at a rally of the entire school.

"Many of my colleagues and students attacked me," he recalls of that incident. "One of the 'counterrevolutionary' statements I had made was that people running a political campaign are like children eating peanuts. First they select the big ones, then the small ones. But eventually the child will eat all of the peanuts. I wasn't angry at my colleagues but I was demoralized by the meekness of the intellectuals as a whole. Some tried to take advantage of the situation to become somebodies themselves. But most were just meek. Only one of my colleagues, also a student returned from abroad, defended me. He told the meeting that I was a great patriot who didn't have to come back to China in 1951. At the end of the meeting he shook hands with me and for that he too was declared a rightist. All of this part of the procedure is called 'debate,' which means 'denounce.' The more you say, the more you get yourself into hot water. And they tell you that leniency will follow if you confess. That's another one of their tricks."

Li did confess that he had made statements that were "reactionary." In April a jeep arrived at the school to take him to a detention house that was attached to a showplace prison. The prison was the showplace, not the detention house. In the company of pickpockets, thieves, rapists, and other ordinary criminals, Li stayed there for three months under circumstances of calculated cruelty. He lived in a cell about the size of a large hotel room. It had a cement floor, a bucket for a latrine, and was inhabited by thirty people who slept in tightly packed rows of straw pallets. There was one bowl of corn gruel a day, and two more meals consisting of four hundred grams of coarse grains, again mostly cornmeal. "At first I couldn't stand it; but afterward, I wanted my food. Only later did I realize that the conditions were designed to break the spirit of the prisoners — to sleep and eat like that. It lasted for fifty days. Because I was a serious case, I was called into a separate room each day and made just to sit there. During the interrogations, they didn't get anything more about me because I had already told them everything. I had nothing to hide. And, in any case, you have no way to prove yourself innocent. Silence is also a crime, however. Silence means resistance."

Li also says that after a few weeks in the detention center, he was psychologically softened up to be taken elsewhere, and, indeed, when he was told that he could go to a "farm" in Manchuria, where he would have all he needed to eat and might, if he had a good attitude, even receive a salary, he greeted the news with relief, even with something akin to joy. And so, in the middle of one night in the summer of 1958, he and many of his fellow prisoners were taken in a caravan of guarded buses to the train station for the three-day journey to Harbin and then to the Soviet border. He remembers that on that journey, the prisoners were treated very well. They were given real wheat *mantou* (steamed bread) for the first time; then in Harbin they got European-style bread. Li was in a good frame of mind when he arrived at what had been called a farm. Soon, he found that it was a swamp. The rightists were to drain it by building a dam and irrigation ditches. They slept in tents; then in barracks that they built themselves. There were nine "farms" altogether with a total population of some ten thousand prisoners. Li had no idea what the length of his sentence was. He was just told that if he behaved, he would be set free. He was a "prisoner for education and cultivation," technical jargon for a noncriminal, that is, a political, offender who, presumably, needs to be taught to believe that Marxism-Leninism–Mao Tse-tung Thought is science. It is a euphemism for indoctrination. "Nobody protested," says Li. "The worst part of it is that they get all the other prisoners to say that you deserve what is happening to you. That was disheartening; I was deserted by my friends."

During the antirightist campaign, the state made nearly no allowances for the families of prisoners, and thus, one problem constantly preying on Li's mind was the difficult circumstances of his wife. The two of them had one son; a second child, a daughter, was born shortly after Li was taken to the detention center. The wife worked as a laboratory technician for a salary of about forty dollars a month, but the loss of Li's salary, combined with the need to buy essentials like food, blankets, and clothing to send to him in prison, put a tremendous strain on her. Then, as if that was not already enough, she too got into political difficulties. She was a practicing Catholic and was denounced for that. She was also criticized for failing "to draw a clear line," meaning that she declined to denounce her husband. At the end of 1958, the central leadership determined that all "undesirable elements" should leave the sacred precincts of the Chinese capital. Li's wife was forced to go to Hubei Province with their two young children.

What followed was a winter of extraordinary suffering and despair. For Li, life in the labor camp was nightmarishly bare and hard. Temperatures dropped to forty degrees below zero Fahrenheit. The very heavy work he was assigned to do consisted largely of cutting and removing the ice from the irrigation canals and then widening them — a task that is done in winter precisely because the water from the canals can be removed in this way. Li remembers with some astonishment that only a few died that winter; he says that, in retrospect, he is amazed that he survived himself. The next winter, however, was to be much worse. It was the first year of the post–Great Leap Forward famine, and many people lost their lives as a result of malnutrition. One of Li's freinds, a doctor, later wrote a dry, scholarly paper in which he described what he called "concentration camp malnutrition." Meanwhile, Li's wife sold the family's furniture to survive. "She suffered terribly," Li says, blaming that period for her weak physical condition of today.

After three years, Li was transferred to the Qinghe Farm near Tianjin, an immense prison camp run by the Peking municipal Public Security Bureau, which, unlike the inescapable frozen vastnesses of the northeast, came complete with armed guards, high walls, barbed wire, and mounted patrols. At first Li and the other inmates were pleased that they were leaving the northeast. But within two weeks they realized that at Qinghe they would be put on a starvation diet, consisting mostlyof salted turnips.

This was the period when throughout China the combined disasters of the Great Leap Forward and several years of bad weather produced a massive famine as widespread and devastating as those of traditional China that the modern, scientific Communist party was supposed to wipe out. Of course, conditions on the Qinghe Farm were worse than they were elsewhere. Two incidents in particular remain engraved on Li's mind as emblems of the bizarre, lugubrious months that he spent at Qinghe. Once, he was dispatched by his section chief to dig graves for the dead. He dug one pit and returned, only to be reprimanded by the chief for not having dug several. He remembers also the horse-drawn carts that were so short bodied that the corpses' legs stuck out with grim comic effect from the cart itself and dangled over the ground below. Because there was so little food, the prisoners were required to write to their families and ask them to provide for them. "China was a country that couldn't feed its prisoners," Li remarks now, "and yet it kept them in jail." Finally, after several months he was able to write to his wife, asking her to come from Hubei to visit him, telling her that it might be for the last time because he was sick and hungry and was not sure that he would survive very much longer. When she did come, however, he was unexpectedly and mercifully allowed to leave with her, paroled for medical reasons. He left in 1961 for Hubei so emaciated that people used to turn and look at him when he walked on the street or on the campus of the school where his wife had found a job teaching.

The following year, 1962, the policies of the center were relaxed somewhat so that, while still supposedly under "the supervision of the masses," Li was allowed to teach at the same school as his wife. He began to live something more like a normal life, though he was still theoretically a rightist of the sixth category, subdivision A. Finally, in 1964, even that stigmatizing label was removed and Li was able to believe that the horrors were behind him. But two years later, the nightmare returned in all of its garish twisted horror. The Cultural Revolution began, and naturally, as a former rightist, as a man with "overseas connections" and with "complicated social relations," Li was one of the first to be discharged from his duties, to be locked up in one of the small prisons known mockingly as cow sheds, and eventually to be hauled off to another rural work camp, this one with the endearingly euphemistic name of May 7 cadre school.

That lasted six years. Then as a semblance of normal political life started to return to China, Li went back to teach again in Hubei — still under "the supervision of the masses." At long last, three years after the Gang of Four was, as the propaganda put it, "smashed," Old Li was allowed to return to Peking. He had been absent for exactly twenty-one years. He had done no wrong, committed no crime, made no mistakes; he was exonerated and given his present, rather undemanding position and paid a modest salary. Indeed, Old Li bears few visible scars from the horrific experience of being an innocent victim. He seems healthy; his face is unlined. He talks about it all with the calm, reflective intelligence of one who has not only retained his sanity but searched in himself for great strengths and found them.

"People make decisions at certain points in their lives as a result of many convergent circumstances," he once told me. "At certain times you can only go one way. That's one reason why I have no regrets. It couldn't have been different for me." Li's fatalism may be an important factor in his political views. While he is not a very avid supporter of the Communist party per se, he remains unshakably patriotic. He hopes that Deng Xiaoping and the moderate leaders of China will succeed in their search for wealth and power, though he knows that they will have to do it without the contribution he might have been able to make.

Once, shortly after his arrival back in Peking after his many long years of persecution, Old Li had an extraordinary chance to test his ability to "be worthy of my suffering." It happened that his old friend, the other Li, the physicist, came from the United States to China for a visit to the motherland. Our Li went to see him and they had a chat about old times, about the divergent paths they had taken and that had resulted in such different lives. Old Li says he wanted to see how he would feel seeing his old schoolmate who had reaped all of the benefits of a brilliant career in the West: the money, the fame, the international prestige. And, he says, he did not experience envy; he accepted as inevitable what had happened. But he did feel a supreme irony. Here, after all, was the physicist Li being lodged by the state in a luxurious suite at the Peking Hotel. He had a Red Flag limousine at his disposal. He was ushered into the presence of the top leaders for cordial conversations. Laudatory articles were published in the press presenting him as a model for other successful overseas Chinese whose hearts still belonged to the motherland. And what Old Li thought was that for nearly thirty years it was the physicist who had played it safe, who had not returned as an idealistic, patriotic, and talented youth to help build the country. While the physicist was heaped with praises and honors, Old Li, who had followed the call of patriotism, had become a poor, obscure, exonerated rightist.

So it is that China, under Mao, committed the crime of wasting the lives and talents of its best and its brightest. The irony is summed up by a bittersweet piece of conventional wisdom that passed among China's intellectuals as they watched the grand receptions accorded those who came from abroad: to have become a revolutionary early is not as good as to have become a revolutionary late; to have become a revolutionary late is not as good as not to have become a revolutionary at all.

What stands out for me in Li's terrible story is not only the waste of his talent; it is also the betrayal of his altruism and of his hopes. In this sense, he stands as a stark emblem of the principal failure of three decades of Communist rule in China. When Mao Tse-tung climbed the reviewing stand at Peking's Tiananmen Square on October 1, 1949, and proclaimed the victory of his forces, he was popularly welcomed, not because of his ideology, but because of the luster of his image. Tens of millions of Chinese hoped that Mao and the Communists would accomplish what generations had yearned for, that they would restore the brilliance, the status, the wealth, and the power of one of the world's proudest civilizations. Indeed, in the early days of power, when Old Li was making his fateful decision to return to the motherland, the Communists' image and the ardency of the national desire for restored greatness provided Mao and his legions with greater popular backing than perhaps any Chinese government had had before them.

The tragedy of the Chinese revolution is that the aroused goodwill of people like Old Li was neglected, misused, destroyed. It is not, of course, that communism's failure was total; it was relative. Like most nations, China since World War II has made a degree of material progress. It has built industries, expanded agriculture, increased literacy, and spread better basic health care. These are, however, by no means the unique accomplishments of the Chinese government; they are the result of the general worldwide sweep of development and modernization that, to greater or lesser degrees, has affected most countries of the globe. Meanwhile, for its very modest postrevolutionary achievements, China has paid dearly with what are the now admitted blights of the recent past: the prison camps, the ruined lives, the desiccation of the national culture, the loss of private rights, the deadly sluggishness of the world's largest bureaucracy as it tries to pilot the cumbersome ships of central planning and state monopoly. Communist history in China can be seen as a deterioration from hope and vigor to the twentieth century's familiar totalitarian malaise, in which power is held less and less by popular consent and enthusiasm for the common purpose and more and more by thought control and police surveillance.

Now, as the Western press has amply reported, China's post-Mao generation is promising still another new beginning. The claim again is that a formula for renewed greatness has been uncovered and that it consists of a reinvigoration of the socialist system, the "correct" policies of which were subverted by Mao's mistakes, by the Gang of Four, and by the ideological illness known as ultraleftism. By the year 2000, China is supposed to emerge as an advanced, modern state with a per capita income four times as high as in 1980 while at the same time showing a florescence in the arts and culture, in education and science, encapsulated by the slogan "Let a hundred flowers blossom."

We can well hope that China succeeds. As Europeans and Americans across oceans and continents from the ancient Middle Kingdom, we have nothing to fear from Chinese prosperity. Indeed, it will benefit us, not least in our own efforts to balance the threatening might of the Soviet Union, one of whose greatest concerns is a genuinely resurgent China on its southern border. A China that offers its people the benefits of higher standards of living and that releases their skills in the cultivation of the arts and sciences can also improve the quality of our very small world; it can deeply enrich our own lives just as China has already done by virtue of its extraordinary heritage of greatness. Thus the West's instinct to help China, to exchange goods and experiences, is the correct one.

The important question, however, remains; can China under its more flexible, pragmatic masters finally realize its ancient goal of restored greatness? Clearly the nation has been aided by its decision to shake off the irrational and destructive components of Maoism, the constant campaigns, the notions of revolutionary purity, the extreme xenophobia that left the country without the benefits of international contacts. That alone should enable China once again to benefit somewhat from the creep of modernism as it makes its slow pace across the globe.

But what else is it realistic to expect? China's current leaders, in their hopeful reconfirmations of "the superiority of socialism," reflect what has become a standard cliché of the totalitarian left: that while socialism has not proven superior in other countries, that is because the policies pursued by those countries do not conform to true socialism. We, the adherents of this notion never stop repeating, have found the right key to the socialist future; we are doing something never tried before and it will lead the way to a perfect amalgam combining the egalitarian justice of socialism with the flexibility, the creativity, and the dynamism of a system of free activity.

Unfortunately, China shows few signs of this ideally happy marriage. For there to be greatness, the state must allow a sufficient degree of independence and freedom for the individual to create without political fear. Yet, while China's propaganda pays lip service to this twin need — just as it adheres in theory to freedom of speech and of the press — it remains a society where the imperative to control, and the concomitant inclination of the creative individual to play it safe, interferes with any theoretical respect for the rights of the individual to be bold or to be different. Despite the concept of revolutionary change, China remains encumbered by precisely those aspects of what is called "the old society" that led to national decline: the conservatism and caution of the bureaucracy, the intolerance of things new or heterodox, the jealous grip on their monopoly of power and on their vested interests by the ruling class, the assumption that it is the right and the responsibility of supreme power to impose its visions and concepts on the amorphous mass.

"We Chinese," a friend of mine in Peking once commented, "are a lovable people and we have a lovable culture." This comment was not a paean of praise for China; it was, rather, a cry of regret over lost hopes and opportunities. My friend, who was in her mid-thirties, had, like so many of her generation, been crushed by the revolution. Bright, witty, attractive, and idealistic, she had spent ten years away from home, the whim of the party having provided her with a long term of labor on a rural commune. Her education had been wrecked; far from her normal environment and from the people she knew, she never met a suitable man and thus remained unhappily single; she worked day to day for a publication, editing the numbing, self-satisfied prose of Communist propaganda and earning a grand total of twenty-six dollars a month.

We used to meet from time to time on the streets or, occasionally, in her parents' home. She loved to tell me about ancient poetry and operas, about abstruse literary games and works of visual art; that is, about the greatness of China. And though she masked her situation with a veneer of spirited cheerfulness and good humor, it was easy to see that, at thirty-five, when she should have been entering into the full productive stage of adult life, she was bored, unsatisfied, trapped in a system that gave her little chance to control her own life.

Like most of the Chinese I knew, like, for example, my friend Old Li of another generation, this friend was entirely lovable. Every time I met her and came away with another small pearl of Chinese culture, I reflected that it was the neglected duty of the Communist revolution to provide her with something better. Just like the other lovable Chinese that I knew, she deserved more, more of a chance to be herself, more of an opportunity to contribute to the country that she continued, despite everything, to love, more of a chance to hope that after all these decades of decline, of misdirection, of mediocrity, China might one day be great again.

Index

X